LAND AND LANDSCAPE

LAND
AND LANDSCAPE

Evolution, Design and Control

———————

BRENDA COLVIN

JOHN MURRAY

First published 1947
Second edition enlarged and reset 1970
Reprinted with amendments 1973

Printed in Great Britain for
John Murray, Albemarle Street, London
by William Clowes & Sons Ltd
London and Beccles
0 7195 1800 8

To
Geoffrey and Susan Jellicoe

Contents

Illustrations

Acknowledgements

My thanks are extended to the organizations and individuals listed below for their help in providing illustrations and for permission to reproduce them. The sources of the photographs and the pages on which they appear are as follows:

Aerofilms, 17, 25, 31, 35, 73, 76, 82, 105, 116, 142, 204, 226, 263, 270, 283, 288, 297, 323, 375 (both), 376, 377
Architectural Review, 289 (photo: Dell and Wainwright)
Archiv Ruhrtalsperrenverein, 237
Ashmolean Museum, Oxford, 27 (photo: Major G. W. G. Allen), 28, 32, 57
Barnaby's Picture Library, 16
Bernard Berry, 3
Bodleian Library, Oxford, 49
British Museum, 62
British Petroleum Co., 345
British Travel Association, 45, 87, 320
J. Allan Cash, 64, 215, 217, 229, 256
Cement and Concrete Association, 354
Central Electricity Generating Board, 99, 144, 202, 337 (perspective sketch by Peter Swann from the author's plans), 341
Central Office of Information, 21
Civic Trust, 6–7
Country Life, 50, 80, 83, 85, 91, 185, 188, 285
Ben Darby, 248, 258
Derbyshire Countryside Ltd., 112
Douglas Dickins, 191
Findus Eskimo Frood Ltd., 269
Forestry Commission, 54, 118, 173, 175, 176, 240, 242, 243, 244, 245
R. C. B. Gardner, 273
Leonard and Marjorie Gayton, 68, 119, 351, 372 (top), 373 (top)
David Green, 327
Bodfan Gruffydd, 138, 342, 359
George H. Hall, 311
Mr and Mrs R. D. Hammond, 92 (photo: Harry Smith)
C. V. Hancock, 209
Italian State Tourist Office, 104

F. Leonard Jackson, 253
Japanese Embassy, 131
Susan Jellicoe, 51, 69, 133, 163, 179, 180, 182, 198, 211, 304, 309, 329, 347, 353
Dr J. K. St Joseph, 34, 171
A. F. Kersting, 117, 287
KLM Aerocarto, 264
Sam Lambert, 106
Longmans, Green & Co, 333
Frances Bell Macdonald, 48, 58, 63
Eric de Maré, 330
Mike Marriott, 370
C. S. Minchell, 349 (top)
Ministry of Defence (Air Force Department), 55, 295
Ministry of Transport, 358, 361, 373 (bottom)
Ann Moorson, 208
National Trust, 125
Edmund Hort New, 39
Maurice Nimmo, 277
William S. Paton, 9
The Earl of Pembroke, 78
Picturepoint, 5 (photo: Kenneth Scowen), 38 (photo: John Baker), 302 (photo: Jack Scheerboom)
John Piper and Faber & Faber, 15
Pix Photos, 290
Planair, 255
J. M. F. Riley, 33, 70
Royal Institute of British Architects and Geoffrey Jellicoe, 123
Royal Netherlands Embassy, 300
Kenneth Scowen, 158
M. H. Shepheard, 348 (bottom)
Edwin Smith, 10, 41
Span Developments, 317 (photo: Henk Snoek)
Tom Stephenson, 14
Stevenage Development Corporation, 321
Ezra Stoller Associates, 348 (top)
Studio Lisa, 102
Surrey County Council, 356
Swedish Travel Bureau, 233
Jon. H. Talbot, 372 (bottom)

C. R. V. Tandy, 52, 135, 335
Tayler and Green, 318
Tennessee Valley Authority, 147
The Times, 66
United States Information Service, 95, 96, 279, 355
Whitworth Art Gallery, University of Manchester, 374 (top)
Wimbledon and Putney Commons Conservators, 249

The remaining photographs are my own.

The drawings were all prepared by Richard Westmacott except for that on p. 260, which is mine. The plans on pp. 314 and 360 are based on drawings prepared by me for the Ministry of Public Buildings and Works in connection with the rebuilding of Aldershot Military Town.

I would like to add my personal thanks to the many friends and colleagues who have helped me search for illustrations, often at considerable trouble to themselves, in particular Susan Jellicoe, Cliff Tandy and Bodfan Gruffydd. Without their encouragement and help this edition might not have appeared. Special thanks also are due to Jeremy Steele for his advice and patience during the preparation of this volume, and to Miss Ann Hoffman (Authors' Research Services), W. J. McGowan, James Riley and others who helped with the research needed to bring it up to date.

B. C.

Foreword

It is the proper study and labour of an artist to uncover and find
out the latent cause of conspicuous beauty and from thence form
principles for his own conduct. Such an examination is a continual
exertion of the mind; as great, perhaps, as that of the artist whose
works he is thus studying.

From Sir Joshua Reynolds' *Sixth Discourse*

Sir Joshua's comment referred in particular to painting. It can be
applied with even greater force to landscape design if the last line is
omitted. Since we are studying not only the art of former exponents
of landscape design, but more essentially the processes of nature,
there can be no possibility of exertion 'as great as that of the artist'.
But an examination of the latent causes of beauty is 'a continual
exertion of the mind'—opening ever new vistas of interest and
delight.

In our study of the artistry of our forebears—that is, in the
history of landscape design, emerging as it did from the art of garden
design, we find two opposite philosophical attitudes reflected in the
humanized landscape of the world. Their expression is most clearly
seen in the garden styles which have evolved in various countries.

At one extreme, the placid acceptance of things as they are, with
humanity deferential to nature, as in Eden before the fall, gives rise
to design whose objective is to follow and perhaps to coax, rather
than to coerce nature. This we see expressed in the art, and especially
the garden art, of the Far East. The opposite attitude of self-assurance and will-to-power is characteristically expressed in Latin
countries by geometric and architectural treatment of land and plant
forms. Various gradations between the two occur and may often
associate together happily enough.

The tendency of our age is towards ever greater domination of
nature by man, though we are dimly aware that the last word will be
with nature unless we can adapt our new powers to the crescendo of
evolution without overriding the natural laws ensuring healthy
survival and duration.

It is here that the need for deeper study and adaptation to the processes of nature arises. We understand too little as yet about how those fundamental natural laws may resist our careless use of new-found power. Enormous risks are taken for the sake of immediate material results with little or no knowledge of long-term reactions.

The rate of technological advance has overwhelmed our judgment and understanding, and deceleration seems to be impossible.

The simple instincts which ensure survival and evolution are not, however, lost and can still lead us through the problematical period. By refinement and cultivation of the senses, humanity has reached new depths of appreciation which find their expression in art.

Landscape design is the youngest art, since the refinement of our natural joy of landscape comes late in history. The understanding and perception of the visual scene goes deeper than what the eye sees, and owes so much to scientific knowledge that the study of landscape design must now bridge the chasm between art and science. It is becoming ever more necessary for science and art to come to terms—their isolation and separate development is a danger to society. In spite of the continuing trend towards specialization, leaders in both fields are aware of the need for wider understanding, and perhaps they can come together most easily through the mutual appreciation of landscape.

Since *Land and Landscape* was first published immense changes have taken place in our landscape, in our powers of altering it and in the rate at which changes occur. We have seen also a great advance in the appreciation of the profession of landscape architecture and its role in connection with these changes. There is growing a public recognition of the need for ensuring, throughout the inevitable change, a setting which our senses can enjoy and appreciate; a recognition of the fact that the aesthetic pleasure we get from our surroundings is a response, whether conscious or unconscious, to the laws of nature's balance by which we live.

In 1947, the threat of over-population was scarcely felt, though the rate of general development was already a threat to landscape in these islands and the havoc that might be caused to our land by growing technical power was becoming evident. But now the pressure of increasing numbers of people greatly increases the risk of havoc and makes the remedies more difficult. The problem is national, and indeed world-wide; each and every profession should be considering how best to contribute to its solution. A vast combined operation is needed to prevent the destruction of any small country's dwindling charm and to ensure for its people, in the future, a landscape worth living in.

A new edition of this book is a very small contribution towards that end. Although much of the earlier edition has had to be rewritten for today the pattern and the theme remain.

PART ONE

Landscape Development in Britain

Nature and Man

The control which modern man is able to exert over his environment is so great that we easily overlook the power of the environment over man. Perhaps we just assume that any environment, modified and conditioned by human activity, must inevitably be suited to human life. We know that this is not so, really, and that man can ruin his surroundings and make them unsuitable for future generations, just as he can make war and leave unsolved political problems leading to more war; but we continue to act as if we did not know it, and we have not properly mastered the methods which the elementary knowledge should lead us to apply.

We should think of this planet, Earth, as a single organism, in which humanity is involved. The sense of superior individuality which we enjoy is illusory. Man is a part of the whole through evolutionary processes, and is united to the rest of life through the chemistry of lungs and stomach; with air, food and water passing in constant exchange between the soil and the tissues of plant and animal bodies. J. W. Bews puts it thus: 'Life apart from environment does not exist and cannot be conceived. Life consists essentially of a process of interchange between the life substance, or protoplasm, and the environment.'[1]

The health of this organism is visibly evident in the state of the landscape, just as the condition of an animal's glossy coat, or the face of a human being, reveals the state of health and the condition of the whole constitution.

The earth's surface today exhibits many scars, sores and mangy patches, nearly all due to human activity, but still capable of renewal through human care. Is this civilization yet sufficiently mature to

[1] J. W. Bews, *Human Ecology*, OUP, 1935.

Ancient oaks at Longleat, Wilts. Possibly the remnants of primitive forest which once covered most of Britain: now part of a treasured parkland, well adapted for pasture and immensely satisfying to the human eye seeking release from city life.

recognize its responsibility (before causing further devastation) for the care of this organism over which it ventures to assume control?

Landscape design acknowledges this organic unity of life in its environment and seeks to express human relationship to the whole. It recognizes the power of subconscious and even of traditional motives, but sees the necessity for positive control of the fast-changing landscape now for the sake of the future. The varying circumstances of each project are a challenge, but also the inspiration to the designer to seek that unity throughout the separate parts, in response to the basic facts of our existence.

Primitive man is part of the wild or natural landscape, and fits into it in the same way as any of the rest of the animal population, making little or no impression on his surroundings. At a later stage he begins to alter the landscape, mainly through his agriculture. Agricultural landscapes, in so far as they are necessarily based on natural biological laws, produce a beautiful and satisfactory landscape well adapted to human evolution. Modern industrial methods applied to farming raise new questions. The visual degradation of the landscape is a warning of peril not to be disregarded. When man comes to the stage where he can recklessly create a new system far removed from its biological foundations, he is in danger of contaminating his environment, of destroying the soil and the evolved beauty of the landscape, and of leaving a worthless heritage for his descendants.

Fertile soil must be preserved for food production, and that process may ensure the preservation of great tracts of beautiful scenery. But the spread of urban conditions constitutes a terrible threat until we have learned to appreciate the real necessity for natural beauty in the surroundings at every stage of human life. We must realize, in all its implications, the truth that man does not live by bread alone, and that the full development of intellectual or spiritual life, no less than mere existence, requires contact with nature and natural beauty.

Just as the child needs the care and protection, the love and companionship of the family if he is to develop fully and freely, so does humanity need contact with nature and with the soil, and the comfort and refreshment of natural beauty in the surroundings. At the earliest stages of childhood these influences probably have more formative value than we realize: but as the child develops, the need becomes more insistent. As he reaches out for more friends and a larger community outside the family circle, so will he explore a wider area of his surroundings, and as his expeditions grow in length his contact with nature will, if given the chance, play an important part in the moulding of his character. Rambling or camping with friends and holiday companions, he develops hobbies and interests through which his knowledge of nature and of life expands into a realization of man's place in the scheme of things which will form the proper background to his later thoughts and actions. And when he founds his own family, the human relationships he creates may be enriched by a love of those outside things which all can share.

At the mature stages of life the higher values of beautiful sur-

Harvest near Thornhill, Perth. The familiar farm landscape of traditional husbandry, seen here, is being changed by techniques of higher production on the land.

roundings become more understandable and more eagerly sought. Combined with some scientific and biological knowledge the working and ways of nature provide a standard of proportion which may pervade all thought, helping it to keep on an even keel; and just as the ballast or keel of a ship helps to keep the centre of gravity in the right place on a rough sea, so does that appreciation of landscape, that understanding of the balance which sustains it, enable thought to launch on deep waters.

In old age, a lifelong habit of finding support and consolation in nature's beauty is of greater value than ever before. For the old, perhaps more than for any other section of the community, there is the need for a life close to nature, where the changing seasons and all the various moods of climate and colour can be appreciated to the full: for these are among the blessings which remain to the last.

A scene in the Rhondda Valley. Typical of much of the tragic industrial legacy with which Britain is burdened. The Civic Trust has published a report on this Rhondda problem. The surrounding landscape still makes possible the visual absorption of a newly designed settlement linked to the hills.

At no stage of human development from the cradle to the grave should humanity be deprived of these vitalizing powers.

Through the early stages of his evolution and up to the eighteenth century man had this natural environment and accepted it without thought. Its real importance in the life of the people was not appreciated, however, and the period when changing conditions made the need for it greater than ever before was precisely the period when huge populations, drawn to industry, were cut off completely from their natural surroundings and left to live in conditions of unspeakable ugliness and squalor in overcrowded towns. This is not to say that the countryman's life has been free from misery, poverty and discomfort: the agricultural worker's lot in times of depression has probably been far harder than the lives of city workers, but, however bad their conditions, they have escaped the degrading effects of overcrowding in grim surroundings, and their work in the

open air has given satisfactions unknown to the people of the slums and mining districts, and almost unknown even to those who have escaped to suburbia.

The creation of slums and distressed areas was an outrage against nature—the result of allowing false values to overrule natural laws on a large scale—and the landscape it brought was a measure of its social and ecological results. The lesson has taught us, at least, the importance of good housing, wide streets and adequate parks and gardens: of the maintenance over as large an area as possible of a healthy agriculture adapted to the needs of the population; and of the need for preserving all we can of the wild untouched country that remains to us. But it has hardly brought home to us yet the real need for seeing man as part of his surroundings, nor made us understand our profound relationship with the landscape.

Our failure in this respect has shown at its worst in Britain in our towns: but the reaction from ugliness in the towns has only led us to extend the ugliness into the countryside. In attempting to escape from the towns, the very same mistakes which had made towns unbearable have been extended into suburbs and into most of the more popular country and seaside districts. In all these sad areas of ribbon-development and villadom, as well as in the industrial areas and many of the towns, a new landscape has to be created if our faith in the future is to be justified. That new landscape may be, in parts, different from anything we have known, but it could be fine and dignified, well adapted to an advanced civilization without loss of contact with the earth and its own natural beauty.

In spite of the disastrous extent of 'urban spread', much of the loveliest country is still unspoilt: and how passionately we long to save that in its unchanged condition is a measure of our dissatisfaction with some recent developments. This remaining country is of two types—the 'wild' and the cultivated. The wilder type is not really wild in this country, since nearly all of it is grazed and farmed in some degree, and nowhere is the forest left free to develop as it will. Nevertheless it is the wildest we possess; and of very great beauty. The need for saving as much as we can of this need hardly be stressed. Louis Mumford has expressed it well in *The Culture of Cities:*

> It is precisely because our culture has reached a higher stage of development that we can no longer be satisfied with impoverished conceptions of environment.
>
> ... We respect as never before the infinite variety of nature ... and wish to preserve it to the utmost degree .... It is precisely those of us who recognize the value of mechanization and standardization and universalization who must be most alert to the need for providing an equal place for the complementary set of activities—the wild, the various, the spontaneous, the natural as opposed to the human, the lonely as opposed to the collective. A habitat so planned as to form a continuous background to a delicately graded scale of human feelings and values is the prime requisite of a cultivated life. Where that is lacking, men will fumble uneasily with substitutes, or starve.[1]

The pressure of increasing population and industry threaten the wilder stretches of landscape with extinction. To allow these precious

[1] L. Mumford, *The Culture of Cities*, Secker & Warburg, 1938, pp. 335–6.

Hill farm in Mull. An isolated upland farm maintaining 'marginal' economy by traditional methods under difficult conditions. Such land is now capable of improvement and increased yield. Given more wind protection and the improvement of pasture its production would be raised without going to the lengths of factory farming as seen on p. 269.

solitudes to shrink piecemeal and to let buildings dominate even these, is to murder a vital part of our heritage. It is a destruction of irretrievable resources held in trust for future generations and for which the future will hold us responsible. The extension of agriculture into the wilder uplands, formerly thought to be uneconomic, is becoming a threat to land that must now be regarded as a vestigial relic. The new roads bring cars and car parks; these, and even the hordes of hikers emanating from the access points, all threaten the destruction of the very thing they come to see.

Agriculture in the higher farming areas of Britain was formerly the surest way of preserving a beautiful and almost unique type of landscape. Gradual changes of system and ownership were geared to the need for preserving fertility and biological balance. Today the application of industrial methods of farming have far more dangerous implications for the landscape, and changes can occur much faster

Shaftesbury, Dorset. The small settlement seen within its landscape setting seems to belong to its context, adding interest to its surroundings.

than in the past. Short-term gain is more easily assessed than long-term fertility, and much is being done without any clear knowledge of where it may lead. Warnings such as that of Rachel Carson in *Silent Spring* carry little weight, and perhaps we need a disaster such as an epidemic, to convince us that battery hens and diseased calves are a short-term speculation not to be tolerated by the nation as a whole. Factory farming as we see it now, often debases the landscape —plainly and immediately to be seen. This pointer, or indication, may be more relevant—more meaningful—than the world is ready to understand.

We have reached a stage where the control and conscious design of the landscape has become definitely a human responsibility. No longer can it be left to the hazards and chances of events. By refusing to acknowledge that responsibility we cannot evade it, for we continue to build and to create new scenery. Refusal to accept responsibility means only the extension of a worthless way of life.

Our growing population seems now to need space for recreation rather than for agriculture. But this situation is likely to be reversed quite soon unless some drastic change occurs in the rate of population increase. We have not so far faced this possibility and we act as if still in fear of a falling population. Those planning large tracts of open country for the recreation of an industrial population should perhaps foresee a time when rising world population and food prices will once again put a premium on home products. Some experts believe this may happen within the next thirty years.

Agriculture in its earlier stages alters the landscape through the play of circumstances and not by conscious planning. The first step towards conscious landscape planning is taken when people make gardens: at a later stage the principles first learnt in the course of garden-making are found to be applicable on a different scale to the wider landscape, as happened in England in the eighteenth century and has occurred more recently in America.

The development of landscape planning in its modern form does not favour an extension of garden type into the countryside. Attempts to do that in the days of formal gardens failed and few vestiges remain today. We have realized that variety of character is our greatest asset: wild landscape must remain wild, and agricultural landscape rural. High productivity in farmland creates a characteristic and lovely landscape so long as natural balance is preserved. Beyond that point, when an industrial urban pattern is imposed, the danger-signals are apparent and can only be disregarded at our peril. The scale of agricultural scenery, variable according to farming types in different regions, allows pleasant contrasts and satisfies the eye up to the point when open fields become so vast or so small that the soil itself is threatened. Most of the incidents enriching agricultural landscape, such as tree belts and hedges, have functional values. The farmsteads, even with the larger modern buildings, properly sited in relation to open space and shelter are welcome, but a landscape barren of trees and hedges or overcrowded with disparate sheds and buildings is a warning of danger ahead.

This relationship between the use and beauty of land is the main concern of landscape architecture, which may be defined as the conscious design of man's out-door environment. Landscape-planning should ensure the proper adaptation of land to the use it is to serve, having regard to the beauty of nature as being a primary condition of human development.

The need for conscious design of landscape becomes greater as the risk of imbalance increases with the growing demands on land use. No longer can we feel that any type of scenery can safely develop under natural laws. The changes are moving too fast and the risks are too great. Visual standards and biological values must be combined. The developing profession of landscape design can be one link uniting art and science for the conception of a worthwhile future.

Before passing on to consider how this art should be applied in the future, it is necessary to survey, even though briefly, the evolution of landscape in this country in the past from the time man first began to meddle with it. Its geological evolution is beyond the scope of this book, though clearly of no less importance to those who would take upon themselves the responsibility of planning for the future.[1]

---

[1] The geological evolution of landscape has been dealt with by A. K. Lobeck, *Geomorphology*, McGraw Hill, 1939. See also the Reading List p. 394.

2

The Man-Made Landscape

The expression 'man-made landscape' applied to a highly populated country like England has become familiar, but it deserves some examination. How far does man really create a landscape? Obviously the physical conformation of the land, its contours, its geological structure, its atmospheric and cloud effects, its sea, lakes and rivers are its most dominating features. Nevertheless, because of man's inter-relation with the soil and with vegetation and because of his own power of altering and building on the surface, that superficial aspect is largely within his control and, because of his nearness to it and his identity with it, it looms very large on his horizon.

Biotic Influence

Ecologists use the term 'biotic' action for all human and animal influences acting on the environment. Grazing animals—wild or domesticated—such as rabbits, deer and sheep, exert a powerful effect on the landscape by preventing the growth of saplings and encouraging the spread of grassland at the expense of forest. Beavers may alter the course of rivers and the outline of lakes. Moles and other burrowing animals increase the drainage of the surface. Human beings destroy the forest and drain the land on a bigger scale. They cultivate the soil and grow crops; they make dams and dykes and sea-walls; they quarry and mine, and they build cities. All those influences change the appearance of the surface in varying degrees and react on the rate of erosion. Man's greatest power over his physical environment really lies in his ability to hasten or to prevent the destruction of the land that nurtures him. Man can create a Sahara in a fraction of the time taken by natural causes to bring about the same result.

In so far as the landscape can really be described as 'man-made'

Ancient stone circle, Castlerigg, Cumberland. Many such remains keep us in touch with the ceremonies and activities of early man. This one in the Lake District, beautifully sited on the valley land below the mountain, gives a sense of continuity with the past undimmed by the intervening farm and field pattern.

the activities which have brought about the results are agriculture, religion, war and defence, industry, building, travel and recreation. Agriculture was the primary and most extensive means by which man modified his environment in the early stages, while defence provided points of special dramatic emphasis. Mediæval castles and walled citadels come as occasional but striking incidents in an otherwise agricultural scene. The scars of more recent wars—trenches, tank-traps and concrete emplacements, which looked impressive enough in their day, have left little mark. Today the spread of industry and housing can be seen encroaching on both the open countryside and its monuments, changing the scene as we watch it.

Churches and Religious Monuments

Religious monuments have always been centrally placed at the heart of a community's life, though not necessarily within the settlements. Stonehenge and other ancient ritual-rings served a district and not any single settlement, while the same may be said of the barrows and burial-places usually sited on an important skyline which, in addition to their religious function, served as landmarks. Christian churches have always been the central feature of town or village—the climax of a group of buildings—easily dominating, by the height of spire or tower, all the other buildings of the cluster and often crowning appropriately the surrounding contours as well. Only in recent years, with the decline of orthodox religion, have other buildings risen up to challenge this pre-eminence. It may be thought symbolic of the present state of flux and philosophical uncertainty that office blocks, cinemas, hotels, power stations, and emporia vie with each other by their size for mastery of the skyline. In a land of skyscrapers even the forms of the steeple and tower have

Church, Oundle, Northants. This compact settlement with the church spire as climax, seen as the background of everyday life and in touch with nature through its setting of trees and river, pleases the eye by its composition. It symbolizes a balanced state of human society.

Industrial skyline, Corby, Northants. Chimneys and mechanical equipment dominate the scenery in our industrial towns. Humanity loses contact with nature when large expanses of land covered with concrete and metal are un-relieved by foliage or natural forms. Productivity increases at the expense of all other life, as if man could exist alone.

been borrowed and enlarged, but through over-frequent repetition these forms lose all symbolic significance and remind us only of those tropical ant-heaps, like spires of clay having no particular relation-ship to the land forms on which they stand.

Industry and Homes

Residential buildings and industry in their early stages affected the landscape chiefly by the clearance of forest. The early potteries and iron-smelting works have left little trace: the flint-mines rather more. These, and the houses people lived in when Stonehenge was built, or even when Grim's Dyke was dug, have left faint vestiges of interest to archæologists but of no importance in the present-day landscape. With the increase of population and the elaboration of its needs, buildings come to dominate the landscape, until they may become a dangerous threat to the very life of a people dependent, ultimately, on agriculture.

Recreation calls for special space and design only at the later stages when population-pressure and elaboration of needs have already set in. The earliest vestiges our landscape still holds of sports grounds, as such, include a few Roman stadiums and a few tilt yards, bowling greens and archery butts of the middle ages. Hunting, poaching and the simpler primitive games needed no special sites.

Communications

Travel, even at the earliest stage, scars enduring marks on the land surface. The tread of feet of early man and his cattle, compressing the soil and establishing lines of communcation and rights of

Roman road, Blackstone Edge, Lancs. The solid stone construction remains visible in a few places, and although many modern roads use the Roman routes, the earlier green roads in upland areas have changed less through the ages.

way over long ages, left impressions which may even outlast those of modern roads and railways. The old green roads have been used constantly as farm tracks. Today heavy farm implements tend to damage the surface and farmers often widen the tracks, or give them hard surfaces, making them available to visiting cars. In this way they often lose their ancient character and become in use and appearance much like the modern roads, though they still follow the primitive lines of communication.

Contemporary landscape is scarred, not only by the ever growing demands of wheeled traffic, but also by the aeroplane and all its paraphernalia. However, air travel does provide a new view of the countryside. On departure and arrival the region around an airport draws special attention, and we see a bird's eye view spread out below like a model—a view whose visual quality has received little attention, though it holds so much of interest. This aspect will be considered again on page 376.

The Primaeval Scene

Humanity is a late-comer in a geological and evolutionary sense, even though the first origins of Palæolithic man are lost in the misty past. We know he lived in inter-glacial phases of the Quaternary Ice Age and that his first origins must be sought in Tertiary times. But he can have had little lasting influence on his surroundings at that stage, and the only signs we have of his existence in Britain up to the end of the Ice Age are charred bones of the beasts he hunted and the implements he used for hunting and fighting. What are the earliest enduring marks of human activity? What are the oldest signs our landscape still retains of primitive man? Food-gatherers left nothing, hunters practically nothing, lasting in the scenery to remind us of their activities.

In a book called *The Old Straight Track*, Alfred Watkins, a Herefordshire archæologist, put forward a theory of tracks made by early Stone Age man in Britain. These tracks, in his belief, were sighted from hill-crest to hill-crest, leading in a straight line from inland districts to the coast. The theory requires the assumption that men of the early Stone Age traded in salt or other essential goods and that these tracks were necessary to such trade. They ante-date the green roads along the ridges, made by Bronze Age man, which still exist, by long ages. The evidence for the existence of these first roads is given in the form of photographs which seem convincing in the absence of any other explanation to account for the features they show. How far the theory may be borne out by later research remains to be seen. If the author is right in his deductions, these notches cut in the skyline, with the sarsen stones set up on end, these mounds and ponds which, he claims, all mark definite tracks and are found in strict alignment with the skyline marks across the intervening lower land, must be the oldest vestiges of human action in the British landscape. They are by no means insignificant in the present scenery and were clearly intended to be visible at great distances. Part of the evidence brought forward to prove this antiquity is that they could never have been sighted or marked out at any date after the forest had invaded this country which, in that early stage, was still arctic steppe and moorland. This places their period near the end of the Ice Age.

In order to gain an impression of how long ago that was we have only to realize that Britain was still part of the European Continent. There was no English Channel, and the Dogger Bank was a low ridge of peaty land lying below the great Chalk Down which extended from the South Downs to join the chalk in France. Yet the submergence of that land, finally making this island, was the last geological change of any significance that has occurred, and was, of course, nothing in comparison with the great changes of earlier periods.

But if we measure the time that has passed in terms of human life-spans we realize, perhaps with surprise, that it is not after all so very long. Geologists date the last retreat of the ice at somewhere about 7000 B.C. and the submergence of the continental isthmus at somewhere between 5000 and 3000 B.C. If we estimate a human lifetime at three score years and ten, there has been time for only about seventy-one lives since Britain finally became an island, or 130 lives since the retreat of the ice and the Stone Age. Even if we take a generation of thirty years as the unit, the figures are still low, and we find that we are only removed from the Early Stone Age by some 300 ancestors in direct line, two of whom have been known to most of us in our own life-time. A company not numerous enough to fill the House of Commons, but which could be accommodated in four two-decker buses in a rush-hour. These thoughts should surely bring consolation to sensitive mortals suffering from a realization of human shortcomings.

When for the last time in Britain the ice receded, early Stone Age man was still the dominant human species. Modern science fixes that period at somewhere about 9000 years ago. He must have lived then in an arctic climate in a land of almost treeless tracts. If we accept Mr Watkins's theories, the tracks he speaks of must have been marked out in the first few thousand years after the retreat of the ice, before the birch forest gained an extensive foothold.

The marks of the Ice Age are still clearly evident in our landscape. There are valleys hollowed out by glaciers in all the highland districts of north and west; and there are rock surfaces planed flat and scoured by the moving ice. The direction in which it travelled is unmistakable. There are sediments of gravel at points where the ice was stayed long enough for an accumulation to collect at the melting edge. Drift soils, mostly boulder clay (called after the rounded, ice-worn, travel-worn lumps of rock which it contains), cover much of the pre-glacial rock-formations in the flatter lowlands of the Midlands and eastern England. There is none of this deposit south of a line joining the Thames and the Severn, and the evidence points to that line as marking the extreme southern limit of the ice. The material was collected by scouring, breaking and grinding of the rocks over which the ice moved. All this loose material freezes on to the underside of a glacier and is carried on with the ice until it melts.

For those who can read it, the history of the vegetation since that time is plainly to be read in peat bogs, some of which carry that history back into inter-glacial periods and even earlier. Bog peat, composed of vegetable matter in a condition of arrested decay,

Snowdonia National Park. A landscape carved by ice, with the detritus massed in the foothills and damming the valleys to contain the tarns. The erosion of wind and water is still visibly shaping the steep high contours. Such landscapes are the nearest thing to wild primitive scenery available in Britain.

contains parts of plants many of which (particularly pollen grains) remain recognizable under microscopic examination after many thousands of years. Whenever the snow and ice melted for long enough to allow the growth of low plants, patches of damp ground with impeded drainage would favour the formation of bog peat composed of the remains of mosses and heaths growing in such positions. There, almost unchanged by time since the bogs first formed, lie the pollen grains so lavishly scattered from plants in or near the bog. Pollen grains in spring, dead leaves in autumn, layer by layer, packed close and compressed by time, enable the botanist to count the years, and the proportion of different plants in the neighbourhood, and so to learn how one type of vegetation succeeded another under changing climatic conditions. Our knowledge of human history can yet be enriched by further discoveries such as that of Tollund Man, preserved in a Jutland bog and recently brought to light.

Each recession of the ice favoured the spread of scrub and forest, the birch, and then the pine, being the first colonizers of the arctic steppe. The outlying position of the isthmus, dominated on the whole by oceanic rather than by continental climatic conditions, must have favoured the growth of trees in the long intervals between the icy periods, and early man must have adapted himself to many changes of environment, welcoming when it came the comparative comfort of a woodland life with all the fuel and shelter it brought, but not becoming so dependent on these as to be obliged to move south with the forest in the long bleak intervals.

After the final recession of the ice, about 9000 B.C., the climate appears to have been cold and dry like many of the arctic areas of today, with a vegetation of low alpine shrubs and creeping plants which alone could endure the icy winds and driven snow. In the next 1000 years an improvement of conditions favoured the spread of birch and pine forest northwards; and in the east of England the first trees of the deciduous forest made their appearance. These were hazel, oak, elm and alder. This was followed in the next 1000 years by the 'Boreal' period—a period of warmer weather and increasing tree-growth. Birch forest seems to have held sway over all other vegetation at the beginning of the Boreal times, but pine gained a stronger hold and became dominant towards the end of that millennium: hazel was also spreading very rapidly, probably as the undergrowth of pine and mixed forests when other deciduous trees began to make an appearance. The scenery then must have been rather like that of Finnish and Siberian forests of the present day.

Between 6000 and 5000 B.C. the climate became warmer and damper, favouring the deciduous trees and especially alder, which in the wetter regions became a dominant species. Lime trees show a marked increase at this time and the pines were diminishing in the south and retreating to the west and north. Deciduous trees spread rapidly, but they were checked in some areas by excessive damp,

The Ridgeway, Berks. This ancient track, sited just below the highest ridge of the Berkshire Downs, served a population of herdsmen depending on the well-drained upland chalk, where the surrounding forest could easily be kept at bay, giving way to springy pasture. The track connected the hill forts and burial places along the ridge and today is still in use as a farm track.

which favoured instead the formation of sphagnum moss, peat bogs and heather. Boggy moorland is capable of spreading and driving back the forest, even in the warmer periods, whenever a high rainfall and strong winds act together on a land surface retentive of moisture. So we find the bogs on the flatter wind-swept areas, often high up in the mountains and hilly districts where the rainfall is high, the atmosphere constantly damp and where the full force of the wind is felt. Round about 4000 B.C. the damp warm climatic phase known as the Atlantic period reached its peak, and there is evidence to show that at that time many areas previously wooded succumbed to the spreading bog peat. Human activity probably hastened or even caused the spread of peat in Britain by destroying forest.

Early Herdsmen

Our human forerunners preferred the well-drained soils: and civilization made some of its greatest strides on the limestones and chalk of the south and east. A characteristic of the Neolithic culture is the herding of livestock, and it is by means of his grazing cattle that man first begins to exercise control over the vegetation of his landscape.

This development must have taken place in Britain about 2000 years or more before the birth of Christ, in the 'Sub-Boreal' period which was conditioned by a climate very much drier than had been known since the Ice Age, and dry even by comparison with our own. This dry period favoured the forest at the expense of the bog-peat in the wetter districts, but at the other end of the scale it favoured man and his cattle at the expense of the forest, and much open space and hill grassland must have been cleared of forest growth at that time, thus producing the conditions under which higher forms of agriculture could evolve.

At the 'food collecting' and early hunting stages of his development, man leaves little or no trace of his existence, but when he begins to herd cattle in large numbers he acquires a dangerous power, for heavy grazing destroys forest and, in dry climates, may even destroy the grass and set up soil erosion, making the land in course of time uninhabitable. This we see happening now in the African grassland zone of East Africa. In Britain the climatic and numerical conditions can never have reached the danger point, though considerable denudation of forest must have occurred on upland districts and on the lighter soils.

Hill Camps and Man-made Terraces

It is rather an astonishing fact that the landscape received, during the course of the Neolithic and Bronze Age cultures, more dramatic shaping by human hands than it has known again. All the great earthworks, camps and hill terraces, especially those of the chalk lands, where they are found in most abundance, are on a scale that is almost geological in scope. They present a skyline carved by man as an enduring background to the scenery of today, and they bear witness to that distant and almost forgotten past. However, the power of machinery now makes possible a faster and greater change.

Lynchets on Chaddenwick Down, Wilts. The great carvings of the chalk lands, whatever their purpose may have been, impress us still by their strength and extent. Only with the aid of machines has modern man emulated their impact on the land forms, but often without their grace.

We easily fail to realize how numerous and extensive those early carvings are, and what a vast work of civilization they represent; but even the most careless observer cannot overlook them. Nor can we forget such things as the White Horse of Uffington, the Mizmaze of Salisbury Plain, the great stone circles and other works of mystery and art which still adorn the hills and were probably connected with the people of the earthworks. Whatever the origin of these people and whatever the purposes of their works, they were clearly a people of the hills, shunning the lower lands and the forests, and it is largely on that account that their carvings are so impressive today. They are seen from far off on the highest ridges and skylines—land which, though it is for the most part still clear of forest was, for many centuries, used only for sheep grazing.

The chalk springs rose at higher elevations in the past than they do now, and water presented no problem. The camps themselves, such as Uffington Castle, Maiden Castle, Martinsell and very many others, mostly on the chalk, crown the hills, but the hill terraces or 'lynchets' are far more extensive in number and distribution. If we could be sure that these terraces were evidence of early agriculture, they would indeed be striking examples of the permanence of the work of Cain. It has often been stated that they are the result of Saxon ploughing, but their character and position are in keeping with the earlier hill culture, and to the student of landscape they seem clearly to belong to the Neolithic or Bronze Age rather than to Saxon civilization, which chose the forest clearings of the valley. C. S. Orwin, author of *The Open Fields*, and other authorities, have shown that they could never have been made by the plough alone, and if their use was arable farming, why did these people use the bare escarpments rather than the plateau soils? It must have been hard work carving the terraces out of the living rock (chalk, limestone, red sandstone and other formations): it would have been harder still to have created cultivable soil in such positions. Later on, the Celts cultivated the deeper soils of the plateaux, and the remains of their rectangular fields surrounded by rough banks are still discernible at the present time; but they are not on the scale of the terrace lynchets, and are difficult to find without the aid of the one-

Uffington Castle and the White Horse on the Berkshire Downs. The sculptured ramparts and the figure carved in chalk still dominate the landscape near Uffington. The plateau land, now cultivated, shows a new pattern. In earlier centuries, since man first farmed the downs, all would have been pasture.

Tree belts date either from the eighteenth century or later. Some have been planted in this decade.

The stream which must have formed the 'Manger' or combe below the horse now rises at a lower level.

inch-to-the-mile Ordnance Survey maps, on which they are marked. Some of the Celtic fields have been overgrown by forest, but those on the open downs appear clearly in aerial photographs. They, too, are often referred to as 'lynchets' though it would cause less confusion if the word applied only to the hill terraces whose character and appearance are quite distinct from the Celtic work.

With no knowledge of archæology, but only some knowledge of soils and the economics of soil moving, it is tempting to guess that the people of the earthworks would have grown their arable crops on

Charmy Down, north of Bath. Underlying the stone-wall field boundaries in use today can be seen the older pattern of Celtic fields laid out in small rectangles.

the plateaux, leaving, perhaps, no trace of field boundaries. The purpose of the lynchets remains a problem. Some at least of the more dramatic lynchet groups tempt the imagination to see them as temporary fairgrounds or ceremonial sites, with accommodation for tents or hutments in the terraces overlooking the ritual below. The extensive lynchets on the Ridgeway near Bishopstone, on the northern slope of the Berkshire downs, would be beautifully adapted to such use.

The Plough

The end of the Bronze Age and the beginning of the Iron Age seem to have corresponded with a change of climate. The Sub-

Atlantic period, lasting from about 1000 B.C. to about A.D. 1000, produced conditions probably less favourable to man, but the use of a heavier iron-shod plough, drawn by oxen, made possible the cultivation of deeper soils, and the terrors of the forest waned. Arable agriculture became widespread.

The type of cultivation and of the implements used influence the shapes, sizes and siting of fields. Rough picks or wooden ploughs could cultivate only shallow soils, and on the deeper soils it would have been more difficult to keep the forest at bay. Drainage problems would not have arisen on the chalk and limestone uplands, so one would expect the earliest cultivations to have occurred on the flatter areas of these, probably on land already cleared of forest by pastoral farming. The heavy plough introduced by the Belgæ brought the cultivation down to lower levels, and the harnessing of oxen to the plough changed the shape of the fields from a small rectangle to a long strip. This pattern still extends over vast areas of Europe and can be seen in Britain at Laxton, Nottinghamshire.

When the Romans first invaded Britain they found an agricultural rather than a nomadic people, though the large proportion of the land was still dense forest. Cæsar described the British as a woodland people fighting behind barricades of tree trunks felled across the forest tracks. Nevertheless, there must have been wide areas of open cultivation round the villages, camps and dykes. And these would have given parts of the country, at least, a well-lived-in human scenery.

Roman Occupation

Roman complaints of the British climate surprise us so little that we usually forget that the climate of that time was, in fact, a good deal worse than it is now. The Sub-Atlantic period must have been hard indeed on the conquerors from the sunnier South. It is not surprising, when we examine the climate changes which took place over North-Western Europe, that the 'Dark Ages' ended only after A.D. 1000, coinciding with an improvement in the weather, when the present equable climate set in.

The Romans, during their occupation, made considerable changes in the landscape. They made little use of the existing green roads along the ridges of the hills, but their own more solidly constructed roads have left less impression after 2000 years than those old British tracks, though a few stretches are still visible on the surface. Roman methods of road construction and of transport enabled them to disregard the indications of the contours, so that the pattern of this road system contrasts strongly with that of the British pattern which emphasizes the physical topography of the land. Where the Roman roads are still in use we are reminded of their origin by their long straight lines, but their superficial appearance has changed with the rest of the modern system. Where they are disused they are almost lost. The old British tracks, on the contrary, have kept much of their original character, being in use, nearly everywhere, if only as farm tracks and rights of way.

Much land was drained and reclaimed for agriculture during the Roman occupation, but may have relapsed into forest and fen later. The fact that Britain was exporting grain to the Continent during the occupation proves that there must have been large areas under arable cultivation. Both the Celtic and the heavier wheeled plough were in use, the former by the natives and the latter on the Roman estates.

It was, however, the walled cities and the Romans' architecture which made their most enduring contribution to the British landscape, and give us to the present day that sense of Roman efficiency and thoroughness which we associate with the character of the conquerors. Outside the cities, sites of Roman villas and estates are known in some quantity—most of these are on the foot-hills of the chalk or on other porous rocks—but, unlike the camps, they show up little in the general scenery of the present day. Aerial photography has given the clue to the finding of these as of most of the early cultivation. Much that remains of the past can be seen better from

Watling Street, Yorks. The A66 follows the line of the Roman road built for the legionaries of the northern outposts. The adjoining field pattern has grown parallel to it, and seems to borrow something of its rigid character.

Roman villa, Northleigh, Oxon. From the air the plan of an important home shows clearly. The site remains a settlement, having little regard to the Roman plan.

that distant view—when a large area is seen as a whole—than at closer range.

The British, left to defend themselves against Saxon invaders, made more earthworks on a very localized system, vainly attempting to defend certain areas in a piecemeal way. Such, according to Pitt-Rivers, is the history of Grim's ditch, south-west of Salisbury, and of Bokerley Dyke which cuts across it near Martin, off the Salisbury-Blandford Road.

Saxon Landscape

The Saxon invaders, in contrast to the Romans, were an agricultural people with little use for towns and stone buildings. They brought with them a rural system, already partly evolved, which they adapted to this country and which, developing here, gained a long-enduring supremacy in the south and Midlands. Their log-houses clustered round a church and manor house, also of rough-hewn timber, and the arable land surrounding these was divided into three large fields to suit their three-year rotation (first, wheat or rye; second, barley or oats; third, fallow). Several strips in different parts of the field might belong to one owner. Beyond the fields was an area of rough pasture where grazing animals kept down the scrub and gave the arable land protection from the encroachment of forest. The inhabitants of the village exercised rights in all three: the forest was available to any who wished to take game or timber, and an increase of population and stock would automatically enlarge the

Shilton, Oxon. An integrated village cluster, now built in Cotswold stone, but still typical of the Saxon pattern of settlement. The asymmetry of the grouping seems to fit the surrounding countryside naturally.

Braunton, Devon. An area where open fields still exist and the landscape typical of the old strip-farming system can be seen. The scale of the panels relates to a man's work.

Many European agricultural systems still have open fields giving a similar pattern, but these are usually surrounded by forest on higher land.

grazing area. So long as settlements were few and small the difficulty was to keep the forest and its wild animals at bay rather than the risk of destroying their resources. The arable fields were ploughed by joint effort, each man contributing oxen, implements and labour according to the size of his holding. Cattle were grazed on the common grazing land or on the weeds and stubble of the fallow field, thus manuring the latter for next year's crop. It was an organized system far in advance of the Celtic fields and well suited to the few crops then available and to the simple needs of the time; and it held sway, in the district where it was established, throughout

Scattered holdings in Eire. The pattern typical of Celtic settlements still survives in many western areas of Britain, in strong contrast to the compactly grouped villages of the south and midland areas.

Norman and mediæval times. It was a system which could be extended, when required, to heavier soils: for the furrows dividing off the individual strips could be deepened to carry off the surface water, and the strips between raised into a broad ridge providing adequate drainage for each man's plot, which had no other form of demarcation. This open field system was only finally superseded in 1801 when the General Enclosure Act was passed, and at Laxton in Nottinghamshire it is possible to get a very clear idea of how it worked. Much of the ridge-and-furrow pastureland so familiar in the present day scenery of the Midlands was once arable, and received its striped pattern under the old strip-farming system;

though there is also a great deal of ridge-and-furrow of later dates formed for drainage.

The western and northern parts of Britain never received the Saxon pattern of development. Their inhabitants, mostly of Celtic stock, inherited a different tradition of more individualistic farming which was compatible with the high rainfall of those districts. Water supply was a governing consideration in the siting of settlements in the south and east, where rainfall was low and only some of the strata water-bearing. In the highland and western districts, water being abundant, the Celt could indulge his taste for solitude and individualism. These factors have preserved a distinct difference of rural pattern to the present day. The nucleated settlement, closely disposed round the church and village green, is seen in its perfection in parts of Essex and Hertfordshire and gives way, as we pass westwards, to scattered farmsteads with little or no definite centre till we find, in Ireland, the opposite extreme, making it hard to say where the village lies; and isolated small holdings make up the parish.

In the wetter districts people depended on stock rather than on grain, and we should expect to find that the open field arable system was never established there. Local differences of system were largely due to the tradition of the settlers: the Jutes who settled in Kent never adopted the open field system, and Danish influence may have suppressed and obliterated the Saxon system in East Anglia.

Norse Influence

The Norsemen left less impression on the country than on the towns: and although new earthworks and defences were made by both sides in the course of the Anglo-Danish wars, it was a period of urban rather than of agricultural development. Nevertheless, in the country districts, feudalism and the power of the Christian Church, both of which were in due course to have marked influence on the landscape, were growing.

If the Saxons and Danes cultivated gardens as distinct from agricultural land they have left no mark. But the period of garden-making in England was approaching.

3

Farm and Garden from the Middle Ages

It is not surprising to find that in this country the leisurely and peaceful art of garden-making was nurtured, along with learning and other signs of a maturing civilization, in the monasteries and abbeys of the Christian Church. Garden design, as Francis Bacon observed, is a late development of evolution.

There is nothing to show that the early Celtic Christian Church, the Irish establishments and those of Iona and Lindisfarne developed any horticultural tradition. Probably, like many of the isolated monasteries of the Balkans and Middle East, they preferred a wild and untouched setting: this tendency is seen too in India and Tibet, where isolated temples are built on rocky hillsides or in steep valleys amid wild surroundings whose striking natural beauty lends an awe-inspiring quality of aloofness. The architecture in such cases is often bound into the rocky foundation, so that the buildings seem to grow out of the land itself. The Celtic monasteries were, in the words of Professor G. M. Trevelyan, 'congregations of hermits'. But the Christian movement that spread in the seventh century from the south of England developed differently, acquiring land and imposing a human-use pattern on it, following the tradition already established in Europe.

The Monastery Lands

From early drawings and plans (such as that of St Gall) and from the remains of others in this country (such as the Abbey of Beaulieu in Hants), we see that these monasteries contained land within the precincts which must have been used as gardens in the modern sense, distinct from the vineyards, orchards and farmlands beyond the walls. Besides the Abbey church and the monks' quarters, all the other buildings, such as hospital, physician's house, the Abbot's

A Greek monastery at Meteora, Thessaly. The walls shaped to the form of the living rock seem to grow from it as a flower from the bud.

FECIT MIHI MAGNA QUI POTENS EST ET SANCTUM NOMEN EJUS

The College of St MARY MAGDALEN in the University of OXFORD Founded by WILLIAM of WAYNFLETE BISHOP of WINCHESTER AD 1457

The courtyard system of building. Traditional for monasteries, palaces and universities, it gave open spaces or gardens suited to the requirements of the buildings to which each related.

house, the guest house, school and so on, each opened on to a garden whose use related to that of the building. The garden lay-out, together with the cloisters and courtyard system of the plan, served to link the buildings together and to make of the various units one whole community. This type of close relationship between grounds and buildings can be seen in monasteries and early settlements throughout the world, and still works well in many British College gardens and in large buildings such as Hampton Court. As a model of a sound workable community system it has probably not yet outgrown its usefulness, and though neglected in the interval might well return to favour in the future.

The Benedictine order aimed at being self-supporting, so that agriculture and horticulture were both practised extensively: and horticulture, in particular, owes much to that period. Even those

Orders whose rule forbade agriculture permitted the physic garden and herbarium for medicinal and other essential needs. The monastery gardens were primarily utilitarian, though we may assume that they were also designed as places for contemplation and rest. In any case, the fish-ponds, made for the breeding of carp, roach, perch and dace for Friday's meals; the dipping-wells and other features whose origin was purely utilitarian became the prototypes of more ornamental features, later on, in the gardens attached to manor houses and other lay buildings.

It must have been a long time before garden design made any further progress in this country. It is essentially an art of peace and can be practised only by people enjoying a fairly comfortable standard of living. The unsettled times just before and just after the Norman Conquest would not have favoured its development outside the walls of monastery and convent.

Norman Influence

The tendency of the Norman Conquest was, at first, retrograde. Warlike destruction, both by the invaders and by the ancient Celtic enemy (ever ready to snatch an opportunity for plunder), fell on the agricultural areas and settlements and much land reverted to forest. The Normans also took possession of most of the remaining forest, subjecting it to 'Forest Law', which checked the extension of cultivation and building in those areas. In spite of these events, however, and with the return of more settled times, the population and the settled areas increased, and the reduction of forest continued at an ever-growing pace. The Statute of Merton in 1235, which first permitted the enclosure of forest by the feudal lords—providing they left enough common land for the needs of their villagers—was ostensibly meant to preserve the essential balance between forest, pasture and arable, and to ensure adequate timber reserves. The feudal lords' taste for hunting coincided conveniently with the need for preserving forest, but the statute proves nevertheless that the forest was dwindling and was now regarded, not as an ever-present menace of encroachment, but as a valuable resource to be preserved by law.

Corfe Castle, Dorset. The dominating positions of the Norman castles and their firm emphatic shapes add splendour to the landscape still. The importance of the castle here matches that of the site, and the landscape gains much from their association.

Saxon architecture, using whole or half logs for the construction of walls, had been an extravagant method of building; and a natural outcome of the new attitude with regard to forest was the use of mud and wattle for building, requiring solid timber only as a framework. This made it possible to draw supplies of coppice growth from the same area at comparatively frequent intervals, for wattle is made from young secondary shoots springing from the roots of felled trees or saplings. Two features still characteristic of our landscape resulted from this development—half-timbered houses, and coppice woods.

'High above the wooden huts and thatched roofs of the Saxon villeins towered the great stone castle and the great stone cathedral.'[1] Neither wattle nor half-timber nor even whole logs could satisfy

[1] G. M. Trevelyan, *History of England*, 3rd edition, Longmans, 1945, p. 136.

the Normans themselves. For them stone alone was good enough and, as in the Roman days, the contrast between conqueror and conquered must always have been strongly emphasized by their respective architecture.

Many of the Norman castles and keeps still enrich our scenery— the Plantagenets chose highly picturesque positions for their strong-holds, and the thick masonry and massive poise of these buildings and battlements, crowning the higher land forms, make them seem a part of their surroundings. Like those lonely temples and monasteries already referred to, they seem to grow out of the living rock and to need no conciliating growth of vegetation.

Home Produce

Presumably the manor houses of this period must have had, at least, herb gardens of sorts, though few illustrations of English examples exist. Vineyards and orchards, we know, were cultivated beyond the walls or moats, and it is surprising to realize that for many centuries the vine was extensively cultivated for wine-making in England. Most of the monasteries owned large vineyards long before the Norman conquest, and the Normans planted many more. Even in this inclement climate, the wine-making tradition, inherited from Europe, died hard.

Herb gardens would have been restricted to the small area inside wall or moat; and this fact, together with their practical purposes, would have indicated formal design. Clearly there was no thought of any other type of lay-out until more peaceful times allowed the garden to extend over larger areas and to serve other than purely utilitarian purposes. The first necessities were 'simples' of every kind, and the women of those early centuries had to depend on their garden produce not only for kitchen use but also for medicines, cosmetics, scent and disinfectants. Where, today, one can buy furniture polish, soap, insecticides and all the rest of the household necessities, the woman of that period knew how to make these things out of wild or home-grown herbs or got along without them. Honey was used instead of sugar, so bee-keeping was general, and in gardens of later centuries we find special adaptations of design to accommodate the apiary. Few vegetables were available in the middle ages, but the winter meat must have needed a strong flavouring of dried herbs as a change from imported spices: at that stage of agricultural development it was still necessary to kill animals for butcher's meat in the autumn. Winter fodder was scarce and only the breeding stock and ploughing oxen could be maintained. Meat was preserved by drying or salting. It is not clear when the 'ice house' was first used, but the idea was simple and may have evolved at an early stage: certainly there were ice houses in use until it became possible to feed stock well through the winter. Many of these ice houses still exist, forming a fairly prominent feature, usually outside the garden itself but within easy reach of the manor or farmhouse. They consist of a large mound of earth planted with trees, and having a passage leading from the direction of some pond from which the earth was excavated, into a vaulted chamber, built of brick or stone below ground level, and kept cool by the mound of earth and the shade of the trees on top. During a hard frost ice was taken from the pond and packed into the vault around the meat.

Water for Use and Pleasure

The treatment of wells, pools and water generally, according to its uses, has always been an important motive of garden design. The fish-ponds and dipping-wells of the monasteries were repeated in the secular gardens of the middle ages, but in addition we find fountains and pools of more ornamental design, which may have been introduced originally as drinking-wells or foot-baths, but which indicate a growing use of the garden as a place of pleasure and relaxation rather than as a mere adjunct of kitchen and still-room. This use of water may first have been borrowed from sunnier lands in the East, where the Crusaders would have seen gardens whose main attraction was the sight and sound of running water framed in shady groves, and whose fountains, canals and runnels were the central features. Water was a less urgent need in the English climate, and a little of it went a long way, but its more elaborate display led to other refinements of garden design; we find the gardens growing both in size and in variety of incident as time goes on. 'Tree gardens' may also have derived inspiration from the East, for we hear of them at this early stage, although the prints and drawings of later and more elaborate gardens suggest that they were not a common feature, and the gardens of the Tudor and Stuart periods seemed to make little use of trees larger than pears, apples and cherries.

Games and Playgrounds

Sport and recreation began to influence the lay-out of village and of large estates through the need for tilt-yards and archery butts. Areas specially designed for these activities may still be found in the gardens of a few old manor houses. The tilting-yard was simply a level turfed area surrounded by walls or banks, and the archery butts are sometimes found on long narrow terraces, with a recess set back in the wall by the target for the safety of the scorer.

The village green was probably the usual scene of such activities. 'Idle' ball games and also coursing and cock-fighting were evidently practised, but not openly, since they were frowned upon by the authorities as being valueless for military training. Even bowling-greens were not designed as such until the arrow had been superseded as a weapon of war.

The Black Death

The appearance of the countryside underwent an important change after the Black Death of 1348–9, owing to the very serious fall in the population. In Saxon times such an event would have favoured the forest, and much land would have been lost to cultivation: but the feudal system brought about a different result, and we find, already starting, the modern type of change depending on the prosperity of agriculture. Land which had been arable became pasture, since one shepherd with a flock of sheep could deal with more land than many ploughmen and ox-teams. In this way the lords found they could keep their land in productive use in spite of labour

Chipping Camden, Glos. One of the loveliest of the Cotswold towns enriched by the 'golden hoof', the sheep grazing on the limestone hills. The oolitic limestone, whose texture in itself gives pleasure, was used for buildings and roofing tiles. It is well adapted to fine masonry and the local character of the area is pronounced.

The group, with its glimpse through a narrow lane to a wider expanse beyond, framed by the single tree, satisfies by its simple composition.

shortage. English wool was found to be the equal of any, and when the wool and cloth trades began to flourish the character of farming in this country underwent a permanent change.

The Wool Trade

As the population increased again, many found a better living in the new industry than on the land; but agriculture also received fresh impetus and direction from the growing trade in the towns, whose need not only for food but also for wool, stimulated mixed farming methods. The 'golden hoof' began to enrich the arable land, and the course was set for England to become, some centuries later, the leading stock-breeding country of the world. The climate, so favourable to turf and grazing stock, would probably have indicated this course in any case. The predominant green colour of these islands strikes any traveller from other lands; and that fine natural pasture, with the possibility of grazing even highly specialized breeds under natural open-air conditions through most of the year, has moulded the character of our agriculture, our trade and our landscape.

Sheep had been kept for the sake of their wool for many centuries: the Cistercian monks in Yorkshire had shown that sheep-farming was a profitable way of dealing with light soils, and their example had been widely followed in Scotland and the north of England as early as the twelfth century. After the Black Death, when the south and east took to sheep-farming, it was natural that here too the higher districts should be devoted mainly to sheep. As in earlier pastoral periods of Neolithic and Bronze Age cultures, the chalk and the limestone again became centres of human activity. The Western Highlands remained important breeding-grounds for sheep as they have done ever since, but the woollen trade and the cloth industry developed along the limestone and chalk escarpments of the south and east.

The country towns and villages which grew out of the wealth of the woollen industry are to this day some of the loveliest in England. That first industrial revolution—for such it was in effect—unlike that of the nineteenth century, was very close to the land: it was directly concerned with agriculture and it grew out of the soil. Natural native materials were still the logical ones to use for building, and the changing needs of the population were not such as to out-distance building tradition. Moreover, the feudal system and the City Guilds respectively still provided a form of community cohesion and control well adapted to the rate of development, and both town and country areas were dealt with as whole units, leaving little possibility of the piecemeal development which was the curse of the nineteenth century.

The Awakening

A quickly growing population, with new-found wealth, and in contact with European civilization, took to using stone and brick for its domestic and civic architecture. In the limestone districts, such as the Cotswolds and the Isle of Purbeck, there were not only ideal conditions for sheep-rearing, but also an easily worked building-stone. By the time the influence of the Renaissance reached its height in England, strong local traditions on which it could act had already emerged as the result of the variety of materials available. Half-timbered houses continued to be built for many centuries, especially in districts where timber was more easily obtained than stone, but wattle gave way to brick for the walls between the timbers in most of the clay-soil districts.

The changing needs of the population, the greater distribution of wealth, and the more peaceful times which had followed the Wars of the Roses brought about changes not only in architecture but also in garden design. By Tudor times the garden had spread beyond the protecting wall and moat, and no longer required warlike defences. The space devoted to food production occupied only a small pro-portion of the whole, and lawns, alleys and flower gardens were lavishly laid out.

Elaborate subdivision of the square parterre by means of dwarf hedges gave rise to 'knot gardens', always associated with the Tudor period. In England these knot gardens were usually rectan-gular in shape and were often arranged in groups of geometrical knots, the design being defined by clipped box, lavender or other low evergreen, with the spaces between occupied by low herbs or coloured sand and gravel. The designs are all architectural or geometrical in character, and they never gave rise here, as they did later in Latin countries, to the flowing floral patterns of 'Parterre de Broderie'.

In Tudor England the garden was still an enclosed self-con-tained area; but whereas in earlier times there had been no sign of any interest in the surrounding landscape, a new feature now appeared which suggests that the need for some outlook beyond the walls was being felt. The 'mount' which, in the form of a raised terrace against the boundary wall, may be derived from the battlemented defensive wall, more often took the form of a hillock near the centre of the garden, with steps or spiral paths leading up to a flat space (sometimes surmounted by an 'arbour') which served as a look-out place, from whence the garden boundary could be overlooked.

Sir Thomas More makes the citizens of his Utopia appear as keen gardeners. 'Their diligence herein commeth not only of pleasure but also of a certain strife and contention that is between strete and strete concerning the furnishing of their gardens.' King Utopus, in fact, planned a garden city of flat-roofed dwellings grouped in fine integrated streets. But just as More forecast a type of planning which did not then exist, so also his inter-street garden competitions may have existed only in his imagination. Nevertheless, it proves a widespread interest in, and love of, gardening. Gerard's herbal, written nearly a century later, refers to the 'care of almost all men in planting and maintaining gardens, not as ornaments onely, but as a

Fronteira Palace, near Lisbon. The use of box in wide solid bands is characteristic of Portuguese garden design. The solidity and mass thus given to the gardens has great charm.

New College, Oxford. Most of the building dates from 1386, but the garden court is said to have been the work of Sir Christopher Wren. The high central mount and the walk round the battlemented walls indicate the growing need for views beyond the enclosed garden. The parterres at the foot of the mount no longer exist: their hedges and internal devices were of clipped juniper. The mount has lost its architectural character and is now planted with shrubs and trees.

necessarie provision also to their houses.' It was still possible for a man of learning to know all the plants then cultivated in this country, and their uses; and such knowledge appears to have been general among educated people.

Bacon, the Prophet of a New Style

Our ideas of Elizabethan gardens are derived from early prints and illustrations, and from Bacon's essay *On Gardens*. Bacon's essay, though it must have been written with the knowledge of many contemporary gardens in mind, is not necessarily a picture of what they were, but rather of what he felt they should be. It is evident from this essay that garden design had already become over-elaborate in Bacon's view, but in spite of his advice, topiary and knot gardens were to become ever more elaborate and ornate in the hundred years that followed, and the lawn, to which Bacon gave pride of place, was to fade into a relatively insignificant position. Four acres of lawn, without the help of a mechanical lawn-mower, must have been a serious undertaking. Bacon devoted one-third of his space to the 'wilderness', but this idea, very novel at that time, passed apparently without much notice and had little influence on garden design until the eighteenth century, when the general reaction against formality in garden design set in.

The views expressed by Bacon on the need for wind shelter, on the use of flowers for scent and colour, and on the relative value of sun and shade are very much in accordance with modern ideas of

Packwood House, Warwicks. The Sermon on the Mount in yew. These figures may once have been clipped with greater realism than we see now. They symbolize the apostles and the multitude. The interest of the group lies in its historic rather than its visual quality. It is probably the most elaborate green sculpture to survive up to this day.

Vaux-le-Vicomte, France. Perhaps Lenotre's greatest masterpiece. The gardens are smaller than those of Versailles, where the scale seems almost to overcharge the formal style of layout. At Vaux the rich detail can be more fully appreciated.

garden design, and although we would not care for his fanciful use of coloured glass and hanging bird-cages, his garden would, on the whole, be a pleasant place today, though it lacked big trees.

Bacon's essay confirms the impression of a rather treeless garden which we get from most prints and gardens of the sixteenth and seventeenth centuries. Fruit trees and clipped hedges and tall pleached walks provided the shade and shelter. Bacon refers to the flowers of the lime, but does not state how or where they grow—his pleached alleys may have been of lime—and he excludes trees categorically from his wilderness.

Topiary

That trees and shrubs trimmed to architectural and sculptural shapes must have been far more general in gardens of the sixteenth and seventeenth centuries than in modern gardens is clear from contemporary accounts and drawings. This garden art of 'Topiary' had been handed down from Hellenistic and Roman times and was emblematic of the Hellenic attitude towards art and nature, weaving them together and endowing natural materials with humanistic forms.

For nearly three centuries topiary was a main feature of English gardens, evolving from the simple hedge to the knot garden, parterre, pleached alley, maze and heraldic beast to ever more

Levens Hall, Westmorland. The great yews have grown far beyond the designer's intention. Only in this climate would they have endured so much clipping for so long.

intricate and 'busie' designs, until, towards the end of the seventeenth century, there can be no doubt that it had overshot the mark of common sense.

In France, Lenotre brought the architectural use of plant material as enclosing walls to a pitch of perfection which ensured the art of topiary a permanent place in French affection: but his use of 'green sculpture' was confined to small conventional pieces, used as punctuation rather than as ornament. In the English climate yew and box seem to endure more ill-treatment than elsewhere. Only in England do fantastically clipped trees of very great age remain. The yews of Levens Hall, for instance, probably never intended by their designers to grow taller than the human figure, have shown such vitality and vigour in spite of centuries of clipping, that today they have become giants out of some unimaginable nightmare, with an awful beauty and stateliness lent by time. The yews of the south garden at Hampton Court were not intended to be more than a few feet high.

Trees and Timber

The love of trees for the sake of their own beauty seems rare in Europe until the following century, when poets began to sing their praises, and painters first saw landscape as a subject worthy of notice on its own merits rather than as an adjunct to figures and architecture.

It was probably significant for us in these islands that this development came at a time when Englishmen were becoming alarmed at the rate and extent of de-afforestation in this country. The fear of a serious timber and fuel famine was felt early in the sixteenth century, and in 1544 the first of a series of statutes was enacted to prevent clear felling of further forest. Twelve standard trees were henceforth to be left standing on every woodland acre. This density represents the best spacing for oak intended for shipbuilding, and it established the 'coppice with standards' type of forestry which has been a favourite system up to the present day. Coppice occupies the space under and between the standard trees, providing quicker returns than the big timber, and meeting local needs for hurdles, fencing, handles for tools, ladder rungs and so on. Sheep-farming on the richer lands and in the valleys provided a constant demand for hurdles for sheepfolds.

Enclosures

The open field system still prevailed in most of the Midlands, though many of the western counties, and also Kent, Essex and Suffolk, had been enclosed before Tudor times. The temptation to change from arable to sheep-farming must have been great while the wool trade flourished, and many of the open fields of the Midlands were enclosed for this reason in the sixteenth century, particularly in Leicestershire and Northamptonshire. Other considerations also led both large landowners and small-holders to enclose their land, and it was on lands now enclosed that farmers were able by degrees to evolve the mixed farming methods, the improved system of stock-breeding and the new rotations using newly introduced crops, which finally revolutionized agriculture of the eighteenth century.

Coppice with standards. The type of woodland adapted to timber ships and to houses with wattle panels between the main beams. Modern sylviculture calls for closer stands of the main timber and few uses remain for coppice undergrowth. The open type of woodland had, however, a certain charm.

Enclosure of open fields brings a complete change of landscape to the district. Not only do the hedges break up the open space into smaller divisions, but the new pattern they make is emphasized by differences of colour and texture due to differences in the treatment of each separate field. In the place of three large tracts of open ground, each showing one colour throughout, we get a patchwork-quilt effect of varying tones of green, brown and yellow, each outlined by a broad green band of hedge, punctuated by occasional tall trees. A few hedgerows trees in each field are almost a necessity in the case of pasture or of any mixed farming system where pasture forms part of the rotation, to provide shade and shelter for stock.

Nevertheless, owing to the general scarcity of timber and fuel which was becoming acute in the seventeenth century, it is unlikely that any trees not protected by law survived for long after reaching maturity. Young saplings, growing up in the hedge, would be left to take their place and would soon provide enough shade for stock.

Everything indicates that the landscape of the seventeenth century, outside the dwindling royal forests and some other stretches of primæval forest protected by the great landowners, must have been very treeless. Planting of trees and woodland had not been undertaken to any great extent, and large trees were not, as we have seen, considered essential in gardens. Ideas on this subject were probably still conditioned to some extent by the primitive view of forests as an inevitable menace, and of forest trees as unwanted, out-size weeds, not compatible with good husbandry. The shelter from wind and cold given by the forest was forgotten or overlooked, and to the present day we under-estimate the value of trees for this purpose.

Kilby, Yorks. The ridge and furrow of the older fields can be seen under the existing pattern of hedgerow enclosures. The enclosures were suited to a more varied and productive farming than had been possible in the open fields, but today the scale of the enclosures is too small for modern farm equipment, so hedges are being rooted out and a new pattern is emerging.

4

The English Landscape Style

We have already seen two influences leading to a changing landscape style in an embryonic stage: namely the need for new agricultural systems, less rigid and more capable of growth and development than the old strip farming, and the need for planting trees to keep up supplies of timber and fuel, instead of depending solely on natural regeneration of forest. Also developing was a new appreciation for natural forms and natural landscape, expressed in painting, poetry and garden design, which, in the latter, was in opposition to a standardized and stilted formalism.

Changes of Taste contributing to a New Style

Bacon's suggestion that one-third of the garden might be treated as wilderness, though it met with no response at the time, may have been in the mind of Milton when he described his Paradise, for he wrote not of a formal garden but of

> A steep wilderness; whose hairy sides
> With thicket overgrown—grotesque and wild
> Access denied: and overhead upgrew
> Insuperable height of loftiest shade,
> Cedar and Pine and Fir and branching Palm,
> A Sylvan scene, and as the ranks ascend
> Shade above shade—a woody theatre
> Of Stateliest view.

And he includes

> Flowers worthy of Paradise, which not nice art
> In beds and curious knots, but Nature boon
> Poured forth profuse on Hill and Dale and Plain.

Landscape by Claude Lorrain (1600–82). Paintings such as this inspired the creators of the English landscape style. A new conception of asymmetric composition came to replace the strict symmetry of earlier styles.

In spite of its wildness, Milton's wilderness is really much nearer the Italian garden in feeling than to Bacon's treeless 'heath'. Shade upon shade—a woody theatre—particularly if the trees were cedar and pine and palm—might almost be some ancient and forgotten terrace on a warm Mediterranean slope, rising to a profusion of wild flowers on the open plateau.

It is not really surprising that the revolt from formal to naturalistic garden settings occurred at a time when Classic influences in architecture were still strong, or that naturalistic garden design heralded the romantic movement instead of following in its wake. Although garden design usually follows after other developments, 'as if gardening were the greater perfection', this example is, in reality, no exception. The wilderness had been advocated by the most classically minded of writers: and while Gothic buildings had geometric gardens, the Parthenon and other Grecian monuments had none, but stood in splendid isolation, aloof from, yet dominating, scenery of magnificent wilderness. This sense of aloofness was apparent in the siting of Palladian country seats. Symmetry in

Lake Pavilion, Stowe, Bucks. The English landscape garden followed the appreciation of natural forms evinced by contemporary painters. But what appears here to be a natural lake is no less carefully contrived than the formal pools of sixteenth and seventeenth-century gardens.

architecture calls for an opposite quality in the setting. There is less obvious need for wide, open spaces and natural plant forms in connection with irregularly shaped Gothic groupings than there is in the case of very symmetrical buildings and streets.

Stories of Chinese gardens designed in an irregular, non-geometrical style were heard in England in the seventeenth century, and the knowledge that Chinese art recognized a beauty of balance and form that was not symmetrical was probably among the ferments acting in the direction of a new garden style. It is, however, difficult to trace any direct connection between those traveller's tales and the first actual landscape gardens that were made.

Sir William Temple's reference to Chinese gardens, in his essay on *The Gardens of Epicurus* (1685), is full of interest. 'The Chinese', he wrote, 'whose way of thinking seems to be as wide of ours in Europe as their country does . . . scorn our walks and trees ranged so as to answer one another at exact distances. Their greatest reach of imagination is employed in contriving figures where the beauty shall be great, and strike the eye, but without any order or disposition of parts that shall be commonly or easily observed. And though we have hardly any notion of this sort of beauty, yet they have a word to express it; and where they find it hit their eye at first sight, they say the sharawadgi is fine or admirable . . .'

Claude, Poussin and other seventeenth-century painters were clearly the model for many gardens. The Grecian and Roman ruins depicted in those paintings were reproduced in a scene of wild or pastoral beauty as near as possible to the artist's conception. Landowners and garden-designers aimed at 'the picturesque' rather than at 'sharawadgi.'

Bacon has been called the 'prophet' and Milton 'the herald of true taste in gardening (on account of their introducing natural wildness)', and Addison, Pope and Kent 'the champions of this free taste, because they absolutely brought it into execution'.[1] But this omitted one whose influence on gardens and on English landscape in general must have been at least as great as any of those mentioned, though he was concerned with the need for planting large forest trees rather than with any new style in garden design—namely, John Evelyn, author of the famous diary and of the book *Sylva*, which was first published in 1664.

Sylva was really a 'Grow more Trees' campaign intended to increase the national supply of timber for shipbuilding. It had a striking success even in Evelyn's lifetime, but its influence reached a climax in the following century, just when agriculture and garden design were undergoing very far-reaching changes. It was the coincidence of three movements (agriculture, timber production and landscape design) interacting at a critical time, when so much of the landscape was in the melting-pot, which gave us the rural scenery we so easily take for granted today.

The Landscape Garden

It was in the eighteenth century, in England, that garden and landscape first came together and were seen to be in relationship. The

---

[1] From a postscript to William Mason's poem 'The English Garden' (1772).

idea of deliberately designing gardens as a part of the wider land-scape, and the wider landscape as a garden, was new, and was not fully grasped even in the eighteenth century. Now that we become aware of the need for conscious design on a far broader scale than ever before, the history of landscape and of gardens may be seen as two entwined threads of one theme.

Of the three influences which led to their union perhaps the greatest was the need for timber, urgently felt throughout most of the seventeenth and eighteenth centuries on account of the threat of war. From the days of bows and arrows timber has always been an important munition of war, but at the present time it is wanted in the form of pulp, or for pit props, fencing and so on, rather than for shipbuilding. The vast majority of the trees planted for that purpose in the eighteenth century were never used, and remain to grace our countryside today. Of present-day timber requirements in relation to landscape, more will be said later.

A. G. Tansley remarks in *The British Islands and their Vegetation* that the earliest known reference to the need for planting to main-tain timber supplies in England is found in 1571, when Bodenham drew attention to a custom already established in Spain of plant-ing seven saplings to replace every tree felled. But in Scotland the timber shortage had become acute much earlier, and Acts were passed as early as 1457 requiring the King's tenants to plant trees. The Scotch, still believing firmly that trees impoverished the land, and grudging the space they occupied, resisted this and other sub-sequent laws so that Scotland remained very treeless for many cen-turies. It is doubtful whether tree planting would have become as general in England as it did in the eighteenth century but for the fact that just at that time the two other influences referred to—new developments of agricultural system and of aesthetic taste—synchronized with the pressing need for timber reserves, and that the large landowners of the south were moved by all three con-siderations.

The effects of changing fashion influenced the agricultural changes, but the aesthetic impulse alone could never have produced the results actually achieved. Rational impulse was gained by the practical need for changes in agriculture and forestry, and these called for conscious planning.

John Evelyn had urged the planting of forest trees not only for their timber but also for their beauty. He was interested in trees for their own sake and as features of the garden, and he drew attention to many introduced species till then little known outside the botanical garden. He took a hand in the design of several gardens, and his advice about tree planting was widely followed. Once men's eyes came to regard trees for their own characteristic beauty of form, it is easy to see how the rigid rows and the clipped shapes of the formal garden would lose their hold on the imagination, and inspiration would be sought instead in nature's own groupings or in the art of the landscape painter. The use of bold, irregular tree outlines or foliage masses, and the contrasts of light and shadow in non-symmetrical compositions so dear to Poussin and Claude, must have come with the appeal of a fresh vision, and prompted some departures from formality before the new garden style was fully established. Daniel Defoe, writing in 1714, speaks of a wilderness as one of the features of Wanstead which, for the rest, was a formal garden: he also saw and approved of 'irregularities in the design' of the garden at Sutton Court.

Joseph Addison, writing in 1712 to the *Spectator*, admits that he is 'looked upon as a humourist in gardening' on account of his unconventional views on that subject: he goes on to describe his own 'wilderness' and tilts at the formal garden. He was, however, probably voicing contemporary views fairly well when he said: 'Gardens are works of art, therefore they rise in value according to the degree of their resemblance to nature.'

We get a good impression of what the landscape garden meant to its contemporaries through the words of men of letters such as Alexander Pope, Horace Walpole and Thomas Gray. The design of garden and farm was a subject for intellectual debate. Pope sharpened his wit on the formal garden and, using the weapon of ridicule, finally routed any supporters it might still have had. Horace Walpole's essay, *On Modern Gardens*, vindicates the new form of design and explains its theories. Thomas Gray, in a letter of 1763, speaks of

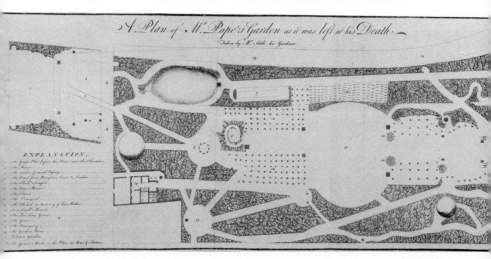

Plan of Pope's garden at Twickenham, Middx. An underground passage crosses the road between house and garden. We see the influence of the landscape style and the departure from geometrical symmetry. The design provides long vistas framed in the woodland belts on the boundary, with much variety and change of mood. The proportion of open space to planted ground gives a satisfactory sense of spaciousness. The general character would seem to be that of arcadian glades in forest surroundings.

'the only taste which we can call our own, the only proof of original talent in matter of pleasure; I mean our skill in gardening and laying out grounds. That the Chinese have this beautiful art in high perfection, seems very probable from the *Jesuits Letters*, and more from Chambers' little discourse published some few years ago. But it is very certain we copied nothing from them, nor had anything but nature for our model. It is not forty years since the art was born among us; and it is sure that there was nothing in Europe like it, and as sure we had then no information on this head from China at all.'

Forty years was an underestimate, as we have seen, for the wilderness as a part of a garden otherwise formal. Before 1720 Bridgman introduced 'a little gentle disorder into the plantations of his trees and bushes' at Stowe (according to Walpole) and had 'banished verdant sculpture though he retained green architecture'.

William Kent, called in to make alterations and additions at Stowe, began his career as a landscape-gardener by doing away with the green architecture and all straight lines in the garden, which remains today much as he left it, one of the best examples of his work. Walpole gives Bridgman the credit for inventing the 'ha-ha' to conceal the boundary and open up the view beyond, but says that Kent was 'the first to leap the fence and show that the whole of nature is a garden'.

Kent had studied art in Italy and had obviously been impressed by the trees in Italian gardens, and by the light and shadow effects they give; and although he rejected formality in favour of naturalistic design, one cannot but think that he drew an inspiration from Italian gardens which was missed by their imitators in earlier and again in later centuries. In the English climate we must be sparing of shade, and our light and shadow effects cannot be as dramatic as those of sunnier lands. But Kent saw that we can nevertheless make good use of tall forest trees and their shadows.

Lancelot Brown was, in a sense, Kent's pupil, since his taste was formed at Stowe when he began as kitchen-gardener. By the time his

Stowe, Bucks. The fine bridge and the straight road contrast strangely with Kent's naturalistic treatment, but they related the earlier Bridgman design logically to the town of Buckingham.

Longleat, Wilts. The work of Capability Brown can be seen as a whole from this vantage point, and gives a good idea of his wide grasp of landscape composition.

reputation as a landscape-gardener was established, the new fashion was at its height; and he is supposed to have destroyed more of the older gardens than anyone else, though he refused to alter those at Hampton Court where he had, for a period, been head gardener.

Elsewhere, many old terraces were rolled out into undulating vales and swelling curves. Innumerable clipped trees and even fine avenues of forest trees were destroyed. Brown changed avenues into isolated clumps by leaving a few trees standing at intervals and adding others to the group to mask the original straight lines of the planting. Sir Uvedale Price complained that he never saw this done with good effect, for 'the spot was haunted by the ghost of the departed avenue.'

Lancelot Brown's work still enriches our countryside. In particular the lakes and waterways he so successfully contrived marked an advance from the small pools and fountains of the past. Dutch influence in the previous century had introduced canals into the scene, but now Brown worked on a larger scale, and showed the immense value of large water surfaces beautifully related to surrounding contours, reflecting the wooded hills and sometimes the stately homes of his clients, to produce completely new landscape.

In spite of his immense and successful practice, 'Capability Brown' appears to have been rather a joke to his contemporaries. 'I hope I may die before you,' said one, 'so that I may see Heaven before you improve it.' We would give much today to see some of the gardens he destroyed, before the 'improvements' had been brought about.

Towards the end of the century, while Brown's successor Humphry Repton was developing garden design a step further, critical voices began to be raised against the landscape style. Some complained that the style aped nature unsuccessfully, others that it was too much like nature and lacking in the intimacy and human interest of formal gardens. The old gardens were remembered with regret, even by Sir Uvedale Price, himself an exponent of the new style.

Repton, influenced by these tendencies, often preserved existing avenues, and even concluded that a level terrace, on to which the doors and windows of a house should open, was a necessity to be permitted in spite of its formality. He was interested in tree forms and their relation to architecture, and his comments on this subject are worth study.

The complaints against the landscape garden on the score of dullness were more difficult to meet. Most of the trees used in the new gardens were slow-growing forest trees; flowers had been relegated to distant walled gardens and there can have been little compensating effect in the lifetime of the owners. Sir William Chambers, although believing that the English garden style was superior to any formal garden, went on to say that the landscape gardens 'differ very little from common fields . . . and a stranger is often at a loss to know whether he be walking in a meadow or in a pleasure

West Wycombe, Bucks. Open treatment of the ground around the house led later designers to provide more shelter planting and other enrichment near the buildings. But the site is protected from the north by the wooded Chilterns, and the sense of parkland extends to the church on the hill.

ground made and kept at considerable expense. He sees nothing to amuse him, nothing to excite his curiosity, nor anything to keep up his attention.' On the strength of his travels in China, though he was obliged to draw heavily on his imagination and on hearsay, he described the wonders of the Emperor's palace in Pekin, which, he said, was naturalistic and picturesque yet never dull. He deduced that a few pagodas would enliven the English gardens, and since this was the day of 'Chinese modes' in all things, he was commissioned to try his hand at Kew. Looking at his pagoda in Kew Gardens today, one realizes that his knowledge of Chinese gardens must have been small: and, in fact, he admitted as much himself in later editions of his book.

Pagodas were not the only 'enrichments' introduced for the

enlivenment of landscape gardens. Artificial ruins, and grottoes were sited as eye-catchers in prominent positions. 'Where objects were wanting', says Walpole (of Kent), 'he introduced temples.' Kent also tried introducing dead trees in a London park, but this was too much for the native sense of ridicule and they were removed. The idea of employing a hermit to sit in meditation by a cave doubtless aimed at recapturing the missing human touch while still preserving a sense of ideal unreality. The poet Shenstone (1714–1763), followed by other amateurs of garden art, held that every garden scene should evoke an emotional response: that places should be sublime, grand, melancholy or awful, and although these effects were at first supposed to be achieved by purely naturalistic means, it was inevitably easier to convey them with the aid of buildings and 'objects' such as rocks, grottoes and caves, particularly on sites which were not in wild or mountainous surroundings. The professional landscape-designers inclined to a smooth non-rugged scenery, and if Peacock's jibes in *Headlong Hall* can be taken at face value, they must have been obsessed to some degree with the idea of easy sweeping contours and smoothly modelled surfaces.

The landscape garden at its best followed the principles of composition as understood and demonstrated by landscape painters. It was held that a landscape painter, by reason of his knowledge of light and shadow values, of composition through the relationship of mass and void and by his sense of line and proportion, would know best how to design garden and landscape. Though few gardens were laid out by painters, unless we include Kent, the influence of the painter's sense of composition was very widely felt, and can still be seen in many lovely gardens of the period still in existence. Few of the earlier gardens and fewer still of later date can be compared in this respect with the best of the eighteenth century.

Except where drastic alteration of contours was needed for the creation of a pool or serpentine lake, the design usually followed fairly closely the existing configuration of the site. Water and trees were used to emphasize the land forms, the trees being grouped with little apparent relation to buildings on plan, but linking them with the land forms in the vertical or perspective view. The trees also served to lead the eye outward to more distant undulations of the skyline. The basis of the whole composition was turf; and although it has been suggested that the French had tried and discarded the idea of the landscape garden as early as 1700, it is inconceivable that it could ever have been successfully carried out in any country not having a natural ground carpet of good turf.

Stourhead, Wilts. The garden with its grottoes, classical temples and lake was designed by its owner in 1741–50. However, many of the conifers and rhododendrons more recently introduced must have altered the sense of open space and the breadth of scale of the original intention.

Wilhelmshohe, Kassel, W. Germany. This part of the grounds with the great lake was laid out as an English Garden in an area where climate favoured this style. It contrasts strongly with other parts of the site where French influence or baroque styles held sway.

The English Landscape Garden Abroad

Whenever English gardens have influenced foreign garden-design it seems that it is the use of turf which is both the objective and the stumbling-block. In sixteenth- and seventeenth-century French gardens, 'le parterre Anglais' was a green lawn; but because French turf could not be walked upon with impunity, it was laid out as separate floor panels, bordered with clipped box, and buttoned down with small topiary pieces, within the framework of gravel path. 'Le jardin Anglais', a term referring definitely to the landscape style, also has to make use of more gravel, more trees and less grass than its model. It therefore misses the character of the original, just as English reproductions of Italian gardens miss the real quality of the latter for climatic reasons. With sunlight at a premium it is not possible to be so lavish with shade.

Use and Beauty combined in Agriculture, but divorced in Gardens

Although the landscape style had a considerable vogue on the Continent and held its own in England for about a hundred years, it was never completely satisfying as a garden to be lived in, as is clear from the mass of contemporary criticism, and from the violence of the reaction which followed it. Gray, the poet, was right in saying that a new art had been born, but it was not realized that the true importance of that new art lay less in its treatment of the garden than

Ferme ornée at Wooburn, Surrey. A contemporary print showing the ideal of farm and garden united in the setting, with no visible division between them. This imaginative objective has practical application in modern landscape design since agricultural use is the economic way of maintaining the land in good order.

in its treatment of the countryside. Large landowners had, in the past, tried to relate the two by planting miles of straight avenues, extending the axis and vistas of the garden through agricultural land. But though that method might be, to some extent, effective in flatter parts of Europe, it was obviously farcical in the undulating country-side of England, where the lines of the avenues, however straightly sited, became curved in the vertical dimension. The freer informal type of design, on the other hand, made possible belts of trees which not only invited the eye outward into the landscape but also provided shelter for stock, crops and game. They improved the land as well as the landscape, without imposing any garden metaphor on agriculture as did the straight avenues. The light poor land, on the higher ground, is usually the best position for shelter belts, and these groups crowning the upper contours emphasize the undulations of the ground. The outline plan of the tree belts might be deter-mined by soil type or by contours in relation to wind direction, or both, and while their value in the scenery played no small part in their general siting, this was not dictated by the axis of the garden plan.

Model farms were laid out on these lines as large landowners came to appreciate the advantages and possibilities of the method. Very far-reaching changes were already taking place in agriculture in general, and any new light on the subject fell on what was already a focal point of interest.

The Enclosure of the Farm Land

The open field system, which in some parts of the country had been giving way to enclosed farming for some centuries by a gradual process but which still persisted over the greater part of the Midlands and south, was clearly out of date and inefficient by eighteenth-century standards. Enclosures were essential for the improvement of both stock and arable farming, and the three-field system, wherever it persisted, acted as a brake on progress by preventing any individual in the area from trying new methods. The selection and breeding of special strains of animals called for fairly small fields enclosed by hedge or wall and having a few trees for shade. Improved arable methods, and new rotations taking in recently introduced crops such as roots and clover, made it possible to feed more cattle throughout the winter, and this in turn meant more manure and greater fertility for the land. Different rotations could not be tried under the open field system.

Much had been learnt, too, about land drainage, and it had become possible to improve all the rich heavy land, and to reclaim much that had been uncultivable waste, by means of comprehensive drainage schemes; but these were difficult or impossible to organize while each man's strips were scattered through the three fields. One owner's land seldom lay together in a consecutive block, and the whole area needed regrouping before drainage operations could be effectively undertaken.

Besides the new Enclosure Acts which, at the beginning of the century, dealt with one district at a time, a great deal of land was redistributed and enclosed by private treaty amongst the owners. The process of surveying, valuing, agreeing the redistribution and planning the drainage schemes, and all the new roads involved, was complicated and costly. Enclosure funds, contributed by the owners in proportion to the extent of their land, met the cost, but although the increased yield per acre made it well worth while for those who could afford to wait, many smallholders preferred to sell their land and be quit of the expense of hedging. 'The method of the enclosures had not taken enough consideration of the small man, and too little had been done to fix the lesser peasantry on the soil as part of the new scheme of things. When similar changes took place in contemporary Denmark,[1] a land ruled by a monarch dependent on his general popularity, the interest of all classes down to the poorest was carefully considered, with excellent consequences in the agricultural Denmark of today . . . .

'In the redivision of the open fields and common wastes among

---

[1] In Germany, at the present time, re-organization of the same type is being tried in a few areas of poor land where very small strip holdings prevail. Hedges are not used however, and the land allotted to wind shelter is cut to the bare minimum, presumably because their value is not yet fully appreciated.

Compton Wynyates, Warwicks. The close relation of mansion and grounds to their farmland through tree groups and hedges is typical of nearly all the great houses, manors and halls in Britain. The system, arising from practical consider-ations such as the need for shelter and enclosure, gives rise to pleasing visual composition.

individual proprietors and farmers [in England], there was no intention to defraud the small man, but no desire to give him more than his apparent legal claim. Often he could not prove a legal claim to the rights he exercised on the common. Oftener his legal rights to keep cows or geese there, or his personal right in one or two strips in the village field, were compensated with a sum of money which was not enough to enable him to set up as a capitalist farmer or pay for the hedging of the plot allotted to him: the compensation might, however, pay for a month's heavy drinking in the ale house. And so he became a landless labourer.'[1]

[1] G. M. Trevelyan, *History of England,* 3rd edition, p. 611.

5

Land Changes in the Nineteenth Century

With the threat of food shortage due to war conditions and the dangers of enemy blockade, at the start of the nineteenth century, the increased yield per acre in this island was of utmost importance, and the advantages of the enclosures were more apparent than their defects. In 1801 the General Enclosure Act simplified the process for all the land still remaining under the open field system: and in 1845 a further Act made the process still easier, till very few districts remained unenclosed.

Enclosure in itself did not reduce the amount of labour needed on the land, except in cases where it was done with the intention of stock-breeding on land which had hitherto been arable. This did happen in certain districts. But where mixed arable farming was the objective, as it was in most cases, there was another new factor leading to rural depopulation even though the improved methods meant more work. Farm machinery was improving, and was gradually displacing manual labour and so preventing the rise of wages which should have come with the higher yield of enclosed land.

The tendencies, together with the growth of industrialism in the towns, combined to shift the balance of rural and urban populations at an unprecedented rate. The growing towns at first provided good markets for home-grown produce: but the time was bound to come when the countryside would suffer for its loss of population.

The Repeal of the Corn Laws

Its weaknesses first began to appear when the Corn Laws were repealed. There had been a long series of Corn Laws, designed not merely as 'protection' against foreign competition, but primarily to counteract the effect of bad seasons in this country and to maintain and distribute as evenly as possible the livelihood of the producer, so dependent on the vagaries of the weather. They served, in effect, the same purpose as a fly-wheel in an engine—a most urgent need in the mechanism of the nation's food production, as every food producer knows. But the townspeople and the landless poor of the country-side saw them only as a means of keeping the price of bread higher than it would otherwise have been in bad seasons. G. M. Trevelyan speaks of the Repeal of the Corn Laws as a victory of the industrial over the agricultural interest, continuing: 'But the agricultural interest, in the wider sense of the term, had in fact been divided on the issue. If there had been a numerous peasantry owning or occupying the land in small portions, the landlords and big farmers would not have been left isolated in the struggle. The landless agricultural labourer, so far as his almost negligible opinion was asked by politicians, on the whole inclined to the policy of the cheap loaf.'[1]

Low wages for the workers in both town and country contributed greatly, therefore, to this result. And although the increasing population maintained the demand for home-grown food for nearly thirty years after, so that the countryside felt no immediate ill effects, the decline of agriculture, when it started in 1874, set in as the result of a series of bad seasons combined with uncontrolled imports of cheap food, and was very difficult to check, with results which showed more and more clearly in the landscape as the years went on.

The Growth of the Towns

However slowly the agricultural landscape was affected by the sudden change in the balance of the population, the result on the towns themselves and the surrounding land on which they over-spilt was immediately disastrous. They grew without control; and the huge changes now made possible by improved communications and new scientific knowledge only added to the confusion, coming, as they did, on people unprepared to direct the new power at their disposal and unable even to foresee the need for direction and control.

[1] G. M. Trevelyan, *History of England*, 3rd edition, p. 646.

Preston mills, Lancs. The dreary expanse of monotonous and ugly building uses up vast stretches with no understanding of man's dependence on nature— or of the ecological basis of human life.

The feudal system and the town guilds, which, in the past, had served as planning units in scale with the needs of their times, had by now practically ceased to function and they broke down completely under the new strain. They should have been replaced by new systems covering larger areas and wider interests. Instead, all sense of collective responsibility was lost, and individuals were left to proceed alone, each going his own way. Under such circumstances individual gain or success becomes an objective out of all proportion to the needs of the whole land. Slums built without regard to humanity or beauty were a symptom of this attitude towards life. The utter disregard of man's dependence on nature, of his need for fresh air and for contact with soil and vegetation, was all a part and parcel of the same attitude, assuming as it did that man can exist alone— separated from the rest of creation. It was a failure to realize that we really are, ultimately, members one of another.

In the case of the distending towns and industrial areas, natural laws were defied both in regard to man's relationship to man and also in his relationship to the soil and to the rest of living creation, and so the landscape deteriorated immediately. Row upon row of small identical houses close packed, in narrow streets sited in utter disregard of land form or any natural feature, seen perhaps at their worst in the north of England, became slums and scarred the landscape. In the case of the countryside, only the structure of the human society had been unbalanced. The new agricultural system in itself was better balanced, better adjusted to natural laws than the old, and the landscape benefited to that extent. But humanity had reached a stage when the social structure required conscious control, and when the failure to exercise that control would gradually outbalance the benefits of improved agriculture even in the countryside.

The belief in the self-sufficiency of the individual, or single family, was probably a root of much extensive ugliness. Where individual importance looms large in proportion to the relationship between the individual and the whole, ostentation and snobbery amongst the wealthier classes tend towards a general debasement of taste through the need for self-advertisement. The possession of costly objets d'art becomes a mark of success, and they come to be valued as status symbols rather than for their intrinsic and universal qualities.

But the adaptation of design to purpose also played a very large part in the æsthetics of the time. Solid, practical utility and comfort ranked high in the assessment of values—too high, if considered incompatible with beauty. Those deep armchairs were the height of comfort, the heavy wardrobes were roomy and well-adapted to the fashions of the period: carpets and curtains were warm and hard-wearing. Superficial ornament was often used to counterbalance an ugliness thought to be inherent in objects made primarily for use. Designers now seek an organic beauty which, in theory, should be inherent in true adaptation to use. But many an eyesore has been perpetrated in the name of functionalism, and nineteenth-century design was functional, even when clumsy: clearly functionalism

Wilton House by Richard Wilson. The garden was designed to be seen as part of the surrounding landscape: later additions and even some of the modern planting show that a need for more intimate detail is felt. From the historic angle, however, the great trees on broad stretches of turf are in better relationship with the building.

alone is not enough. Only sensitive aesthetic design can conceive the beauty of form which may arise from true adaptation to use.

An examination of nineteenth-century garden design throws an interesting light on other developments of the period. It was a sad retrogression as regards appearance, but it was, in part, a reaction towards functionalism in the garden.

If the landowners of the eighteenth century had combined use and beauty in their gardens as successfully and as simply as they did in their farmland, that reaction might have been avoided. Taking nature as their model, they had produced in their countryside an agriculture based on natural laws, but in their gardens they had produced an idealized copy of wild nature which, though it had charm, neglected many of the realities of human life. The landscape garden had been designed as a picture to be looked at rather than as a place in which to live. For the sake of fine views, shelter was sacrificed, and the intimacy of the enclosed garden with all its richness of colour and ornament for close-at-hand enjoyment had been swept away. Flowers had been banished along with the vegetables to a distant, walled garden hidden from sight by trees and shrubs lest its straight lines should offend. ('Nature abhors a straight line' was the cliché governing this removal. Serpentine walls were tried as a substitute for straight ones, but with all their curves they still appeared artificial and never came into general use.) The kitchen garden was so far removed from the house that the owner lost that contact with the soil which comes from actual gardening. The grassland round the 'mansion' provided little scope for the indulgence of gardening as a hobby, so the English love for gardening was frustrated.

Reaction from 'The Sublime'

In his later years Repton had become aware of the need for some more intimate type of garden, and had made provision for flower and vegetable gardens within reach of the mansion, though he continued to conceal them from the open parkland. His sheltered formal flower garden became a prototype for the proliferating middle-class gardens of the Victorians. Repton taught that 'all objects of mere convenience or comfort, if incapable of being made ornamental or of becoming proper parts of the general scenery must be removed or concealed,' thus blaming the objects for incapacity rather than accepting their challenge.

Repton seems to have missed the truth in Windham's view that conformity to use and enjoyment is that which constitutes beauty. Having been an agriculturalist before taking to landscape gardening, he might well have been able to appreciate the beauty of well-used land, but he had followed fashion and taught that the 'shade and colour of cornfields and the straight lines of fences are totally at variance with all ideas of picturesque beauty'. Of Shenstone's model farm, The Leasowes, he said that it 'drew the sneer of great men and the ridicule of the farmer for that mis-application of good taste'; and he deplored 'that constant disappointment which the benevolent Shenstone must have experienced in attempting to unite two objects so completely incompatible as ornament and profit'. He hoped that 'the good taste of the Country will never confound the character of a park with that of a farm, which are so totally incongruous as not to admit of any union but at the expense either of beauty or of profit.'

It was not for nothing, however, that The Leasowes had become 'the goal of sociable pilgrimage', and from that time up to the present day its ideas have influenced the great landowners. In the nineteenth century, farm and garden went their separate ways; the gardens, not the farms, suffered loss of beauty because their objective was artificial rather than organic.

While the agricultural pattern underwent no violent reaction, continuing to weave use and beauty happily together, the garden designers looked to Repton's formal gardens and to the views of Uvedale Price and Richard Payne Knight, both of whom had compared the English landscape garden unfavourably with the formal

Ashridge, Herts. Humphry Repton's design for a rose garden at Ashridge bears witness to the need arising even in his lifetime for more variety and enrichment. He sited small formal gardens behind the main buildings, in order that they should not obtrude on his broader landscape conception of the house surrounded by parkland.

gardens of Italy. Price had remembered nostalgically the old garden he himself had destroyed, with its 'air paré' and its decoration which, 'whatever the advocates of extreme simplicity may allege, is surely essential to an ornamental garden.' Since trees, shrubs and undulating ground are found in wild nature 'they cannot add distinction to a garden'. Knight had said that the art of landscape gardening 'takes away all natural enrichment and adds none of its own'.

Gardens in Victorian Times

Enrichment. That word is the key to much that now happened in gardens. Not only were they to be made more comfortable and usable by means of well-sheltered level ground with gravel walks and good seats, solid walls and steps instead of open grassy slopes, but also there must be enrichment of architectural detail and, above all, of colour.

The landscape garden of the eighteenth century had been limited in its colour effects to varying tones of green and to the soft russets, browns and greys of nature. But exotic plants from sunnier climates had been introduced and cultivated in greenhouses and were capable of giving the brilliant parterres which are often supposed to be the main charm of Italian gardens. In this country they could be raised under glass only, and bedded out in the garden for temporary effects, requiring frequent replacement: but this would add all the more to the 'enrichment' of the garden, and they could never be confused with common flowers.

In the large gardens of the preceding century, garden flowers had been relegated to a place where they would least be seen, and even wild flowers had held little importance. Now the pendulum swung to the opposite extreme, and exotic flowers in the crudest of primary colours found first favour, and were massed trimly in full view of the house. Scarlet geraniums, Reckitt's-blue lobelia, and strong yellow calceolarias in concentric circles, set off by the hardest whites available, were to be accommodated near the buildings. Shrubs as shelter and background could be planted on the slopes so carefully modelled by Kent, Brown and Repton; and flower-beds could be carved out

of the lawn. It was, of course, necessary to have gravel paths, wide
and solid, meandering lengthily around them to ensure their proper
appreciation at close range, and seats for comfort. By the time a few
urns and sundials had been added and the former naturalistic composition completely broken up and obliterated, the desired effect was
often felt to have been achieved, and so many remained until quite
recently as monuments of incongruity. But thinking out new shapes
for the beds had evidently taxed the imagination, and when the
circle, the half-circle, the crescent, square, diamond, and star had been
exploited there was nothing to do but to repeat them.

More co-ordinated results could be had by employing an architect such as Sir Charles Barry, Sir Joseph Paxton or Nesfield to design
an 'Italian' garden as was done at Bowood House, Blickling Hall,

Holkham Hall, Norfolk. The shelter belts along the coastline (seen faintly in the
top right-hand corner) protect the farm-land near the park from the north winds
(see pp. 260–3). Older plantations form the landscape of the park, in which
Lancelot Brown, Repton and others were concerned. The formal garden near
the house by Sir Charles Barry probably met the new need for more colour
and enrichment.

Knebworth House, Herts. This Gothic extravaganza was built about 1843 for Lord Lytton, the novelist, and incorporates a wing of the original Tudor mansion. The elaborate formal layout of the parterre no doubt reflected the relationship of house and garden, but the change of circumstances and taste would call for a different approach today. Not only the problems of maintenance, but also the visual reaction of our period would indicate plain uncluttered lawn as the only foil to such architectural elaboration.

Eaton Hall, Longford Castle and many others; but these scarcely affected the main treatment of the estates, which, for the rest, remained as their eighteenth-century designers had made them. New formal terraces and parterres of elaborate geometrical design, enclosed by walls and hedges, were laid out in close relation to the buildings, but unrelated to the park or landscape beyond. They remain in parentheses, interpolated into the wider conception of an earlier age. These gardens usually depend for their background, skyline and general setting on the results of eighteenth-century planning, without which many of them would be almost wholly two-dimensional. But they are often found in direct competition with a fine view, and since no concessions are made to the subtler indications of the surrounding land forms, the sense of conflict is aggravated and the beauty of the eighteenth-century surrounding is, as far as possible, nullified.

The formal garden of this period was not freed from the dictum that 'Nature abhors a straight line', but paid tribute to it by means of a lavish use of geometrical curves—one of the hallmarks by which it may always be recognized. Curves were 'in': some of them could scarcely be attributed either to nature or to geometry, but only, as was pointed out by a French critic, to alcoholic intoxication.

Gravel paths had always worried the landscape-gardeners of the eighteenth century because they never looked natural and, when curved, tended to be ungainly: they had used them as little as possible. But now, twisting paths, winding through shrubberies and doubling back on their tracks, were found to be capable of making a place seem larger in extent than it really was. Every device capable of enlarging the apparent size of the private garden was tried, and skill in this matter was regarded as the garden-designer's main function.

False Perspective

Many of the garden developments of the middle and end of the century came as the result of attempting on comparatively small sites effects previously designed for large estates. False perspective had been introduced in a broad way by Kent and his successors as the natural result of the picturesque attitude. But now, applied on a smaller scale, it became nonsense. The ha-ha, which can be effective only under certain limited conditions and which needs very careful handling, was now adopted in the hope of making the place seem larger, in many an inappropriate position.

Foreign conifers were being introduced from America, and were in great favour for their exotic and rich appearance. The monkey-puzzle appears to have been first favourite, a horticultural expert having expressed the view that no gentlemen's demesne could be complete without it. Newly introduced trees, such as *Sequoias* and

Clandon, Surrey. The introduction of exotic conifers and other plants greatly changed the character of English gardens during the nineteenth century. Gardens of this period are still identifiable at a glance by their wealth of introduced trees, and often they now seem to be too closely planted. The thinning and removal of rare specimens presents a problem.

Cupressus first planted on the great estates, became status symbols; and to some extent they can be regarded in this light to the present day. Their unmistakable spiky outlines are visible from afar, marking private estates and gardens well maintained for at least a century. Their introduction coinciding generally with the nineteenth-century Gothic revival led to their frequent association with pointed gables whose forms they echo. Repton had favoured contrast, and not harmony, between the forms of architecture and plants, saying that rounded tree forms were the best foil to Gothic architecture. If that was true of the Strawberry Hill Gothic of his day, it was even truer of the Ruskin Gothic, but his warning had been forgotten and no new voice was raised in protest. The pointed trees and pointed gables still remain in association in countless places to prove that on this Repton's judgment was not at fault. (See drawing on p. 200.)

The heavy furniture of the nineteenth century and all the knick-knacks and ornaments overcrowding the rooms found counterparts in the garden as the century wore on. Heavy shrub planting, much of which was redundant, was monotonous and dull. Often it obtruded too near the buildings and encircled too closely small open spaces, making a stagnant and claustrophobic effect. 'Objects' were never lacking, and the clarity and simplicity of open spaces were overlaid. The objects might be raised flower-beds representing vast baskets with the sides and a gigantic arch forming the handle made of wire trellis, draped in ivy. The baskets would be planted with brilliant hothouse flowers in concentric rings. Other devices were clocks and sundials (figured in carpet-bedding) on a gigantic scale. It was as if machinery, not nature, was the model to be idealized in gardens. The art of topiary was revived in both its sculptural and architectural form, but it was the former which gave the greatest scope for the display of originality and which, when originality flagged, drew the heaviest censure. The habit of clipping bushes, once contracted, easily becomes a vice, and the results could be seen in the serried ranks of green, gold and variegated plants, neatly trimmed to standardized shapes, but often cut to within an inch of death, which appeared not only in private gardens but in parks, railway stations and other public places. To clip groups of shrubs such as these into single specimens ruins their value as shelter or background, and brings them into restless competition for the limelight in the centre of the stage. The practice is an attempt to substitute skill for design, by individuals blind to the need for good design.

Just as the abuse of green sculpture had been a main cause leading to the reaction against seventeenth-century formal design, so again, at the end of the nineteenth century, it proved to be the formal garden's weakest point and became the main centre of the new revolt against formality led by William Robinson (1838–1935).

English Cottage Gardens

Yet the art of green sculpture had one invulnerable stronghold in England, where it was never misused and whence, one hopes, it will never be evicted. The cottage garden, through all the ups and downs and the changing fashion of taste in the large estates, kept serenely to its own unchanging tradition, using a profusion of flowers. There were preserved many of the garden plants which might otherwise have been lost to cultivation in the vicissitudes of aristocratic and intellectual controversy, and there too, at least on the chalk and limestones, the art of topiary was honoured. Chalk and limestone was the native home of yew and box: on the river silts clipped holly was often used instead. The cottage garden had never attempted to appear natural, because it was natural: natural to man, fulfilling specific needs of body and mind. Flowers, fruit and vegetables grown within neat, clipped hedges and bisected by the essential path of stone, brick or gravel were its constant features. But where the native evergreens were holly, box or yew, countless cottagers had trimmed one or other of these into a huge and gloriously non-functional ornament, each generation faithfully performing its annual

Cottage garden at Leckford, Hants. The tradition of the small front garden in English country villages remains unchanged. A mass of flowering plants in gay profusion dominates over the ground plan.

service of clipping and perhaps adding something to the design as the size of the tree increased. These village topiary pieces are usually seen singly, or at least in very small numbers. To add to them would ruin their effect. They dominate the gardens in which they stand, often overtopping the cottage and giving character to the whole street.

The voice of Robinson, fuming against the practice of clipping hedges or any growing plants, never reached the villages, and these outstanding examples of topiary remain unscathed. He made no exceptions in their favour and probably classed them, in his mind, with the rest. But in some other respects he advocated a return to cottage-garden traditions.

Throughout the eighteenth and nineteenth centuries, cottagers were apparently the only people who could indulge a taste for amateur gardening. The people of these islands are innate gardeners, and love to potter in the garden, propagating and watching plants

Cottage topiary. Clipped yews in cottage gardens prove generations of devoted care, giving a sense of duration in history. The low wall enclosing front gardens, so characteristic of English villages, gives spatial continuity to vistas often composed of individual house types.

grow, especially flowering plants, for the sheer pleasure this brings them. Yet for two centuries the well-to-do had deprived themselves of this simple pleasure. Flower gardens, removed from the general life of the household in the eighteenth century, had regained their old position in the nineteenth century, but the carpet-bedding system was not one in which the amateur could interfere. It was too precise and too mechanical.

The Horticulturalists' Garden

This was another of the vulnerable points in the system attacked by Robinson, and by urging the use of hardy plants he could appeal to a very fundamental need in the British character. Plants from all parts of the world were now in cultivation at Kew and other horticultural centres, and whereas in the early part of the century interest centred round conifers and tropical plants, it was now veering towards flowering shrubs and perennial plants, many of which were hardy in our climate. As a gardener Robinson was interested in these, and as a journalist he was able to convey his interest to others. Realizing, however, that they did not look their best in the formal beds designed for carpet-bedding, he became convinced that formality of any sort must be avoided, and he embraced the landscape faith. But he advocated a very different type of treatment from that of the earlier landscape-gardeners. Flowers were now to be a main theme, and all the rest merely a setting for those flowers.

Nature was to be the model again, but nature in her more flowering and less austere moods. The shears must be banished and hardy shrubs and herbaceous plants must take the place of carpet-bedding and greenhouse plants. Nature's method of disposing these hardy plants was to be the guiding principle of garden design.

Robinson himself had instinctively much feeling for constructive design—he used his material well. But he modestly assumed that the virtue lay in the material, and that a sound knowledge of horticulture and ecology would make a good designer of any man. The belief, still very generally held, that garden design consists of growing beautiful plants in suitable conditions and in their natural form, was

Hidcote, Glos. A view in the wild garden at Hidcote. Planting of the type advocated by Robinson is the feature of this scene. Rough paths, interesting foliage and a complete absence of architectural material may be compared with Sir Edwin Lutyens' lay-out at Marsh Court (*opposite*).

probably due to his influence and to his own excellent work. He understood so little of the motives underlying his own sense of design that he was quite unable to convey them to others, and most of his imitators were content to grow interesting collections of flowering plants without troubling further about design. A blaze of colour and an absence of geometrical lines did duty and passed for garden design. Nevertheless, the use of newly introduced hardy plants, together with many old favourites now rescued from oblivion, focused attention on the possibilities of well-blended colour schemes of a beauty and subtlety unknown to the era of carpet-bedding.

Architects' Gardens in the Early Twentieth Century

The weakness of design in these horticultural gardens, however, stimulated new champions of the formal style, and the architectural profession, throwing itself into the breach, took up the gardener's challenge. A fresh attack on the naturalistic treatment of garden space was led by Sir Reginald Blomfield (1856–1942), Inigo Thomas,

Inigo Triggs and Sir Edwin Lutyens (1869–1944); but none of these, any more than their opponents at this period, saw the matter in its wider application to the land in general, partly perhaps because the private gardens they were considering were smaller than those of last century. The architects, each tackling the subject in his own way, agreed on the whole that the British version of the Italian style was not a good line to follow, and that inspiration should be sought rather in our own formal gardens of the older period, before the over-elaboration of these had led to their eclipse. They appear to have overlooked the real importance of landscape design as a 'new art' applicable to the wider landscape, and attacked it only in its less important aspect. In this country little or no attempt was made to

Marsh Court, Dorset. This garden by Lutyens is an open-air extension of an architectural conception. Plants are used as interior ornaments, not as the structure of the design. It is perhaps an extreme case which led many to the opposite method whereby living plants form the main structure.

Jessups, Kent. Many modern gardens such as this combine the architectural and the horticultural type of design happily enough. Here clipped hedges relate the lawns to the house, and the Robinson-type planting in the foreground relates the group to the countryside.

prevent the loss of landscape through the encroachment of industry, railways, and the new settlements related to them.

In earlier centuries, whenever the question of formal versus informal garden design had arisen, one or other of the opposing theories had had an easy conquest, swaying the whole fashion of an age; but now the balance of opinion was more even, and the debate was pursued with fierce antagonism and virulence. Each side had its fashion and its fanatic following. Robinson's preface to his book, *The English Flower Garden*, and Blomfield's *Formal Garden in England*, may be taken as fairly representative of the two points of view.

Gertrude Jekyll

Gertrude Jekyll (1843–1932) found a bridge between the two camps, and showed by her books, and by her planting work in many of Lutyens' gardens, that the two were not incompatible. There was a place for both in most gardens, and the formal gardens of the architects needed the softening effect of informal grouping of hardy plants no less than the naturalistic garden. She showed how well-designed colour schemes and naturalistic planting were applicable equally to geometric or free arrangements of the main design. But her discovery far from checking the wrangle, only served to convince each side that they alone were right.

Lutyens was lucky to find, in Gertrude Jekyll, an artist sensitive enough to give his gardens an interior decoration harmonizing with his own intention and a remarkable unity was achieved. Her work was the perfect counterpart of his own: yet that unique case contributed, perhaps unfortunately, to the architects' conviction that construction and planting were separate, unrelated subjects, and that after the architectural framework was designed, the planting could safely be left to other hands. They did not all find a Gertrude Jekyll: the architectural garden of the early twentieth century tended to lack harmony owing to the emphasis on brick and stone, and a wrong use of plants.

The horticultural followers of the Robinson school thought of plants as the *raison d'être* and the essential material of gardens, overlooking the need for structural design. They failed to realize that if brick and stone are banished, plants must be used structurally. There was often a sound basis to their criticism that architectural gardens were unworkable owing to a lack of knowledge of garden routine. Just as the design of a kitchen calls for a knowledge of the cook's routine, so the design of the open space calls for a knowledge of maintenance routine. Witness the case of a gardener who indented for a helicopter to carry mowing equipment into internal courts. But the gardener's gardens, in spite of the wide appeal of their lavish use of plants were often restless, lacking structure and cohesion. They depended too far on interior decoration.

In the course of the debate, however, both sides made substantial contributions to English landscape design. The application of ecological principles and the consequent development of special types of garden for different plant associations, such as the alpine garden, the woodland, water and bog garden, were an important advance to the credit of Robinson and his followers; and to the credit of the architects was the move in the direction of the more rational design of gardens as places to live in—intimately linked with the buildings they served. The architects' gardens were open-air extensions of the buildings themselves, designed as a setting for human life rather than for plants.

In so far as the cleavage between the two ideas obscured wider issues it had unfortunate results. Everyone interested in the design of gardens became partisans of one side or another, overlooking the fact that the enormous increase of plants available to cultivation, together with the growing need for planning outside the private garden, had produced a problem which could no longer be approached from the angle of horticulture or of architecture alone, but required a special fusion of the two, such as had occurred for that short period in the eighteenth century.

The Landscape Style in America

A very different development was taking place in the United States of America, where gardening knowledge was less widespread, and where a rapidly expanding need for parks and gardens, and for new roads, brought suddenly to the fore the need for designers specializing in these subjects.

Then it immediately became evident that special training was necessary, that such training could not be superimposed on either of the two other professions, and that it must be wide enough to cover the design not only of private gardens, but also of parks, 'parkways', and other public open spaces. Schools of landscape architecture were started and were scarcely able to meet the huge demand for the new profession. An experimental stage of bewildering plagiarism of other garden styles was a short phase only to be expected at the outset: the

Central Park, New York. Olmsted designed this park to create a sense of natural country within the confines of the great city. Tower blocks now dominate the skyline in some areas but the sense of calm remains, and from many parts the surrounding town remains unseen. Outcrops of natural rock and groups of native trees bring the character of the countryside into the centre of New York.

worst of its results were confined mainly to private gardens. The designers of public parks and parkways chose the English eighteenth-century landscape garden as being the logical inspiration for large-scale planning, and that tradition, transplanted from its native home where it had lost favour, developed naturally and consistently, along with the American 'Colonial' architecture.

In America the idea of country planning emerged from that beginning, a fact which has stood the country in good stead ever since. It is only now with the expanding development in Britain that we are feeling the extent of the loss due to that break in our own tradition in nineteenth-century England, and are realizing that we must borrow back experience from across the sea, since we have built so little of our own in the interval. We are faced with an unprecedented need for the services of qualified landscape architects, and an unprecedented eagerness on the part of young people to study the subject and make it a career; but our training facilities cannot yet meet the demand, and the supply of qualified landscape architects falls short of the numbers needed.

Today, the demand for professional design of private gardens has shrunk: the profession has moved instead into the wider field of landscape design. National and regional projects, new towns, local authorities, nationalized and other industries are seeking the services of landscape architects, either as independent consultants or as salaried employees. This tendency, begun in the last century, has gained momentum since the end of World War II.

Hutchinson River Parkway, Westchester, U.S.A. The Westchester Park System owes much to landscape architects such as Gilmore Clarke following the Olmsted tradition, which in turn derived inspiration from the English landscape treatment of parks. They mark a stage in the progress from garden design to landscape planning.

6

The Changing Scenery

Throughout the nineteenth century and early part of the present century, while the argument between the upholders of 'formal' design on one hand and 'wild gardens' on the other proceeded, British scenery was changing rapidly in the wider field. Architects and horticulturalists alike failed to see the need for a new alliance to defend the countryside from desecration. They continued the argument about gardens while vaster areas were being despoiled. Perhaps like Nero they may have felt the conflagration was beyond their powers to stem. We now have this fear in our minds, but we are proclaiming the possibility and need for controlling the flames, whereas the idea does not appear to have occurred to any of the 'arbiters of taste' in this country until the first quarter of the twentieth century.

Was the cause of the trouble in part due to the belief so warmly upheld by Repton that use and beauty were incompatible? Landscape has always suffered from the attempt to keep ideas on different subjects in separate, watertight compartments.

Railways in the Landscape

Belief in the incompatibility of usefulness and beauty had been fostered, and its bad effect increased, by the fact that so much of the industrial development was of a recalcitrant type, not easily woven into the landscape even if that had been an objective. The gradient necessary for railway lines cannot be gracefully moulded to the contours of undulating land, and it was railways above all which had extended industrialism. In America, the idea of the 'fitted highway' was emerging (that is to say, roads sited and designed for their landscape value as well as for efficiency); but even there the railways had defied such treatment. The practical requirements of the railways are so uncompromising that all hope of improving their appearance seems doomed. Once that view is accepted, everything to do with railways is assumed to be inevitably ugly, and the whole thing—stations, yards, sidings, embankments and cuttings, rolling-stock and fittings—is given free rein to be as ugly as possible.

Much could actually be done to improve the design of railway buildings and to assimilate the whole thing into a fine landscape. But their influence has been devastating and has driven home the belief that such ugliness is inevitable, making us all endure without protest conditions which should arouse violent reactions. This applied also to mining districts and factory areas. The black country and derelict areas generally are the legacy of that attitude. It is far easier, as we shall see, to maintain respectable landscape in the course of industrial changes than to restore it after uncontrolled development.

Seeing and Perceiving

Since the 1946 Planning Act the principle of restoration by the industry concerned with development has been recognized, if not always successfully operated, but the damage done earlier without control will not be remedied without vast expense and long delay. It has created an aesthetic resistance to all change even harder to overcome than the practical and economic difficulties involved. Remedies will have to be applied when the wastage of these areas makes itself more apparent as the population grows. But unless these are designed with sensitive regard to their visual landscape, restoration of such areas can easily create new extensions of slums.

Protests and violent reactions against dereliction and ugliness are, unfortunately, often wrongly directed. People tend to like what they know: the gift of visualizing something new and unknown, as it could be at its best, is extremely rare, and the fact that so much of the new is ugly reinforces the mistrust of new landscape or of the unfamiliar. Objects which were useful yet visually acceptable dating from before the industrial revolution, such as windmills and lighthouses, are appreciated, but more recent innovations are suspect. If we had never known windmills, and they were to appear as new

Windmill near West Burton, Notts. Familiarity can in some cases breed appreciation and reverence. The ancient monument on the left might appear as an obtrusion if seen for the first time today, and in the future the cooling towers may become treasures of the countryside. Today they enliven a flat landscape.

features in a familiar landscape, they would probably cause an outcry no less agonized than that against electric pylons. Viewed objectively, judged by the eye alone, certain windmills and certain transmission towers in certain positions are beautiful: but the eye is influenced by mental associations and memories—perhaps of other pylons, ugly because of clumsy design or bad siting—and thus a purely visual perception is rare and difficult to achieve. The eye is so prejudiced by ideas and associations that the beauty of unfamiliar objects is often unseen. Special discipline is needed to distinguish between the visual impression and its associated ideas.

The landscape architect's training and experience should enable him to *see* in several different ways. He should consider first the purely visual effect—unprejudiced by ideas; then the effect influenced by association of ideas; and thirdly the effect influenced by his own knowledge of scientific and biological factors. He must see it from the points of view of the artist and of the scientist, and as an intelligent member of a human community balancing the value of these different viewpoints.

The changes taking place now are far greater and occur faster than any in history. We must increase our power of controlling them —we must realize that completely new landscapes will emerge; that these could be visually satisfying, and that unless they fulfil that requirement they will fail in their functional objectives. They will fail to give us a world worth living in, and will increase the force of the resistance to all change.

The new road system presents a new view of the country. Much has been learnt in the early stages of this development, and we have profited from foreign experience. We may regret the passing of the old winding narrow roads and may hope to preserve the country lanes, but at least we can see improvements in the alignment and 'fitting' of the new wide motorways into the landscape through which they pass. The general acceptance of the fact that roads laid out like railway lines are dangerous, is a step towards the acceptance of good landscape standards in design. Logically, this realization should be applied to every form of land use design.

Agriculture and Landscape

We have yet to appreciate fully that every loss of agricultural land is a menace to the future, both from the point of view of fine landscape and because, if the world-wide population explosion continues at anything approaching its present rate, the time is not far distant when home-grown food will become more essential than car parks. We squander our limited land space for short-term needs without thought of this threat to the future. It would be wiser to keep the possibility in view throughout the siting and planning of all the new developments. Essential these are now, but a very different situation might develop even before the end of this century.

Taking the short-term view, it appears that agriculture can produce more food off less land than formerly. Mechanization and new systems have raised production not only on rich land but also on land hitherto regarded as marginal or uncultivable, and we feel that vast areas can now be spared for development, recreation and car parking. No one knows where the impact of the rising population figures will first strike. The pressure up to the present has been felt only very mildly in regard to road space, and shortages of power, water, gas, gravel and other resources. Scarcities and temporary breakdown of these are attributed to exceptional circumstances of climate or accident, and it is not generally admitted that all are related to the basic fact of rapid population increase, which is outgrowing our capacity. As the increase is world-wide, overseas supplies cannot be regarded as permanent manna from the sky, and the land might once again be our shield against famine even in this country.

Even if this eventuality is discounted, the need for preserving landscape and the balanced environment is reason enough for checking extravagant overspill and preserving open country.

Urban Spread

The squandering and uncontrolled urban and suburban spread has been checked by planning legislation in this century, but the pressures on open space have grown. We have yet to learn to look at the whole problem from a new angle and to realize fully the implications of the changes taking place.

The first reaction from overcrowding and industrial squalor produced the Garden City, aimed at giving industrial populations rural areas. Ebenezer Howard may have been right in thinking that loss of agricultural land could be more than compensated by increased productivity in small private gardens, though this was not the way the English normally use their gardens. Gardening is still one of the most popular spare-time hobbies of the industrial worker, but by growing flowers rather than vegetables, whenever he can afford it, he demonstrates that his most compelling need from nature is of the spirit rather than of the flesh.

Welwyn Garden City, Herts. This was a first step towards building whole towns at one time. The terrace groups are compact, but the layout is more open than in our later new towns. It was the reaction to overcrowding in the industrial development of the nineteenth century. Higher densities sought today are more convenient and space-saving.

Suburbia

However the small individual owner strives to make his own plot beautiful, he can never achieve the fine landscape he really needs. On the scale of modern housing there is little possibility of giving either the illusion of wild nature or the dignity of broad urban treatment; and the series of identical plots extending beyond the boundaries, though stimulating the desperate desire for originality of a kind, stamps each with an inescapable die. The series of water-tight compartments occupy so much space, and the occupants are so far removed from real country or from active city centres, that a special expedition must be made to enjoy either of these pleasures.

The wealth of blossom and the wide range of plants in the sub-urban garden fails to produce a unified landscape, in spite of some undeniable compensations for the individual owner. There is a monotony of scale and of material that makes for dullness; there is an absence of bold grouping, of real spaciousness; and the repetition of meagre and identical forms makes an extremely unsatisfying skyline which somehow conveys a sense—not so much of confinement—as of suffocating isolation and powerlessness. This feeling is reflected in the lives of the occupants. In the new housing estates, community life does not flourish as it does in a country village, or as in a setting designed for community living (as, say, a university, a kibbutz or other communal establishment): far less indeed than in the old slums where close quarters and common difficulties shared produce a kindly neighbourliness. The greater the number of similar dwellings grouped together, and the greater their separation from work, play and shopping centres (with all the variation of architectural form and size these involve) the poorer the quality of the landscape, and of social community life.

Judging by the landscape criterion alone, even if it were borne out by no practical and psychological considerations, it would seem that human dwellings can become a beautiful part of their surround-ings in two different ways. They may do so either as isolated units in open country, as in the case of crofters' cottages, farm buildings or important country houses; or else in larger, more compact and closely integrated groups with broad open spaces well related to massed architecture, as in the case of country villages, certain country towns (Bath, Bradford-on-Avon) and parts of larger towns such as the Mall in London. Universities and other large-scale institutions can achieve the effect very well. Many foreign towns, especially the compact market towns of mid-Europe and the hilltop towns of Greece, Spain and Provence, also prove the value of compact, in-tegrated grouping.

Large numbers of separate houses, close enough to be seen to-gether but unrelated by mass variation of form, can never create fine landscape, and their offence is doubled when they sprawl over and destroy larger areas of open space and of agricultural land than would be required by compact design.

In so far as the suburb, the garden city and the 'overspill' town

Spoleto, Italy. Close-grouped buildings with narrow streets lead up to the climax on the high contour. The important buildings are silhouetted above the general group, and the whole town is contained within a clear outline set in its landscape. Compare this with the toothy roof lines formed by small semi-detached pairs in monotonous sequence which mark our scenery and sprawl over too much good land in Britain.

fail to enrich rural life, the objectives of Ebenezer Howard and others whose aim is to repopulate the country have not materialized. The new towns are finding better systems of grouping, but the loss of rural population continues and much good land is still being engulfed at the expense of landscape and of country life.

The Machine for Living In

Le Corbusier's solution of the problem was a purely architectural one. He visualized his towns and buildings in fine natural settings, easily accessible to the occupants; and he assumed without question that this setting would remain unchanged. In fact, it is rarely possible to place a large building on any site, without some adap-

tation of the context. The Le Corbusier type of building makes little
provision for man-as-a-part-of-nature, but only for man-as-master-
of-his-fate. Such a conception seems incomplete and immature,
ignoring far too much of the nature of things as they are. It is not
enough to select pre-existing sites and insert something completely
alien into them—the building and its surroundings must fit together,
must be a part of a whole. This involves a different attitude to the
plan from the start. On a different scale from the garden city, the
'machine-for-living-in' tends to keep too many things in separate
watertight compartments and to ignore essential relationships.

The most satisfying examples of modern architecture are those
which do not ignore human dependence on natural beauty, but
which provide for as close and constant a relationship as possible
between natural and man-made forms.

Our new towns, perhaps the most striking accomplishment of

L.C.C. housing at Roehampton. The buildings have been fitted into what was
formerly fine landscape with as little disturbance as possible. Yet the necessary
adaptations to ground form and layout were extensive and the success of the
scheme is largely due to a recognition of the importance of the setting from the
outset.

Students' Halls of Residence, Queen's University, Belfast. Modern tower blocks tend to dominate their surroundings. Preservation of existing tree groups, and careful ground shaping with very broad simple treatment integrates them happily into the landscape. Close co-operation between architect and landscape architect is needed from the outset.

our century, are finding ways towards that relationship through the integration of open space and built up areas, the system of footpaths keeping some sylvan quality separated from the roads, and the traffic-free precincts. But the value of contrast between compact building and open space has yet to be re-learnt. Housing groups sprawling on the outskirts seldom achieve either the convenient urban quality of the old towns or the friendly grouping of a country village.

Architecture in the Landscape

The future development of landscape design is probably more closely bound up with that of architecture than was its past, owing to the growing tendency for building and open space to be combined in an interlocking design, rather than as two separate unities. The 'outdoors' is drawn into the building, and the 'indoors' extended into the grounds through a sequence of subtle graduations: wide, low windows form a lens better adapted to the shape of the outer landscape and to bifocal human vision than upright windows. And if plant forms are used inside the windows, they become almost a part of the view or at least its framework. Then a loggia or pillared gallery, with sliding doors to be closed or open according to the weather, may give access to a sheltered courtyard or outdoor hall, roofless, but still within the area of the ground-floor plan. In the case of domestic architecture this 'outdoor room' probably belongs to an individual family as much as the indoor part of the house. It leads on to the community garden or precinct which should still be closely linked with, or surrounded by, a group of buildings; and finally there is the general landscape beyond, whether it be town, green belt or open country.

Landscape Design in the Future

A new style of garden design well suited to a setting for contemporary architecture is emerging. Christopher Tunnard pointed out in the 1938 edition of *Gardens in the Modern Landscape* how inappropriate were the traditional styles. Changing styles in the wider landscape are less marked, since some of the best-designed landscapes are still so close to nature that they do not appear to be artifacts. Nevertheless vast changes in the general countryside are inevitable, and new landscapes will appear; to landscape architects will fall the problems not only of preserving some part of traditional landscapes but also the creation of new types and patterns of landscape in the areas of changing land use.

Landscape is alive and growing. Its rate of change has in past periods been almost imperceptible in terms of human life-times, but is now accelerating so fast that control becomes essential if life is to be worth living. The landscape architect's training is designed to understand this changing medium, to visualize past and future aspects of the land and the various intermediate stages of development. No other profession emphasizes, to the same extent, the need for continuity from past to future—the need to ensure a smooth flow of evolution so as to reduce the shocks of sudden change and to minimise the effects of imbalance.

Nature must be served rather than mastered, for man is a part of nature and of his environment. In so far as he can control that environment, he is responsible for the safeguarding of his own future existence.

Humanity cannot exist independently and must cherish the relationships binding us to the rest of life. That relationship is expressed visually by the landscape in which we live.

In the visual surroundings, the partnership between art and science will be reflected in the consciously controlled new landscape of developing areas. The scientific adaptation to changes of land use needs to be tempered by visual satisfaction. Some give-and-take between art and science is essential if human enjoyment of the scene as well as healthy progress is the aim.

Natural land forms resulting from slow geological processes appear asymmetric. In living creatures symmetry is subtle and not always self-evident, though some of their products such as the spider's web and the honeycomb have obvious symmetry. In the design of the living organism itself there is usually a coalescence of symmetry and asymmetry such as we see in the human body. Each hand alone is asymmetric; together, as in prayer, symmetry appears.

This association of symmetry and asymmetry has served for most of our human inventions, especially those concerned with movement and time—from the sundial to the aeroplane. In the broader scale of landscape where the land forms provide the rough block of the design, symmetry as we understand it is replaced by a different rhythm—a balanced life cycle embracing life in all its forms, and through which evolution proceeds.

Imitation of nature, or of portrayals of nature, is no longer the objective, but the design is still inspired by nature through the climatic and geological indications of each site allied to the proposed use. The indications may suggest geometric or free treatment, or both combined. The 'style' is important only so far as it succeeds in relating function to environment, to produce that organic unity and balance from which beauty itself arises.

The model is to be found in the structure of living organisms

rather than in their products. Certain constant characteristics of
living things are those we seek in our work. There is that relationship of function and environment, interpreted in the case of landscape design in terms of the needs of the people using the site, related
to topography and climate. Then there is the building up of separate
but interdependent units into a group, the groups uniting to form
larger groups eventually merging into a whole with clear relationships, order and sequence in the distribution of the parts. While the
individuality of the units is retained, there is a unity of character
common to all, demonstrating their membership of the whole.
Recognizable qualities of line, angle, pattern or expression are seen
throughout, without overlaying the individuality of the minor
ingredients within that whole.

In design of this order, function and aesthetics are combined.
Science and art are seen as two aspects of the same thing, and just as
bodily beauty plays a part in procreation, so beauty in the surroundings of human life stimulates and tempers human development,
nourishing the spirit. The higher the stage of evolution, the greater
the need for this response to natural beauty. In that sense beauty is a
function of evolution.

One of the strongest reasons for preserving and creating fine
landscape is the rights of posterity. This fact tends to be overlooked
because it is not easily reconciled with the immediate needs and
greeds of the present population. Our instinctive love of fine landscape is thwarted and suppressed by evidence of economic necessity,
often put forward on humanitarian grounds, but without regard to
long-term needs of humanity in coming generations.

There is a changing pattern of life in villages and countryside,
not only in the lowlands within easy reach of cities, but also in
the distant highlands and coastal regions of our wilder and more
dramatic scenery. Cottage and croft alike are being taken over as
holiday homes or for retirement by professional people not dependent on the land for their living. Adaptations of the existing
crofts and cottages, and new homes being built are often of urban
or suburban type unsympathetic to the surrounding simplicity,
and the change usually leads to neglect of the former small holding

and the land. The change may be welcome to the locality because it helps the economy and replaces a dwindling population of the older type now drawn to the towns, but it introduces a surburban character into many of the loveliest remaining areas. This unfortunate development could be avoided by compact grouping and sensitive design of the new homes — but we see few examples of how well this could be done. The change is a world-wide symptom of a new way of life, and some of the more successful attempts to meet the new need with deference to the old system can be seen in certain hill villages of Provence in France.

The greater and more rapid the changes affecting the landscape, the greater must be our powers of adaptation. The designer must understand the past and the influences of tradition, but must also be free from limitations no longer applicable to our time, and ready to embark on new courses. In landscape design this means being truly responsive to the spirit of place, and alive to the need for new uses to which places are to be put. Environment and purposes must be brought into relationship.

Landscape design approached in this spirit, whether it be on the scale of urban areas related to buildings or on the larger regional scale, will inevitably be dynamic, changing to meet new conditions and essentially of its own time. The landscape architect must always be looking forward to the long-term outcome of his design. Immediate economic factors may conflict with the longer view, and here the landscape architect's duty may be to demonstrate the longer view, or at least to show that short-term economic factors are not the only ones to be considered.

The greater the scale of the project, the less likely is the new landscape to be of marked 'period' style. The designer wishing to impose his own style, or to demonstrate striking originality, will be well advised to keep to small urban projects, where the vagaries and quirks of fashion may be indulged. True individuality arises naturally from thoughtful adaptation to the circumstances of each project, not from self-conscious efforts to display 'originality'.

PART TWO

Principles of Landscape Design

7

Science and Art Related in Landscape Design

Landscape architecture, like architecture itself, is concerned with the design of human environment. The two forms of design have much in common but differ profoundly in that architecture deals with man-made roofed-in structures of static material, while landscape architecture deals with the open-air, outdoor surroundings of human life, and with ever-changing materials. They differ, too, in other important ways, particularly in their scale.

Structure

The materials, in the case of landscape design are, broadly speaking, two: first the land itself, with its rocks, soil and water; and secondly its vegetation, ranging from forest trees to grass and the lowly mosses and lichen.

The land forms, whose surface we see, are determined by the underlying rocks: these are the skeleton giving the country its basic shape. Soil and water are the flesh and blood, moulding the outline. Vegetation is the skin—the living robe clothing the surface and providing all that variety of colour and texture which means so much to the human eye.

The history of how the rocks were formed, and how they came to be where they are, with all the vast changes which have brought

Dovedale, Derby. The materials of natural landscape are the land and its vegetation. The rocks and the water that springs from them are important features of the natural land forms. Human activity now adds new features—roads, bridges, buildings—all capable of dominating and concealing the underlying form. Landscape design should help to keep us aware of our relationship to nature: conservation of the best in its natural condition is essential to human understanding of that relationship and our part within it.

about the land as we see it today, should form the background of the landscape-planner's outlook. With it is bound up the story of the soil, and of the origins of life itself. Soil, supporting life, was engendered through the action of weather on the rocky matrix. An understanding of that long geological history and of the life that has evolved on the surface helps us to realise the effects of what we do today.

Contemplation of our landscape based on an understanding of the origin and structure of the visible land can bring a new vision and a deeper love of its infinite variety. Greater depths of meaning and significance unfold themselves, and the land that is lovely even to the superficial view reveals, through this closer study, a personality and a spirit of ageless beauty.

Under the earth's crust lies a mass of material about which human knowledge is still at the conjectural stage. Its history is astronomical rather than geological, and to extend the organic analogy it may be compared to the subconscious mind. There, hidden from our sight and knowledge, is stored the memory of past ages, linking us with the sun.

Geology merges into biology at the level of the soil: and the history of landscape at that level evolves under the influence of weather and of living organisms. Variations in the plant and animal communities of the different types of country, or grouped on the different rocks, provide unending interest in natural landscape, and a further means of tracing the underlying structure and of appreciating the harmony of nature's design.

Ecology, that branch of biology which deals with the relationship of living forms with each other and with their surroundings—or the mutual reaction between living communities and the environment—is the science of landscape. It takes into consideration geology, climate, soil (especially in relation to human needs), as well as the associations of plants and animals and lower forms of life.[1]

Vegetation has changed through the ages almost as much as the

[1] See A. G. Tansley, *The British Islands and Their Vegetation*, CUP, 1939.

rocks themselves. Primitive types evolved and became extinct, to be replaced by higher forms. The familiar trees of the deciduous forest —oak, ash and beech—are of comparatively recent origin. In Britain many of them arrived long after early man and were preceded by the conifers; all in turn colonized the land as the ice retreated, many coming as invaders from the south-east across the land neck which then joined England to the Continent.

Man began to make his marks on the landscape soon after his first appearance, and his action grew until we have now that well-lived-in appearance sometimes called 'the man-made landscape'—an expression which tends to overlook the importance of the underlying rock forms.

Only in his mining, quarrying and rock-boring processes has man touched the bone: his action in the main has been confined to the surface, and most of it, till recently, has been done without thought of the appearance: it has been simply the outcome of adaptations called for by his agriculture, his travels, his wars, his religion and his industry, with all the earthworks, roads, buildings and plant growth entailed in this development.

Conscious aesthetic design of the landscape is a very late development. It starts with the construction of gardens; and this can be appreciated only in peaceful and comparatively civilized surroundings. Francis Bacon first pointed out that garden design marks a later stage of evolution than architecture: 'A man shall see that when ages grow to civility and elegance, men come to build stately sooner than to garden finely, as if gardening were the greater perfection.' A yet more advanced step, first taken in this country in the eighteenth century, is that of extending conscious design to the countryside as a whole. That step, that phase of adolescence, was forgotten and retracted in later years, but fortunately its imprint was firm and remains with us in great measure to the present day. Now we are gathering strength and resolution for a more definite step in the direction of independence, of conscious control of our own destiny. The conscious control of landscape having regard to its visual quality will be a sign of new maturity.

Chanctonbury Ring, Sussex. Eighteenth-century plantations sited as important landscape features, to be seen from afar, were a first step towards the conscious design of the countryside. These beech clumps crowning the high contours are characteristic of the English landscape style. Natural regeneration on the chalk escarpment is here forming new woodland to link with hedges and woodland in the richer valley scenery.

The Materials of Landscape Design

Land and vegetation are the two main materials of natural land-scape. Each, in a different way, contributes to those solid masses and open voids which make up any composition. In the case of the land itself, hills, mountains and convex forms make up the 'masses', while the valleys, plains and water surfaces form the obverse spaces or 'voids' of the composition. Man lifts his eyes to the hills and rests them in the valleys; and instinctively he classifies 'mass' and 'void' in relation to the scale of his own figure, whether he is looking at land or plant-forms. Vegetation provides 'masses' in the form of groups of trees and shrubs larger than man, and 'voids' of turf, low plants and farm crops which his eye can dominate.

The interplay of these four themes, land and plant forms, masses and voids, dependent on existing contours and influenced by basic indications of climate, soil type and land use, provides all the variety

and pattern of landscape. In nature, or in agricultural landscape produced by the play of circumstances, there exists a harmonious
relationship between land forms and vegetation resulting from underlying facts of ecology and geology. It is the task of the planners of
the future, if our landscape is still to serve (as Bacon said of gardens)
as a 'refreshment to the spirit of man', to study those relationships
and those basic ecological facts and to follow the same cosmic
principles.

To take a single example: there is the tendency in many of the
best farming districts for land and plant masses to coincide, in contrast to a parallel coincidence of valley and low vegetation—as when
wooded hills give shelter to low-lying farms, water surfaces and
meadows. The opposite effect occurring in upland districts where

Lantic Bay, Cornwall. The natural landscape pattern—even when, as in this
case, depending on land form without important vegetation—is composed of
related mass and void: the rounded convexities contrast with the open flatter
areas, and define their shape.

woods are found growing in the shelter of the valleys and the hills are given over to rough pasture above the tree line, indicates a wilder scene. The upland soils are thin and poor; but in so far as it might be possible to improve the farmland by planting shelter on some escarpments, and cultivating part of the deeper soil of the valley, wildness is a confession of human failure, much as we delight in the naked grandeur of the heights.

Different underlying rocks and geological formations give different characteristic forms to the surface; and although the type of weathering and denudation which has occurred may greatly influence those surface forms, these characteristics are sufficiently marked to be easily recognizable in the landscape. The chalk hills, for example, show quite different outlines and curves from those of the Devonian sandstone or the granite outcrops.

Symonds Yat, Forest of Dean, Glos. The contrast of land form is underlined by the difference of land use: farmland on the valley floor with pasture and forest on the steep slopes. The river defines the shape of the lowest contours.

Scafell Pike, Cumberland. The highest mountain in England is typical of our granite scenery. Above the tree line only low vegetation such as grass and heather grows, together with a few plants to be found only in these highland spots.

Natural Plant Communities mark Landscape Variety

Certain groups of plants show a preference for certain soils and rocks, and although no single member of such a group is necessarily confined to one formation, collectively the group 'community', resulting from a set of conditions of which the underlying rock is an important factor, gives each region a character of its own. Study of these groups and of the causes giving rise to their association is a branch of ecology of vital interest to the landscape designer if he appreciates the native character of our landscape. Nothing is easier than to introduce foreign plants of outstanding beauty and to grow them where we will (having due regard to their likes and dislikes); but to spread these recklessly over the countryside is to overlay the existing subtle variations of our land and to lead in the end to a deathly monotony. We shall be wise to confine this horticultural kind of treatment to parks, gardens and towns where the architecture and the work of men's hands already dominate over nature to such an extent that the native character of the soil is lost; keeping the wider countryside to the natural plant groups. This would not necessarily mean excluding, even from the wider countryside, all but 'true' native species. Since every plant is an intruder or immigrant at some period in history, how can we say that the sweet chestnut, introduced by the Romans, and the sycamore, probably a much later immigrant, are still foreigners in our land? But it would mean limiting our choice in the wider landscape to plants which have established themselves as part of that landscape and are able to hold their own as members of one or other of the native plant associations.

Various systems of plant grouping which have been practised at different times, in different countries, are discussed in a later chapter. Groups which may please the artist may seem entirely incongruous to the botanist, and the Eastern sage may find both the artist's and the botanist's groupings insipid because they lack symbolic content. The landscape architect should understand these different approaches, whatever his own predilections. The problem is further complicated in this country by the fact that our climate allows us to use plants from such a wide area, and the material available for use in Britain is of such colossal range and is still increasing so rapidly that any designer who attempts to keep abreast of that side of the work can have no time left for other aspects. Nevertheless, the landscape architect needs an intimate knowledge, not only of the native plant associations of his own countryside, but also of a large quantity of introduced plants and varieties of garden origin, selected to fulfil his needs and to provide given effects on various soils. In making his selection he will need both the relevant botanical and ecological knowledge, and a keen appreciation of the sculptural qualities of plant form, enabling him to build up groups well related to land forms and architecture. The historic character of certain sites may be underlined by using only those plants which would have been available at the period of the structure.

Architects, town planners and other designers have been apt to think of trees and shrubs as an additional ornamental feature, especially in built-up areas—a final touch to be added when all else was complete, the carnation in the buttonhole of an immaculate lapel. Plants have been used as applied ornament no less than those decorative tiles and elaborate window-panes on detached villas, the 'half-timber' applied to the surface of the pseudo-Tudor gable, and all the rest of the tragic unrelated ornament intended to make pretty something which itself is felt to be unsatisfactory and incomplete. Flowering plants, trees and shrubs used only to serve this same pathetic function unrelated to the main design represent a sentimental attempt to meet a genuine need—a longing for some real and fundamental value beyond the range of the designer.

The Structural Use of Plants

Growing plants are an essential structural material of landscape. Trees and shrubs are used by the landscape architect as stone, concrete and steel are used by the architect and engineer. They may form the boundaries and partition walls defining the open spaces of the design. They may serve as shelter from the wind and weather, smoke and noise, or give shade from the sun. They may be used as screens either to delay a view of a given area until the appropriate point, or to shut out an undesirable scene. They may serve to lead the eye and interest towards a given climax, and above all they can be used to relate buildings and other man-made features to the land.

This functional use of plant material in landscape design is discussed more fully in Chapter Eight. Here it is intended only to distinguish clearly between those plant groups which, in conjunction with the ground itself, form the basic structure of the design, and those which are added merely as superficial accessories.

Flower-beds and borders and some few flowering trees and shrubs 'interior' to the main structure may be compared with the interior decoration of a house. They are needed to make the place habitable, to give comfort and to satisfy our feeling for colour, and they can only fulfil this need if used as part of the main structure. Too many gardens and parks are designed as if furniture and hangings alone can meet our needs.

The amount of planting of a purely ornamental character which can be happily admitted, and the importance of such planting in relation to the main structure, is largely a matter of scale. Scale in landscape design is not, as we shall see, purely a matter of three dimensions.

Scale, Movement and Time

Landscape design, at certain periods of its history, was regarded as an art concerned above all with the means of making parks and gardens appear larger than they were in fact. Designers themselves always took a wider view of their art, but it is true that many tricks of false perspective had been tried in those periods. William Kent, early in the eighteenth century, used the device of the converging avenue with groups of trees irregularly spaced, very wide apart at the near end and narrowing at the farther end. The spacing in both horizontal dimensions can be planned to give this effect, and, to complete the device in the vertical dimension, trees of varying heights could also be used, but it is doubtful whether Kent carried the idea to these lengths. His use of the ha-ha or sunk fence to conceal the boundary of the garden, however, gave the impression that the meadows beyond were part of the lawn.

Repton advocated the use of breeds of diminutive cattle or ponies grazing in the park, saying that the eye accepts familiar animals as a scale of size and therefore animals smaller than those to which we are accustomed make the park seem correspondingly larger. Gertrude Jekyll's colour scale worked on the principle that blue conveys a sense of distance, while warm colours bring objects closer to the viewer.

False perspective was tried out in many ways, but the difficulty about most of them was that, seen from the wrong end, the device was revealed in all its absurdity, and once the mind knows the truth, the trick fails.

The same objection applies to the 'surprises' so much in vogue ever since the eighteenth century. Peacock's question in *Headlong*

Hall is unanswerable: 'What happens the *second* time you go round the garden?'

At Versailles there is an avenue of poplars designed to be seen from the Palace as one pair of giant trees. This effect is even more startling in the garden of the Villa Barbarigo at Valsan Zibio.

Villa Barbarigo, near Padua, Italy. The avenue of cypresses climbing the hill behind the house appear when seen from the front garden as a single pair of gigantic trees dwarfing the tall house.

The tricks are of doubtful value where they aim at increasing the apparent area, but the exaggeration of plant form by the use of these avenues holds its magic effect each time we see it.

Scale and proportion in the open landscape are very different from those of architecture, and need special study. They resemble those of architecture only in so far as they relate to the human figure, and they differ in so far as they are affected by speed and movement, and also in their relation to the width of the horizon.

Bifocal human vision takes in a wide horizontal angle of view, and landscape in general has a wide rather than an upright tendency (witness the photographer's use of the words 'landscape' and 'portrait' to distinguish between the horizontal and the upright shapes of illustrations). Modern architecture makes allowance for this simple fact, and that in itself calls for closer relationship between the surroundings and the interior of buildings.

The horizon is very wide by comparison with the height of trees or other objects appearing on it at a distance; and even when we are concerned with a comparatively close skyline, on level ground the vertical limit is set by the height to which trees will grow, whereas no such natural limitation rules the horizontal dimensions, and these, depending on quite different factors, tend to be much larger—with the result that our eyes are accustomed to, and expect, great width in comparison to height. On sloping ground or in hilly country, trees and other plant forms are a less important scale-factor, though they serve to emphasize or to counterbalance the ground contours.

Trees, when suitably spaced in relation to the ground plan, have the effect of multiplying the two-dimensional area by their height, so increasing the volume of cubic space contained within their height as do walls and ceiling in the case of buildings. The absence of this effect, resulting from open spaces very large by comparison to the height of their trees, is a defect in the case of parks or gardens intended for rest or leisurely movement, but may be desirable in other cases, where the use is different; as in agricultural landscape, or where the speed of movement is greater (as in the case of playing-fields), or on slopes or undulating ground where the vertical dimension does not depend on trees alone. (See drawings on p. 191.)

Flat sites, however, offer tempting opportunity for lavish and grandiose design, and the human factor is all too often forgotten. Recent town-planning schemes in more than one country have included vistas and squares of such majestic proportions that the courage of the mere pedestrian quails at the thought of crossing from one side to the other. Ponderous monuments, vast civic buildings and gigantic open spaces surrounding them are a means by which powerful rulers seek to immortalize themselves at the expense of posterity. The use of such a scale, so far as the open spaces are concerned, can be justified only on the assumption of complete mechanization of the populace. If the speed of movement is that of the bicycle or motor-car rather than human walking-pace, the grandiose scale may be appropriate. But it is to be hoped that populations are not to lose, completely, the use of their legs; and Francis Bacon's essay on gardens again comes to mind—where he says: 'The alley

A lime avenue, Clumber Park, Notts. The scale of such avenues is adapted to the pace of horse or pedestrian rather than the motor car. At faster speeds the repetition of the trunks is confusing to the traveller.

will be long, and in great heat of the year or day you ought not to buy the shade in the garden by going in the sun through the green.'

For several reasons, not all quite obvious at first glance, a more spacious treatment is called for in the open than in the framework of a building. Wider steps, wider paths and gateways are needed partly because the sizes of open-air spaces are usually large compared to the area of buildings. We find, however, that even in small courtyards these things call for more generous treatment than they do under a roof. Some psychological factor is concerned here, probably connected with the habit of speeding up our movements in the open air. The out-of-door walk is more brisk, the stride longer and the whole tempo of existence undergoes a slight change. There is a similar change—perhaps of less degree—at the boundary between the garden and the wider landscape beyond.

Speed of movement, then, is clearly concerned in the matter of proportion and scale. An avenue of familiar proportions, having evenly spaced trees, is inappropriate for fast-moving traffic. The trees, flickering past the eye like the earliest attempts at motion photography, have a physically tiring effect. Spatial proportion, at least in landscape design, turns out to be a four-dimensional problem.

Of all arts, architecture is perhaps best calculated to develop a power of thinking in three dimensions—a power of visualizing mental conceptions 'in the round'—a most valuable and necessary power for anyone concerned with physical planning. In landscape design, however, as we have just seen, the time-dimension calls for a further development of the powers of visualization, and this is apparent, not only where scale and physical proportions are concerned, but also in all cases where plans take time to develop or where seasonal and other changes occur. Like town-planning, landscape architecture is an art of four dimensions: and it provides a sure and comparatively easy approach to a four-dimensional habit of thought and of four-dimensional visualization, because its materials are never static. Trees take time to grow—their life is longer than that of man and many times longer than much of his building created under current short-term policies. In addition, there is seasonal change, and all the constant alteration of growing things under the influence of environment.

The Plan takes Time to Develop

Trees grouped together develop a character and shape unlike the same species growing as isolated specimens. Trees exposed to wind will grow differently from those given shelter. The knowledge that our ultimate conception, in so far as it depends on the planting of forest trees, will take upwards of fifty years to mature, leads the designer to visualize all the intermediate stages, and to provide where necessary some temporary substitute. Long- and short-term planting schemes may be needed together, say alternate trees, of which the fast growing types will be cut out gradually as the ultimate conception develops. To this end it is not enough to ensure that the planting is correctly done in the first place; it is of vital interest to ensure the evolution of the designer's intention—the continuity of the original conception through those responsible for maintenance. The designer can feel little security unless the mechanism for ensuring continuity is as well designed, as efficient and workable as the plan itself.

It is possible to avoid these complications to a great extent, and to reduce planting almost to a three-dimensional problem by using

W. H. Smith warehouse, Swindon, Wilts. An existing tree lends maturity and frames a view of the new buildings. Newly planted, quick growing species, on slightly mounded contours to assist drainage on the heavy clay soil and to increase their height, will soon reach the sizes shown by the white dots. On the other side of the building mature and semi-mature trees make a quicker effect in the early years.

only fully grown trees and shrubs—an ancient practice now widely revived with the help of mechanical methods; but although the use of large semi-mature plants has many advantages, and is well worth while in certain cases, the ultimate results are not the same as and may be less satisfactory than traditional methods, particularly in the case of shelter planting. The choice between the slower system or the ready-made planting should depend on the circumstances of each site. In many cases the two can be combined. For a designer to depend always on 'instant planting' is to change his four-dimensional approach to one of three dimensions—as if a sculptor were to limit himself to working in bas-relief, or a painter to forgo the use of perspective.

The pleasure of watching things develop in time, and of noting and enjoying each different phase as it appears, is not to be relinquished lightly—to miss out these intermediate stages is to lose one of those contacts with the soil which our period can ill afford; and the artificial completion of the project at one stroke is one of those means by which 'civilization' (or that sophistication which we call civilization) impoverishes the realities of living in time.

Planning for Growth and Development

All planning for the future calls for the power of thinking along the time-dimension—of foreseeing results likely to arise from given causes, and modifying present action affecting those causes. In the case of physical planning, in so far as it deals with things which take time to develop, the three spatial dimensions must be visualized as changing elements in the time-dimension. This means developing a power of visualization of new calibre.

Traditional standards of design are no longer the sound guide they used to be in the past, owing to the increasing tempo of change, or at least of human evolution. When, as the result of new sources of power and new scientific inventions, designers were called upon to make the first railway stations, the first radio sets, the first aerodromes, there was no tradition to look back to for guidance and inspiration, and the forward-looking power of visualization had not been developed. It is clear that in future we must depend on our powers of looking forward in time rather than to our knowledge and memory of the past, which is tradition. This is not to say that knowledge of the past and historic background is any less valuable—it is indeed more essential than ever; but we must give up depending on habits and customs of the past as guides in dealing with totally new developments. We need instead a forward-looking instrument which will seek inspiration in its power of foresight and adaptability to change. The new implement is at hand if we can learn to use it, but we are not yet fully awake to the method of applying it. A study of landscape and landscape design may serve to train the mind in four-dimensional thinking and four-dimensional visualization (just as a study of architecture disciplines the mind to three-dimensional thought and visualization), for the reason that vegetation, one of the essential components of landscape, is itself an ever-changing material.

8

The Foundations of Design

Apart from the practical necessities which influence design, and which will be discussed in Chapter Nine, there are whole worlds of traditional thought and belief influencing the design of open spaces. These inevitably react with the necessities such as the use of space, the climate and topography of each site, but they nevertheless override the rest, and can be seen as constant characteristics of national styles.

As our western cultures develop, and as the taste for gardens and landscape grows, there seems to come a stage when the inward-looking enclosure is felt to be inadequate, and a growing interest in the view beyond turns the garden inside out, so that where formerly we had enclosed courtyard or walled garden relating solely to the building to which it belongs, we now find the grounds serving as introduction to the wider landscape and a link between architecture and natural scenery.

Growing appreciation of landscape composition as seen by painters develops after the painters themselves have come to see landscape and figures as related objects. This influence was clearly marked in the case of the eighteenth-century landscape style in Britain, although the later phase of 'naturalistic' design here arose rather from a love of plants and gardening at the turn of the nineteenth century, and owed little allegiance to the art of painting. Nor did it arise from reverence for nature, that impulse so potent in the Far East.

Landscape and Garden in the Far East

Chinese and Japanese garden arts both deriving from early Chinese culture, quite independently of western influences until recent years, differ profoundly in some ways from their western counterparts. Their similarities however, throw an interesting light on the aesthetic factors common to all landscape design. The classic gardens of the Far East have a universal appeal, however different their style and technique from those of the West.

Natural forms, often scaled down and controlled to suit the design, are idealized by gentle unobtrusive trimming. To cut plants into architectural forms would be considered irreverent and presumptuous. Reverence towards a bountiful nature which should be served is a key note: in so far as nature is conquered in Japanese gardens it is done with exquisite delicacy and tact, flattering and emphasizing nature's characteristic beauty.

The object of increasing the apparent size of gardens explored by Repton and others in the western hemisphere was achieved in many Japanese gardens by reducing the whole scale, and by giving free play to the imagination of the viewer. It is a game to be played without any intent to deceive, to see spaces which may be small in themselves, from the worm's eye view—or from an Alice in Wonderland individual reduced to miniature size. The game can by played anywhere by projecting oneself in imagination into the body of a small bird, searching through the undergrowth in the garden, or into that of a mouse in the hayfield.

A use of a scale smaller than real life in the design of courtyards and little gardens is probably stimulating and flattering to the human intellect, once the effort of imagination has been made; it is well suited to anyone requiring a thinking place rather than a sports ground. The appeal of the famous Ryoanji garden in Kyoto where there are no plants, but only patterned sand and subtle groups of boulders, is to the mind and the imagination in contemplation rather than to bodily exploration.

The Japanese garden as it has been exported (to western tea-gardens and willow-pattern plates for example) is characteristic only of certain superficial aspects of its design. Eastern influence might be felt more in the future, however, through this use of natural forms, and the skill in scaling down the design to make the most of limited space. Now that the world increase of human populations threatens to engulf even the wilder solitudes, we may need to create more compelling counter-attractions nearer home. 'It is now impos-

Nanzeni Temple, Kyoto, Japan. The Abbot's Hall Garden. The raked sand represents water. The placing and form of the stones reflect a symbolism unfamiliar to Western thought, but none the less pleasing to the senses. Meticulous trimming of the plants preserves the designer's intent, and customary good manners keep visitors to the pathway.

sible for our multitudinous private landscapes to be splendidly extrovert . . . . It seems therefore that like the Japanese we should do well to concentrate upon the design of the very small space, creating an illusion in it and excluding the environment.'[1] The cult of 'littleness' may prove to be the corollary of the cult of 'bigness', and the cult of 'inwardness' that of the exploration of outer space. It is unlikely that we in the West should enjoy an actual reduction in scale, for our view of ourselves is less self-effacing than that of the Japanese. But there is much to learn from the Japanese control of the extension of space.

The symbolism of the stones and other features in Japanese gardens is perhaps for some Westerners, as for the Japanese

[1] G. A. Jellicoe, *Studies in Landscape Design*, vol. 2, OUP, 1966.

themselves, the most characteristic aspect of their use of space. The universal importance of this, however, is the fact that the result is visually pleasing even to those ignorant of the symbolism. Modern, impressionist, surrealist and abstract painters are exploring ideas which seem to have been expressed ages ago in Japan in designs such as the Daitoku-ji Temple garden. The subconscious appreciations seem to originate deep in the tap-root of human evolution, and are part of a common heritage.

The need to see and enjoy the landscape beyond our own patch is evidenced in nearly all countries in very different degrees. Few Japanese gardens provide this luxury. Instead they create their own world within the confines available. Contemplation of the object close at hand compensates for the distant view, and develops appreciation of natural variety in both ground form and plant form.

The Japanese design some gardens to be looked at from special viewpoints, or from a particular tour of the grounds rather than as places to live in. This is unlikely to appeal to the British with their innate love of gardening for its own sake. It may be well suited to grounds attached to hotels and restaurants or in any case where the garden can be treated as a picture into which we have no need to enter.

It seems more likely, however, that landscape design comes increasingly to see humanity in the landscape, as a part of the environment, and to design landscape with figures.

The naturalistic treatment of trees and shrubs in China and Japan does not arise from any horror of using the shears: the growing material is most carefully pruned and trained into the desired forms, but those forms are such as might be supposed to have occurred in nature, and are not representative of architectural or sculptured forms made in other materials.

The Influence of Rome in the West

In the West, the Latin races adopted the opposite course of imposing human art forms on living plants. Italian gardens to the

Villa Marlia, Lucca, Italy. The Italian use of clipped evergreens as part of the architectural structure influenced Lenotre and others in France, though the cypresses and evergreen oaks gave way in France to lime, hornbeam and other deciduous trees.

Green architecture here combines with balustrades and a rich stone grotto to enclose the reflecting pool. In the tubs are orange trees or flowers as interior decorative detail.

present day depend much on tall clipped hedges forming green extensions of the architecture to which they relate. In France the zenith of this system is seen in the gardens of Lenotre, such as Versailles, Vaux-le-Vicomte and Chateau de Champs, where all the growing material is treated as if it were masonry enclosing space and forming architectural shapes. No single tree, flower or foliage plant is allowed to flout the order imposed: by massed use the plants become, as it were, architectural building material.

The typical Lenotre garden consists of a series of open spaces extending the indoor living space, carved out of surrounding woodland. Nearest to the main terrace are the '*Parterres de Broderie*' laid like carpets or embroidered panels of elaborate design carried out in clipped box and sand. Broad gravel paths surround and intersect these carpets, and some small clipped topiary pieces punctuate the pattern like green sculpture. The whole is enclosed by green walls rising above the colonnades of tree stems. Near the summit of the trees the close clipping ceases, allowing a fringe of inward branching foliage to form the cornice and so to make a ceiling of the sky itself. Behind the colonnades are the shaded woodland walks, green vaulted corridors leading to secondary open spaces or 'salles,' each having its fountain or sculptured nucleus.

Spanish gardens, such as the Alcazar and the Generalife in Granada derive from both Eastern and Western gardens. The green walls dividing separate enclosures are of clipped cypress or evergreen oak, in the Roman tradition, but within the enclosures the eastern influence of Persia dominates the design. Plants with fine sculptural foliage are displayed in contrast to the smooth green walls, and as individuals worthy of appreciation. This mixture of clipped and natural forms together shows a pleasant meeting between East and West. This use of the individual plant form reminds us of Japanese flower arrangement, but the use of the freely-grown specimen placed sculpturally against a tonsured background is typically Spanish.

The Common Denominator

However national styles may differ and whatever the systems of thought from which they spring, certain features are shared by classical examples of all ages and places. A common denominator underlying creative design, no less evident in landscape than in other arts, is the search for compatibility between unity and diversity. An over-all 'oneness' of character throughout is a hallmark of conscious design. On every artifact is stamped (through this unity) evidence of its origin in place and time, and often also the signature of the designer—his recognizable and unique script. That 'oneness' assimilates and reconciles variety in the parts so that each part, individual as it may be, is clearly related to and in sympathy with the rest. Unity, if it imposes monotonous repetition and conformity, is

Generalife, Spain. Free plant form is here seen in strong contrast to clipped hedges which form the structural partition between the various enclosures.

sterile: the dynamism that is life involves change, movement and individuality within the greater unity and throughout 'duration'.

Had leaders of religious and political systems sought as ardently as the artist for the true relationship between Unity and Diversity, the hope of God's Kingdom on Earth might by now be nearer fulfilment. In that Unity (we have been told) there are many mansions.

Conditions governing Landscape Design

The landscape architect having studied his art and thought about it for himself will be steeped in the ideas and traditions of his culture, but in these times of accelerating change must be also reaching out for new ideas and fresh influences. The facts and conditions of each individual project will, however, set a definite framework and provide preliminary ingredients for that project. They will set limits to the possibilities and these limits themselves become a source of inspiration, no less than the aesthetic impulses of the designer.

All design springs from definite sources. Firstly there is the *need* for the thing to be designed; secondly there are the conditions influencing or qualifying that need; and thirdly, there is the designer's power of assessing and weighing up that need in relation to those conditions. The designer (if consciously planning ahead and not merely under the play of circumstances) also makes a definite contribution of his own, arising from his special knowledge and training and from his own inherent appreciation of proportion and composition: of scale relationships, of colour, form and texture relationships, of balance, punctuation and rhythm. He contributes a quality of design based on his whole knowledge and experience.

The designer's function is therefore a dual one; he must approach the subject, firstly, as a scientist, examining, analysing and weighing with factual accuracy all the circumstances and conditions of the site. Secondly, the application of that other quality of good design calls for the power of judgment and the artist's creative urge. In landscape design the artist must understand also the basic scientific approach, and the scientist must also be an artist: without the aesthetic sense, the scientist lacks control over his material and cannot make full use of it. Landscape architecture must build a bridge between Art and Science.

What are the conditions and facts whose examination should provide the designer with the preliminary ingredients? First, there is the use for which the site is intended. Secondly, there is a group of topographical factors such as the size and shape of the site and its relationship to surrounding land, the influence on buildings connected with the site, and any trees or water existing on, or visible from, the site. Thirdly, there are climatic and geological factors such as temperature, wind, soil, aspect and moisture conditions. Fourthly, there are historical factors, general or local. And lastly, economic factors reacting on and modifying the effect of all the others.

Design related to Function

The use to which the site is to be put is the most important single factor governing the design. Compare, for instance, the requirements of a children's playground or a play park, with those of a market garden, a cemetery or an open-air café. The size and shape of the main divisions or sections of the ground are determined largely by their function, especially in the case of areas devoted to games or to the growing of crops and other produce.

The likes and dislikes of the users—the psychology of the client —are important factors falling under the heading of function, since it is the intended use of the space which is under consideration. Every landscape project, like every building, is essentially a work of collaboration between the designer and the client. In the case of a park or other public space the client is the authority financing the scheme; but as this is being done in the interests of a section of the public, it is the needs of that particular public which are to be considered. At the outset of any new project, the landscape architect should examine these needs in association with the architects, engineers, town planners or other designers concerned.

In England, in the past, landscape architects have been employed largely by individual owners or by institutions such as schools: there was a marked difference between the needs of these two types of client. In general, the individual owner showed an anxiety to have quick effects, while the committee acting for an institution has been inclined to take the long-term view, planting for posterity rather than for what they hope to see in their own lifetime. This difference would not have been so marked in any earlier age—in fact, the great landowners of the eighteenth century clearly planted for their descendants with little thought of the immediate result. The individual, being mortal, must take a shorter view than the members of an organization whose own interests are not at stake, and the eighteenth-century landowner only rose above the individual viewpoint through his sense of family ties and security of tenure. Since the finest landscape effects must take very long to develop it is obvious in the interests of landscape beauty that the client's interest should not be limited to his own lifetime. If public institutions or the nation, as representing, collectively, the people, become the clients—if, in other words, the sense of family expands

Art school at Des Moines, U.S.A. An important modern group of buildings designed by Sarinan, dominating the land forms on which it stands gracefully and without aggression.

to a sense of community—a more dignified treatment of landscape should be one of the results.

Topography

The topography of the ground and the buildings connected with the site react on each other so much that they cannot be considered separately. Their influence on the design of the ground form near buildings may be in opposite directions, as when an important building calls for a setting of wide flat space, though the slope of the ground suggests long narrow terraces. Or buildings and contours together may be in conflict with some climatic factor, as when a prevailing wind blows from the direction in which buildings and contours face. The buildings to which the site 'belongs' must be given pride of place, exercising clear dominion over the lay-out, but the topographical context should influence the siting of buildings.

Climate

Climatic factors are often thought to be of secondary importance as acting on plant material only. But it will be shown that plants are the material of the design itself, second only in importance to the ground, and that both land and vegetation are subject to climatic influences. Moreover, climate has a vital influence on the whole character of garden style through the proportion of light and shadow —of open space and planted area—so that climatic factors must be recognized as being a fundamental influence on all landscape design.

History

Historical factors influencing landscape design may be general or local. A knowledge of the history of landscape evolution and of its conscious control by design should be a general background in the designer's mind, against which he views each modern site and each individual case. He sees these in relation to their surroundings and their past; he understands the stratification and drainage of the region through his knowledge of geological history, and is able to judge, by the type and condition of the vegetation, the purposes to which an area has been put by man through his knowledge of the general evolution of landscape. The historic background of agriculture, of architecture, and of landscape design all contribute to the understanding of a given site and to the recognition of its essential character. This general impression colours his whole conception and, deriving as it does from both scientific and artistic sources, may have much to contribute to the ultimate design.

In addition there may be local features of historic interest either on, or visible from, the site, or to which the designer wishes to draw attention in order to give an added interest to the site itself. He will arrange the access and layout accordingly.

Economic Factors

Economic factors include cost of construction, cost of maintenance, and income (if any) to be derived from the use of the land. In cases where a fixed sum is available for construction, the possibilities of the design are strictly limited thereby, and all the other limiting factors are involved—as when the topography of existing ground calls for high levelling costs, thus reducing the amount available, say, for wind screen planting or for swimming pool construction.

Maintenance costs affect the design no less: landscape projects depend on a long period of growth before they reach maturity, and even when fully mature require a far greater degree of care and skill for their continued existence than do architectural constructions. To some extent it may be true to say that maintenance costs can be reduced by extra outlay, or that cheese-paring on construction may increase the cost of maintenance, particularly in the case of materials for roads, paths, pools and architectural construction; but the reverse is often true in the case of plant material, since the native trees and shrubs which may eventually be able to hold their own against the competition of weeds are also the cheapest in the first place.

In any case it is useless to launch schemes unless effective maintenance (including adequate labour) is fully assured: and although this remark may sound like a truism there are, unfortunately, many areas which have become derelict through neglect of this fact, proving that provision for maintenance has been overlooked in a spasm of emotional enthusiasm. These forgotten spots include, incongruously enough, 'memorial' gardens.

When income is to be derived from the use of the ground (whether through produce grown and sold, or amenity charged for), a higher outlay on construction may be justifiable than in cases where the whole cost of maintenance and construction must come from other sources. The bearing of good design on the money returns tends to be underrated.

Five main groups of factors modifying and determining the design have now been mentioned. As has already been shown, their indications are not necessarily in agreement, and conflict often arises from different factors of a site as, for instance, when the problems of levelling limit the area that can be allowed for playing-fields, or when a fine vista or open view of an interesting skyline feature is found to be incompatible with good wind shelter. Such conflicting indications provide the designer with some of his worst difficulties: the resolving of these conflicts and the surmounting of the problems they present call for his special skill and experience. He must value and assess the opposing needs in just proportion, and find means of reconciling them in such a way that the conflict is not apparent in the design, but that all needs are met, in some degree, in a harmonious whole.

These main groups of factors will be found to recur again and again in different combinations in every kind of landscape design, whether it is a regional scheme with National Park, forest and agricultural land and arterial roads, or whether it is the small back courtyard of an individual house. A set of existing factors of greater or less importance will create a special problem for each project, and these factors, by the very limitations they set and by the existing nature of their demands, should provide the basis of individual and special character in the design.

These limitations serve as the inspiration, providing in themselves many of the motifs on which the designer will act. That self-conscious 'originality' so often sought is, in the case of landscape design at least, usually a sure proof that the indications of site conditions have not been really grasped. No amount of fanciful invention applied superficially will ever give that appearance of 'inevitability'—of essential rightness—or that innate, natural and functional individuality which are the hallmarks of good design.

Let us now consider in greater detail, use, topography and climate as fundamental influences of landscape design.

Corby, Northants. Great extents of land used for large-scale industrial working now have to be restored to agricultural or other use. In some cases, as here, forest trees have been planted without remodelling the hill and dale formation left by the extraction of surface iron ore. Methods leading to better use are now being developed.

9

Use of the Land

Of all the conditions governing design, the use to which the site is to be put is obviously the most important, providing the *raison d'être* for all the major divisions of space, and often, as in the case of playing-fields, indicating their actual size and shape without regard to other considerations.

The uses to which open land is put fall, broadly speaking, into the following main categories: productive use; health and general well-being; recreation; educational and scientific use; industrial use; and communications.

Productive use covers by far the largest area if we include under this heading all agricultural and forest land as well as market gardens, orchards, vegetable gardens and allotments. Water-catchment areas, sewage farms and certain other undertakings, should also be classed under this heading.

Health and general well-being may be said to cover all land to be preserved in its natural or wild state, including beach, foreshore, moor, mountain, common and cliff, in so far as these are not in agricultural use, as well as amenity space in built-up areas, parks, gardens, village greens, etc.

It may be criticized that the word 'design' is not applicable to land preserved in its wild state. In one sense this is true, but unless all such land is fitted into a general plan it would soon cease to be wild. Moreover, maintenance and forethought must be applied even to wild land under present conditions—a point which is dealt with at greater length in a later chapter.

Recreation includes sports grounds, playing-fields, bathing-pools, footpaths and running or riding-tracts; golf courses and athletic clubs, camping sites, fairgrounds, etc.

Scientific and educational use includes nature reserves, botanic and zoological collections, arboretums and grounds attached to research stations, agricultural colleges and farm institutes; demonstration centres, and children's gardens where horticultural instruction is provided; meteorological stations and experimental farms, field study centres, etc.

Industrial use includes all the space connected with factories and works or with mining and quarrying operations. Much of this has hitherto been lost land so far as landscape was concerned: the possibility of reclaiming industrial waste, spoil-heaps, gravel-pits and all the derelict space surrounding mines and industrial undertakings, and re-endowing them with positive beauty, is now coming to be realized. The area of 'non-operational' land owned by industry represents an important proportion of British landscape.

Communications: all roads, railways, canals, aerodromes, with the road verges, footpaths, embankments, yards and parking-places connected with these, come under this heading.

As has already been shown, man's first conscious attempts to endow his works with landscape beauty began in the garden, which, but for this development of conscious aesthetic design, is just domestic agriculture. It was only when the need arose for some ground to be devoted to purposes other than food production that

Drakelow power station, Staffs. In the grounds around the main buildings there is much 'non-operational' space now planted for landscape value but including other uses, such as woodland and pasture. A 'nature walk' planned in consultation with local schools is a very popular feature. The encouragement of interest in wild life is an insurance against vandalism and widens the children's appreciation of landscape conservation.

conscious design of the space became necessary, and that beauty was seen to be a necessary component of that design. Flowering herbs and shrubs, first grown for their medicinal value, led men to love plants for themselves; and then the fish-ponds, first used for food production, and the orchards, first grown for fruit, were used in gardens laid out for general enjoyment and pleasure. Tilt-yards, archery butts and bowling-greens needed for recreation were included, so that gardens combining four or five of the uses on our list called for careful planning. The ever-increasing variety of use and the need for integration of various uses elicit landscape-planning, and necessitate considered design.

Where one kind of use alone is under consideration the need for deliberate landscape-planning is less evident. In the case of agricultural land, technical necessities rule and govern the treatment of the ground to the apparent exclusion of all other considerations, and the landscape which it produced in the past had a loveliness of its own for two very good reasons. Firstly, the main materials of agriculture were the same as those of natural landscape—land and vegetation. Secondly, it is a biological science, beholden to the laws and facts of nature. The same thing is true of land devoted solely to scientific use. When we come to other classes of land use having different materials and operating under different laws, such as industry, the landscape produced by technical necessity alone, unchecked by the compensating balance of those other uses, produces a horror of which we must be thoroughly ashamed.

Yet when that ugliness is examined and analysed it turns out to be the result, in the main, of waste space and waste material: space which is being wrongly used or not used at all, having been rendered unusable by waste products or chemicals. In other words, land surface wasted through ignorance, or wilful ignoring, of the scientific facts relating to soil and ecology. The buildings and surface apparatus required by the industry are not in themselves the cause of the ugliness—suitably surrounded and suitably grouped they could in many cases have beauty and character.

A cement-quarrying industry, which must of necessity be sited on limestone and which thereby threatens a magnificent rural district, will, so long as the production of cement is its single objective, continue to devastate and ruin the scenery. Once its objective is extended, however, to embrace the needs of its workers for healthy enjoyment of their leisure hours, it immediately becomes apparent that the ground previously littered with waste products or left derelict after quarrying of limestone and clay must be brought back into use according to its capacity. Top-soil must be respread and playing-fields constructed. Gardens, allotments and grazing must be established. The worked-out clay pits must be made into lakes for bathing, boating and fishing, and these must be suitably set in turf, trees and wild flowers. Shelter must be provided by belts of trees, and any space not otherwise in use can be given over to forestry, which will yield coppice products soon, and eventually timber. The possibilities for new beauty are seen to be immense, and now the quarry itself must be so controlled and arranged that the natural beauty of the site is preserved. People from villages in the surrounding countryside are drawn to take part in this new life, and the contact between an industrial and a rural population, which must be of immense ultimate value to the nation, becomes possible.

The restoration of the landscape should be planned in advance of the extraction work, and phased for application throughout the operation. Planning conditions can ensure this under the 1946 Planning Act. It is far more difficult to restore quarries and other surface mineral workings made before the Act and left derelict since, or where consents obtained before the Planning Act are still operative.

The Tennessee Valley Authority in the U.S.A., and many other foreign undertakings, go to prove on a far larger scale the point here emphasized. Whereas exploitation of the land surface for one purpose alone may ruin the scenery (except in cases where that use has a biological basis), well-planned multiple use improves the possibility of creating fine landscape. In other words one may say that correct biological balance in the widest sense, comprising the whole life-cycle, through soil, plants, animals and man, must be applied to the whole land if it is to remain beautiful. Under modern conditions man himself must understand and adjust this balance. The time is long past when it could be left to nature or to blind chance.

Humanity's need for natural beauty and fine surroundings is a symptom of dependence on that balance. It is for this reason that landscape values can become the reconciling factor integrating and combining the other uses—the link correlating and unifying other functions.

Almost every landscape plan involves a close study of the technical necessities and psychological factors involved by the use or uses to which the land is to be put. In the case of a cement works, for example, the designer has to understand the methods of working the various quarries, and the circulation of traffic, within the area. He has to know a good deal about the workers' needs and their likes and dislikes, and his work, as in the vast majority of such cases, is essentially a work of collaboration with the owners. All this preliminary study must be undertaken along with the physical survey of the site before any attempt at a solution of its problems can be under-

Dam and reservoir, Tennessee, U.S.A. New landscapes are formed by the introduction of structures such as this in response to the needs of modern life. Well sited in areas vast enough to absorb them, they may add to the quality of the scene. Some of the more successful have shown that if visual considerations are allowed their influence from the outset, obtrusive new features can be more happily related to the surrounding land forms, for example by curving dams and burying some of the installations underground.

taken. This is equally true of almost any other case one may consider —it will be enough to refer briefly to a few typical cases to illustrate the point. A public park, for instance, involves a study of the population of the town which it is to serve. The type and activities favoured by the townspeople, the numbers in all the various age-groups to be catered for, and the needs of all these must be considered in relation to other parks and open spaces available in the area. Towns vary enormously in individual character, and the recreations needed, say, in an inland industrial city might be quite unsuited to a coastal holiday resort. To take another example: in order to make a school garden, the designer must know the numbers, ages and sexes of the children, and any special needs resulting from the character or locality of the school; the number and needs of the staff; the requirements for home-grown vegetables and fruit (and possibly for other things such as dairy and poultry produce). The horticultural knowledge needed in order to lay out a kitchen garden and orchard calls for an extensive knowledge of cropping systems and of all the routine working of vegetable and fruit production. It is so highly specialized that a horticultural consultant may be needed. In order to design a bird sanctuary, the feeding and nesting habits of the various species it is hoped to attract must be known, so that food is assured and the right amount and type of undergrowth and shelter shall be provided. In order to design a cemetery or crematorium, it is necessary to study the system of operations adopted in each case, the psychology of mourners and of undertakers, and to know quite a lot about legal and technical matters concerned with disposal of the dead.

The landscape architect must either specialize in certain fields or consult with experts in fields in which he has not specialized. Or else he must acquire the habit and capacity of studying any given subject to the fullest extent necessary from his own particular angle. In any case he must be armed with profound humility, for it is quite certain that he will be dealing constantly with people who know far more about the particular subject under consideration than he does himself, at least in regard to the use of the site.

10

Landscape Design in Relation to Topography

The enclosed garden of primitive type turned inward, away from the surrounding landscape, flattening the interior levels and creating its own horizon, self-sufficient, within its boundaries. Today our horizon widens to link with and embrace, or become part of a wider concept.

Survey and Landscape Evaluation

A well considered landscape analysis should be a first step in any major project for town or country. Topographical and geological maps are used as the basis of the visual scene. Recent advances in aerial photography and survey provide tools for the appraisal of land form and landscape quality which, though no substitute for personal inspection and judgement, greatly increase the designer's understanding of the land. The exact relationships of existing features on, or visible from, a site enable us to appreciate and demonstrate the importance of skylines or views, and of areas which because prominent and seen from many positions, must be accorded special treatment. The survey will indicate sight lines or vistas worth preserving and unsightly items to be screened. Existing features of special interest or value whether man-made structures or mere groups of trees and hedges, whose importance might influence future changes, are pinpointed.

Associated with this landscape survey, an ecological study of vegetation, soil and climate is highly relevant, as providing many pointers for future design. Well sheltered areas or wind funnels and frost pockets can be noted, indicating the requirements for shelter planting or frost drainage. Rare plants or habitats worthy of con-

The sweeping quality of the landscape and the attraction of the skyline have been emphasised by removing some hedges and trees, and reinforcing existing clumps. Some earthmoving in the foreground has given direction to the view and planting has screened the sub-station.

Note how the skyline is formed by objects in the near and middle distances as well as by distant objects.

servation may suggest special treatment of the design.

Landscape site analysis is an instrument for the planner: its full value and use has been much neglected, but its importance, once appreciated, can revolutionize our approach to new development and make possible new landscape as fine as any of the past.

Ground Contours

The shape of the ground, in a land of small undulations such as ours, should be given full expression. In special cases it may be necessary to flatten out the land to accommodate industrial buildings, but on too large a scale this kills the character and individuality of places. Far better to limit the flat areas so far as possible, and to emphasize the major bumps and hollows, relating them whenever we can to the wider horizon beyond our immediate boundaries, and so increase interest and anticipation. The flatter a site may be to begin with, the greater the need to use such inequalities as it may provide. No site is perfectly flat, and an exact knowledge of its undulations is needed in order to relate these to external horizons. A line of vision from dominating positions to lower views can be improved by removing intervening bumps, and making interesting features of the sides of the cutting where the new contours rejoin the unchanged levels.

The skyline holds a special attraction for the eye, which is irresistibly drawn towards it. More than one skyline may be visible from some positions, one formed by the outlines close at hand and the other by the land forms and other distant objects seen through, over or beyond. There may also be other important horizontal lines such as those formed by hill-crests or ridges, which though they do not actually reach the skyline are clearly defined and hold their own interest, secondary only to the main horizon. In open country there may be others still, such as the lines of a river, or of hedges, roads and other man-made incidents—or by some abrupt changes of level or of agricultural use. Each of these lines holds its interest for the eye, and their variation is a source of delight. Too close an echo between any pair or more of them is, conversely, displeasing and may suggest variation in the foreground to give the necessary contrast of form. The main skyline usually provides the principle theme, the others forming an accompaniment and, like different melodies in musical harmony, their relationship, no less than their individual beauty, is of vital importance. Our power of blending the near and the distant horizon provides wonderful possibilities, yet it is often overlooked.

The point of junction where vertical and horizontal lines meet also attracts the eye—for example, the base of buildings and especially of tree stems, where the normal lie of the land gives way to subtle undulations at the tree root, and there is a sense of disappointment or frustration if these are concealed. The eye seeks the upper limit and also the base line of a group of trees or buildings, and objects placed just beyond and below a horizon so that the base line is lost seem incomplete. This emphasizes the need for relating vertical masses—whether of architecture or vegetation—to the land forms.

Replacing part of the hedgerow with a light fence has revealed the boles of the trees and the subtle undulations at the tree roots.

Siting

In hilly land there arises the question of siting main building groups with regard to the surrounding landscape. The detailed placing of the buildings on a selected site is referred to later in this chapter, but wider considerations, concerned in choosing the site itself, come first.

The 'Viewpoints' marked on certain tourists' road maps illustrate an opinion commonly held that the more extensive a view the better. This idea leads many to choose sites on the highest available ground, where a narrow strip of foreground is often the only introduction to an extended distant view and expanse of skyline. Living in such sites, people usually realize in course of time that this advantage of the distant view is outweighed by the lack of middle distance. Experience teaches that if the choice between middle and distant views is possible (but not the possibility of enjoying both), it is the middle distance which gives the more lasting and real pleasure. This can be tested by an unprejudiced eye, by starting at the summit of a plateau, where we see only the near foreground and the distance, and walking gradually down over the brow of the hill till we reach a point where we have the middle and far distance in view, and then on again until the distant view is lost, and where the horizon is limited to a distance, say, of several hundred yards with interesting and pleasing lines composing that shorter area. (See next page.)

Other advantages of siting below the brow of the hill are that better shelter will be available, access to roads, towns, etc., better; and, above all, that the buildings in that position will merge more easily into their surroundings. Buildings on summits should be only those having very definite, even dramatic, shapes, such as towers and spires related to horizontals.

It is not enough to think of the view as seen from any building or group of buildings. The effect of those buildings as seen from elsewhere is important to a larger number of people than the occupants themselves, and the siting ought to be influenced by this fact.

The placing of the trees or the retention or removal of existing

View from crest of hill

View from brow of hill

View from hillside

This series of views seen by someone descending from the top of the hill show that it is the middle distance which gives the most enduring pleasure.

trees should also be considered from other points of view from which they are visible besides that of the site itself. There is seldom any conflict of interest on this point except in the case of trees over-shadowing immediate neighbours.

Existing Trees

Existing trees, if worthy of preservation not only in the distance but also on the site itself, should be included in the design, and, in fact, they may often indicate its general treatment. A new park or garden, a new road or housing estate, may gain so much from well-grown forest trees that the site plan should be designed to make the most of them wherever they exist, remembering that it would take upwards of fifty years to gain the same effect with newly planted trees. In this way we can borrow beauty from the past for the benefit of the future. The new lay-out must then be adapted to the position of any tree so used, and to the exact level at which they grow, since the roots must not be exposed, nor any of the stem buried, by levelling operations.

Water in the View

Any possibility of revealing water surfaces in the view greatly adds to the interest. In many cases glimpses of distant water can be opened up by re-adjustment of nearby ground levels, or by trimming trees and other vegetation interfering with the sight lines.

Alteration and remodelling of the contours and damming of the outlet to raise the water level and create a new or enlarged water surface may add magic to the scene.

Land and vegetation have been referred to in this book as the two main materials of landscape. Water is, however, a third material of almost equal importance. The surfaces of still water contrasting so sharply with those of land and vegetation in form, colour and texture, its power of bringing an image of the sky to earth, are among the more subtle delights of landscape. The duplication of reflected forms, whether natural or man-made, in still water, and the difference of its

Lowering the ground level around the water's edge has revealed the water surface to view.

behaviour when in movement, as if in response to different laws, give a special fascination in landscape. The perfectly true level of water surfaces is in such strong contrast to all the slopes and curves of earth and vegetation that it has the power of presenting us with a new vision of the earth forms by its emphasis on a single contour, bringing out a sectional view of existing forms which the eye could never detect for itself. The outline of a lake, depending on the height of the water-level, gives a sense of the land forms which we get from nothing else.

Another of its charms is the level stretch at the lowest point of a landscape. There is an essential 'rightness' in having that datum—that open flat space lying in the lowest hollow of the scene. Canals and dykes raised artificially above the surrounding contours lack this quality. They never look *right*, though a canal whose level is apparently normal can be as lovely as a river.

Still water reflecting a scene, yet giving it a different aspect and a new quality, provides fascinating opportunities for the designer. Repton first showed how the level of the water and the shape of the bank or verge can be controlled to reflect the pictures required, and the importance of working out these factors correctly from the out-set. Equality of the angle of incidence and the angle of reflection is the basic factor, but the width of the surface, the position of the observer and the modelling of the banks have all to be considered and, as in

A similar effect to the one shown opposite can be achieved by raising the water level. This also increases the extent of the reflection to include the whole tree (A-C) instead of only part of it (A-B).

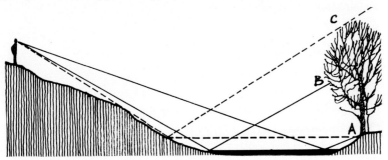

Duddington Mill, Northants. The reflections double the interest of the group and bring the sky into a new relationship at ground level. The smooth water surface contrasts sharply with foliage and masonry.

the case of sloping ground, sections drawn to scale give the required indications.

Moving water—fountains, mills, streams—provides interest of a different quality, referred to again in Chapter Eleven. The contrast of still and running water, as of a waterfall and lake, adds a special enchantment to any landscape.

Siting of Buildings

On any site containing buildings of importance it is almost inevitable that these should form the main feature of the lay-out. Their position and design should relate them to their surroundings. The main buildings should be sited so that the lines of the surrounding ground plan flow outwards from, and inwards again towards, the

architectural climax, and this calls for proper adjustment to site contours and to the visible surroundings. The relationship of important
architectural groups to similar groups in the surroundings, or to a
skyline (whether distant and natural or close and artificial) are
aspects of landscape design too often overlooked. Minor differences
in the position or level of a building, and small modifications of
orientation, may make possible effects which will give totally different results in the lay-out. Opportunities of using the contours to the
best advantage, or of bringing some incident on the distant horizon
into prominence, may be lost through lack of such foresight: and
where, on the contrary, such opportunities are fully used they add
not only to the pleasure to be had from the grounds but also to
the likeable qualities of the building itself.

Flat Areas

The tendency to site important groups on grassy slopes with no
flat platform is apparent today in certain large projects where entry
to the buildings is provided only at limited points. The treatment of
the contours and ground modelling around these presents new problems of construction and maintenance, as the slopes must be related
to varying floor levels, and must be maintainable in a reasonably
tidy state by harrassed ground staff.

The need for a terrace, or at least some level area round buildings
or groups of buildings, on to which the garden doors may lead, has
almost always determined the treatment of their immediate context.
Only before the need for gardens was felt at all, and again, for very
different reasons in the eighteenth-century landscape garden, was it
usual to find buildings standing on the natural slope of the ground.
The eighteenth-century landscape school, in their anxiety to avoid
all formality, tried placing the house as an isolated object standing
alone on sloping turf, but the lack of any dry walks or flat sitting-out
space must have been very inconvenient; and when once Repton had
so far flouted nature as to reintroduce the terrace, the idea slid into
usage again. The present architectural attempts to omit the terrace
areas are likely to be equally unpopular.

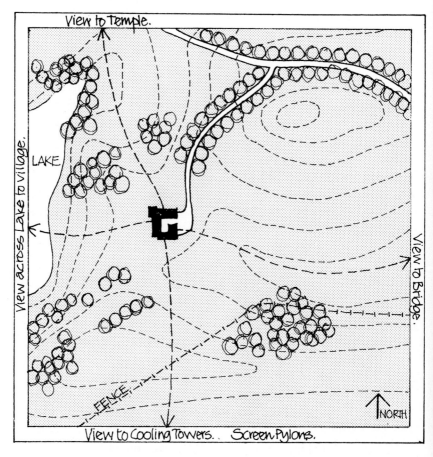

Present-day trends towards a more interlocking treatment of ground plan and garden, bringing open court and living-rooms into close relationship, dispose, to some extent, of the need for a terrace in the conventional sense, if open-air living space is provided within the shelter of the walls. But there often remains the need for a flat walk all round a building, connecting its various doors (usually a necessity for service reasons if for no other), to give that appearance of stability which is gained by a building standing on a well-proportioned level platform. The level of this area, whether we call it 'terrace' or not, needs to be carefully considered in relation to the floor-level of the building, the surrounding contours and any distant

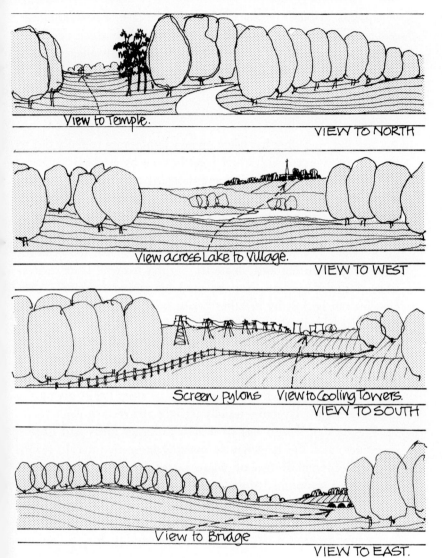

View to Temple.

VIEW TO NORTH

View across Lake to Village.

VIEW TO WEST

Screen pylons   View to Cooling Towers.

VIEW TO SOUTH

View to Bridge

VIEW TO EAST.

A large building is sited in parkland to take advantage of views
and natural features.

viewpoints visible from that position. In the case of new buildings, co-operation between architect and landscape architect is needed at the earliest stages of the design to ensure that full advantage is taken of views both outward from and inward towards the buildings.

Ground Modelling

Ground modelling has taken on new importance recently due to the comparative ease with which it can be done by mechanical means, and to the high cost of carting and dumping surplus material. Here again, where buildings or other man-made structures are concerned, close collaboration between landscape architect and the designer of the new structure, whether he be architect or engineer, can be of great value. The landscape treatment should obviate the need for importing or carting away material. Surplus material from excavations, foundations, etc., can be used by raising contours—deficiencies can be lost by creating pools, lakes or concave contours, giving greater visual interest.

Ground shaping has always been of first importance. In the creation of traditional terraces or playing-fields made by methods of 'cut and fill' the system often resulted in a series of flat surfaces on different levels linked by retaining walls or steep banks giving the basic lines of the lay-out—usually straight and rectangular.

Present-day design has to deal with larger areas and greater quantities, and the tendency is towards more naturalistic forms. Making economical use of waste material leads us to a new, grand-scale sculpture, often with biological undertones as in Geoffrey Jellicoe's design illustrated opposite, which can be seen from the A40 near the underpass entrance. The possibility of new landscape, creating a new sculpture, is emerging for further development.

Of the two materials, land and vegetation, land must come first so far as construction is concerned, though they are obviously to be considered in their relation to each other. Plants and ground forms are complementary aspects of one sculptural whole: the designer visualizes them together. Trees may crown the high contours, low

Guinness Hills, Park Royal, London. These hills were formed using material excavated from the A40 underpass which was being constructed at the same time. The saving on transport of the waste material covered the cost of the landscape work on the Guinness project, including the consultant's fee, and left a balance which was generously presented to the Institute of Landscape Architects library fund. The contours please whether or not we seek for symbolism in their sculptural form.

shrub masses may modulate the outlines, or turf alone may give clean-flowing silhouettes in contrast to the upland tree group.

For all such design, it is clear that a detailed and accurate survey is needed, giving the existing contours at close vertical intervals, while the positions and levels of any existing trees or other vegetation to be preserved must be known. To attempt to do detailed designs for ground modelling without an adequate three-dimensional survey is rather like trying to make a garment for a ghost.

In the vertical dimension, a few inches more or less may make a vital difference to a sight line, and to what may be seen from a given point. Sectional drawings to scale, taking lines from eye-level at various given points to other features of the site or surroundings, provide very valuable indications as to the general treatment to be adopted.

The sight line sweeps directly to the horizon across the contours. The path winds down the hillside parallel to the contours.

Compaction of New Ground Contours

The consolidation of newly formed levels must be very carefully done—enough to preclude the risk of future subsidence, but not so much as to damage soil structure or drainage. Over-compaction by machinery and vehicles is difficult to avoid when the material is clay or heavy loam. Subsequent aeration by cultivation or drainage is a slow and difficult process, but by some means the porosity and texture of surface layers must be ensured if grass and other vegetation is to be established.

On sloping ground, levelled open spaces tend to follow the contours, and so to be narrow in relation to their length. The cost of levelling (for, say, a tennis court) on sloping ground is halved if the length can be parallel with contours, though the need for north-south orientation may require the higher cost. The need for a wide view or vista crossing the contours may suggest walks at right angles to the slope. The eye enjoys a wider angle of vision from a hillside, so that the more important sight lines tend to be at right angles rather than parallel to contours. These contrary tensions often produce a cross movement in the design.

Walks (like roads) on sloping ground involve special treatment of the levels, whether crossing or following contours, and in most

cases some extra width or 'shoulder' is needed on either side at the
same level as the walk if the latter is to be comfortably dovetailed
into the main slope.

Terraced Gardens

The traditional terraced garden, perhaps seen at its best in Italy,
evolved in response to the two different magnetisms referred to
above. The main axis, flowing out from the house, cuts across the

Generalife Gardens, Spain. The broad lower terrace calls for the high retaining
wall; its drama is increased by the tall cypress and massive planting on the
terrace above. The direction of the terraces parallel to ground contour lines
gives views of the encircling range beyond.

contours in the direction of the view, with lateral walks at right angles following the contours along narrow terraces. The central axis provides an open way, inviting the eye in the direction of the distant view, and serves to lift the imagination until, airborne, it can soar above and hover over the landscape. The actual construction of the garden, on the other hand, is subject to the laws of gravity, and the majority of the walks must cross and re-cross the central axis, providing the platforms and stages into which its great stairway is divided, and expanding only at those intersections to allow the observer to indulge in imaginative flight. The width of terraces is governed by the gradient of the original slope, and where extra width is wanted for any single terrace, it can be gained only at the expense of another above or below—an effect used with dramatic results in gardens such as the Gamberaia near Florence.

On very flat sites changes of level can be introduced to provide interest. Flat ground makes for monotony, probably because we miss the joint effect of land forms and vegetation. One of the partners in the duet is out of action, throwing the whole responsibility on to the planting. Very slight surface modelling may be enough to bring the second partner into play again. For instance, on a small scale a lawn made slightly concave (in transverse section only) or sunk slightly below its rim, with suitable planting at the sides to emphasize the change of level, will have far more character than if it is all quite flat. Such effects can be useful, too, on mild slopes.

The eye is very easily misled by sloping sites—a fact often not appreciated. We generally tend to under-rate the gradient of ground on which we are standing. The larger the extent of visible slope, the more we minimize its angle—as if the eye, expecting a level horizon, adjusts itself to the slope in order to bring it nearer to the norm. A level tennis-court constructed on such a slope, seems, by contrast, to rise in the opposite direction. This suggests that it is wiser to avoid true levels, if possible, when all the visible surrounding ground is sloping. 'Running levels' or ground having a slight fall in the same direction as the rest of the slope are more satisfying and more economical to construct, besides being better for drainage. Bowls and certain other ball games call for true levels, but a mild fall often suits the eye better.

The one thing that invariably corrects this faulty judgment of the eye is a still water surface. We readily accept the evidence of this datum in preference to our own sight, so that where a true level tends to look as if it was running uphill, the impression can be cancelled by means of a pool; and, on the contrary, wherever still water is used, there is no possibility of deceiving the eye by means of 'running' or mildly falling levels.

The eye commonly makes another wrong judgment, in an opposite sense, with regard to things seen on a distant horizon. We exaggerate the size of figures or the height of hills on the horizon in relation to near-by objects. The sun seen directly overhead may suggest the size of a shilling, but on the horizon it assumes the proportions of a cart-wheel; and in the same way a hill whose slopes seem mild when we are standing upon them, takes on the significance of a mountain seen against the distant skyline. A case may be quoted in which a distant hill, hidden from a given site by trees on the site itself, was believed to be so high that nothing less than removal of the trees would reveal it to view; whereas in fact, the removal of a few lower boughs was all that was necessary. The trunks and higher branches of the trees then served as an effective frame, focusing interest on that point in the horizon: the focusing would have been lost had the trees been cut down according to the original intention.

The science of optics can give a logical explanation of why the sun seems larger on the horizon than elsewhere—when, in fact, the angle subtended by its diameter, measured instrumentally, never varies. But are there perhaps also more deep-seated psychological factors involved—atavistic memories of ages when men found their way through trackless country by means of landmarks on the hill-crests, and the shape of the skyline?

The general tendency to exaggerate the size and importance of incidents on the distant skyline can often be turned to good account. Such incidents give spontaneous pleasure to the eye for one reason or another, though the casual observer may fail to find them for him-

self without some directing and prompting. Various methods of drawing attention to such points and of focusing interest on them from given positions are available, as shown in Chapter Twelve. The designer can draw the skyline interest into his sphere of operations and distil its fullest essence.

Drainage and Underground Services

Drainage, both the main drainage of buildings and that of surface water, and all underground services must be taken into consideration at the outset. The design must be adapted to meet the essential requirements of these unseen convolutions; and drainage arrangements must be related to the lay-out and levels of the site to be con-

Removal of the lower foliage has revealed the distant view without destroying the value of the trees as a frame.

sidered at the outset. All underground services call for consultation between the various designers, and the landscape architect needs information at the earliest stages. Inspection pits should be sited in hard-surface areas where the covers can match the rest of the material in inconspicuous positions. The technique of drainage and other services is fully covered in *The Techniques of Landscape Architecture,* published by Heinemann in 1967 for the Institute of Landscape Architects.

11

Design and Climate

Climate, Soil and Vegetation

Climate influences the landscape in many ways: to a large extent it determines the type of soil and vegetation, though these are also influenced by underlying rock types. Design of landscape is more directly influenced by climate through temperature, moisture and the quality of light and atmosphere.

Fertile soil being a basic material of landscape design, an understanding of soil structure and its effect on vegetation is essential to the designer. For this reason a short appendix dealing with the subject in simple non-technical terms is given at the end of this book, and for a more thorough study of soil, readers are referred to books listed in the bibliography.

The influence of climatic zones and of temperature and light must be considered as part of the basic foundation of any landscape plan.

World Zones of Vegetation

The broad zones of world vegetation, each of which is associated with its typical soil or group of soils, show a pattern on the globe which is clearly related to climate rather than to geology, proving that, in the broadest sense, climate is more influential than geology in the determination of soil type. But within each of these broad climatic zones the nature of the underlying rock counts for much.

Associated with glaciers and ice sheets in polar regions and on mountain tops—wherever plants can breathe on the fringes of the melting ice—lives a hardy little group of plants known as arctic-alpine flora or 'Dryas' vegetation, after one of its most characteristic plants. The group includes certain mosses, liver-worts and lichens,

Conifers in the Lake District. Thin podsol soils favour conifers rather than broad-leaved trees. Perhaps for this reason many would prefer to see these areas treeless. Yet the absence of dark masses to contrast with lake and pasture would present a poorer composition, and the conifers themselves provide an interesting variety of colour. From both visual and economic aspects the mutual benefits of varied land use should lead to pleasing distribution of plantation and open space.

conifers), including evergreen oaks, olive, laurel, bay, arbutus and all the aromatic shrubs of the maquis such as lavender, rosemary, cistus and myrtle. This flora results from drier and warmer conditions than the deciduous forest, and its typical soils, though very fertile when irrigated, are intermediate between the brown earths and the desert sand. The desert zone is not continuous, though it marks a fairly distinct world zone. It supports a limited flora of palms, cactus and other plants especially adapted to long seasons of drought and great heat.

The equatorial zone is characterized by damp tropical forest and a deep, rich soil, supporting luxuriant growth of broad-leaved ever-green hardwoods in vast quantity. The foliage of this flora is larger and more superb than anything in the other zones, and we may well be envious of its sculptural qualities. This group depends on an even, high temperature and heavy rainfall.

All the northern zones are repeated, or can at least be detected, in the southern hemisphere, but because there is less land they do not appear to form continuous belts of vegetation. There are magnificent conifer forests in New Zealand and the araucaria forest of Chile, while in Australia the eucalyptus or gum tree and its associates represent the equivalent of the Mediterranean flora.

Altitude, as well as latitude, fixes the distribution of the zones of vegetation. On equatorial mountains one may climb up through several series, starting from tropical forest, going through deciduous and conifer zones and out to the treeless tundra or alpine region and eventually reaching the perpetual snows. In the Swiss Alps the lowest regions are in the deciduous zone, but the upper series are very clearly marked, each belt giving a completely different type of landscape in the near foreground, yet merging into a typical zonal pattern in the distant view. The upper limit of forest in Britain at present is around the 1500-foot contour line.

Shifting Vegetable Zones in Britain

For a reason not yet clearly understood, these zones have shifted about the globe in different geological periods, and the land that is now Britain has experienced them all at some time or other in the dim past. Tropical forest gave us the coal measures, desert conditions bequeathed the red sandstone of Shropshire and Warwickshire. The Ice Age left a land of tundra and Dryas vegetation which in turn gave place, first to conifer and then to the existing deciduous forest.

Geographically, Britain lies within the conifer zone at the present time, but her position as an island gives her an oceanic rather than a continental climate, and the influence of warm ocean currents has favoured the growth of deciduous forest at the expense of conifers. We appear to be still in a state of transition, for although the only remnants of pine and birch forest are in Northern Ireland and parts of Scotland, almost all the soils of the highland districts, including Wales and parts of the south-west peninsula, are still of the podsol type usually associated with conifer forest. Deciduous trees have colonized most of these areas and the pines have retreated, but the hardwoods are not able to develop their full stature in these soils. A mild temperature has favoured the deciduous forest, but the damp atmosphere and high rainfall combine to prevent the formation of 'brown earth'. In the lowland districts of the south and east and midland England the deciduous forest has held complete sway for thousands of years and formed the soils which have now become agricultural land.

Our climate favours an exceptionally wide range of plants. The deciduous-forest zone itself, extending over a vast area of the globe, gives us quantities of foreign species suited to our conditions, and besides these we can grow most of the northern conifers as well as the three which are native here (pine, yew and juniper). We have a few native broad-leaved evergreens, notably holly, box and ivy; and under cultivation we can grow many of the Mediterranean species,

A glade in a hardwood forest. It is preserved for amenity. The interlocking of open space and close plantation in forest areas contributes to good design. This is true even if the open spaces result only from periodic clear-felling: but multiple use in forest areas, including farming, footpaths and amenity camps etc., makes possible a more interesting pattern over a wider area.

Parkhill, Forest of Dean. Softwoods flourish better than hardwoods in many western regions of Britain, and our climate favours many foreign trees. The majesty of mature conifer forest is more appreciated in countries where it forms the normal climax as in parts of the U.S.A., Germany and Switzerland. This stand of Douglas firs, a Forestry Commission plantation, shows how fine they can be in Britain.

though these are less hardy than our own natives, and do best in the south and west, some requiring shelter from cold and wind. In parts of Western Ireland the arbutus or strawberry tree is a native and is thought to be a remnant of a Mediterranean flora which may have flourished before the Ice Age and have survived that period owing to the warmer conditions of the west.

The Mediterranean flora includes a number of conifers belonging to a different series and not included in the northern conifer zone—notably certain pines and the Italian cypress. Two cedars, the Lebanon and the Atlas Mountain cedar, are found in the Mediterranean area, but at high elevations, and may therefore be considered as belonging properly to the conifer zone, as does the third representative of the cedar family, the Himalayan deodar, which grows with typical northern conifers at high altitudes.

Of our British conifers, the Scots pine is the only one belonging to the conifer zone. It is believed to have been completely displaced in the south by hardwoods in early historic times and to have been re-introduced from Scotland at the time of the union under James I. The other two native conifers, yew and juniper, are trees of the chalk land and do not associate with the northern conifers unless planted by man.

'Biotic' Influence on Soil and Vegetation

The type of vegetation, and therefore the appearance of any given area, is determined by the three inter-related factors—climate, soil (with all it derives from underlying rock) and history; history, in this case, being the use or treatment which the land has received at the hands of living creatures, chiefly man and his grazing animals. Land not cultivated or grazed in any way reverts to forest, fen or moor according to climate and soil conditions, but moderate grazing tends to encourage turf at the expense of trees and other plants, while excessive grazing denudes the ground of all vegetation, and hence leads to soil erosion. Land insufficiently cultivated or grazed, or left to go wild, reverts to its natural condition gradually and in a definite sequence or order of succession, the first stage consisting of low prickly shrubs, not relished by the grazing animal, which provide an opportunity for larger shrubs of the next stage to take root. In this way taller and larger plants gradually establish themselves and the area of turf is reduced. The soil, made deeper by root action and by surface dressings of dead leaves, becomes capable of supporting small trees and finally forest trees. As the taller plants grow the smaller ones give way, killed by their more vigorous successors or driven to the fringes and open glades. The term 'climax vegetation' is given to the species or group which finally proves to be the highest capable of holding its own under local conditions. On peat moors the climax may be heather; on clay soils it is often oak forest; and on chalk the beech tree usually forms the climax.

The chalk provides the most interesting example of this process in England, and the whole series of different stages can be seen in the course of a walk over downland that is not closely grazed. Juniper, thorn or dogwood often forms the 'pioneer' community. Dogwood has no spines, but the sharp ends of the young shoots, bitten off by sheep or rabbits, gives protection to seedlings of the second-stage community, which may consist of wayfaring tree, privet, spindleberry and blackthorn. Through this grow taller plants such as buckthorn and whitebeam. Yew trees soon establish themselves and are able to push the smaller growth out of their way with the exception of the saplings of ash and beech, which drive up in any available open spot, demanding no lateral space until their tops reach above the yew, when they spread a shady canopy over all beneath. The beech canopy is closer and denser than the ash and reaches higher. So finally the beech holds solitary sway, defying all competition. No other tree of that height can grow in shallow chalky soil. Beech roots penetrate the chalk to some extent, but no very deep soil ever forms on the chalk escarpments because of the extreme porosity of the chalk, which causes the humus to leach down away from the surface. Deep loam can only form on the flatter areas.

The Court of Myrtles, Alhambra, Granada. The cool enclosure of this courtyard in the Moorish tradition is a comforting relief from hot sunlight without. The water surface nearly at pavement level fills the floor space with a play of light and shadow reflected from the colonnade: a fountain gives the welcome sound of tumbling water.

Climate and Garden Design

The effect of climate on traditional garden styles is a fruitful study for landscape architects, whatever the scale of their work. Both in urban and domestic grounds, and in the broader landscape, climatic factors combine with other factors which are more purely psychological or functional. Climatic influences act mainly through the varying needs of people for light, shade and shelter: they affect, too, the type of plant material which can be grown. Climatic influences appear less potent than human fashion in the matter of garden design, and on a superficial view one might be inclined to discount climatic factors as having no very distinctive influence on garden styles. Yet a careful analysis shows that climate has a profound influence on the character of design rather than on 'style'. Its influence is felt through the varying proportions of the elements of composition—above all in the size of the open spaces in relation to

Shalimar Bagh, Kashmir. A Moghul garden deriving from the same tradition as the Spanish Court of Myrtles. When the style reaches towards the Himalayas the space devoted to shade and water is reduced: the canal (empty at the time of the photograph) is narrow in relation to its surroundings, and the great Chenar trees are widely spaced. The flower beds are probably a recent introduction, but one can see how much the view would be improved with water, fountains playing, and expanses of grass reaching unbroken to the trees.

massed plantings, and in the resulting amount of shadow in relation to sunlit areas. Another feature which varies in fairly constant degree according to climate is the use of water in the design. In hot countries running water is felt to be essential; canals with fountains and falls take a central position and extend throughout the garden—the sight of water being no less important than the sound to give an impression of coolness. In cold or damp climates, on the other hand, the sound of water may be all too common a fact of existence, and, if used near dwellings, a little goes a long way. The appreciation of the sound of fountains and running water is probably in inverse ratio to the rainfall. The sight of water, river, lake or reservoir is welcome in any climate, but doubly so in hot countries.

The gardens of Persia and of India, both in the same tradition of 'earthly Paradise', illustrate the extent to which shade and water are valued in hot climates. The designs of Moslem gardens all follow a well-established tradition of formal lay-out, with canals and fountains as the central theme. But the area of open space and the width of the canals varies with the latitude of the site. In extreme examples all the open space is occupied by water, the lateral paths flanking the canals coming under the shade of trees, which fill the remaining space and which form an admirable setting for delicate

Alhambra Gardens. The central canal is quite narrow here and the rather small scale of the enclosures is characteristic of Spanish gardens deriving from Eastern styles.

The emphatic shapes of the two cypresses seen through the curved arch (of clipped cypress) give a touch of drama. The flower beds flanking the canal are a recent introduction.

pavilions and garden-houses whose open halls look out over cool vistas of water and dappled shade. In the Shalimar Bagh of Kashmir the traditional design is adapted to cooler summers—the canals are narrower and room is left for a wide expanse of turf on either side between the water and the trees.

Early Spanish gardens followed the same tradition, but the central canal becomes smaller and narrower and is reduced in some cases to a mere runnel or rill, and although the open spaces are still small compared with those of more northern gardens, the planting is far less dense, so that their eastern heredity is not striking at first glance.

In no country has better use been made of a brilliant clear atmosphere and the need for shade than in Italy where, with a sure instinct for the dramatic value of strong contrasts in the garden, light and shadow are interlaced and interwoven so subtly that the pattern they form becomes a principal theme of the design. The size of the open spaces or sunlit areas is comparatively small, as we should expect in a country of hot summers; but the distribution of light is so variable, so full of interest, and so often unexpected that the amount of planting

Villa Lante, Italy. Sunlight and shadow contribute, with the sculpture, to enrich this water court, designed to give cool relief in a sunny climate.

Shade and water at Vaux-le-Vicomte, France. These fountains serve a double purpose in the design. They are placed at the ends of the long canals closing the vistas of the secondary axis which cross the main central axis, but they also enliven the shady walk round the encircling woodland. Seen from this angle the water catches the sunlight and gives it a dancing movement against the shadow.

never seems too heavy. It must be realized that the close planting of trees, and the narrow walks often designed to produce these results, would not have the same result in a less sunny climate, and although equally interesting effects should be obtainable with different proportions of light and shadow, few designers have made full use of this theme in cooler climates.

Strong contrasts of every sort seem to be the keynote of Italian gardens, water and shade playing an important part. Still water contrasts with rills and fountains. Sudden splashes of vivid colour, provided by flowers in pots or parterres, are all the more telling for the fact that they are rare and that most of the design is built up of green foliage and the neutral tones of masonry and tree stems. An immense view suddenly bursting upon our vision is made all the more exhilarating by means of the sheltered alleys and small enclosed spaces that have led up to it.

Travelling northwards we find the area of sunlit open space increasing. In Northern France, Versailles and Vaux-le-Vicomte are typical of the great gardens of that area. They provide very large central divisions of space open to the sun, surrounded and sheltered by woodland whose walks offer a shady alternative on hot days.

In England sunlight is precious. We rarely have too much of it, and it is very easy to overdo the shade—a fact which has led many designers to overlook the necessity for shade and shadow as a component of design. The dripping moisture from damp foliage is an unwelcome sound in a cloudy country with high rainfall, and on most days of the year we want all the light we can get. In this comparatively mild climate, the need for shelter planting has not limited the size of the open spaces—though it is obvious that many of our parks and gardens would be far more comfortable and hospitable if shelter planting had played a larger part in their design.

One of the outstanding characteristics to be found in many famous English gardens is a feeling of spaciousness, resulting from large divisions of space with little or no massed planting defining them. One section leads on into the next with little break, and the view is not confined to one at a time. This is particularly true of the eighteenth-century landscape garden and all its progeny: it is no exaggeration to say that that style could only have arisen in our climate, or rather that in other climates the causes which produced it would have led to something of a very different character. The excellent quality of the turf—also an outcome of climate—made possible those wide stretches of open space: without that green groundwork some different treatment, on a smaller scale enriched with more incident, becomes inevitable.

Small divisions of space, well enclosed, give a sense of cosiness and comfort conspicuously absent from most eighteenth-century landscape gardens and parks. Where, as so often happens, cold winters and hot summers go together, the smaller divisions with massed tree planting are needed to give shade in summer and shelter in winter. This tendency is well marked in gardens of the eastern United States, and arising out of it a typical garden style is developing, distinct from those of any of the European styles from which American gardens derived inspiration. Cold winters also call for

Polesden Lacey, Surrey. The spacious open treatment on the south side of the house is typical of the English landscape style. The house is beautifully framed by trees and turf, and the contrast between cedar and beech stems is magnificent. Nevertheless the open treatment of this period led later to the need for some sheltered flower garden as open-air living space.

the use of a high proportion of evergreen trees and shrubs, and hot sunshine reconciles us to them in summer. In our soft island climate evergreens in quantity may become oppressive, and we need a carefully balanced combination of evergreen and deciduous planting to give us the right degree of comfort, variety and satisfaction. But with a brighter light and greater extremes of temperature, a much higher proportion of evergreen is felt to be right. In the eastern United States the deciduous planting is often limited almost to the 'interior decoration' of a garden. Very cold winters mean, of course, that the evergreens must be mainly coniferous, whereas in warmer climates broad-leaved evergreens serve instead.

The influence of climate affects the use of colour in gardens in two ways, the first acting through the available flowering plants and the ease or difficulty of their cultivation, the second acting through the quality of light. By far the most brilliant colour effects can be obtained in tropical countries where water is plentiful and where there is an even, high, temperature throughout the year—the conditions of the equatorial rain-forest zone. There, framed in bold, luxuriant, evergreen foliage, and set off against dense shadows, a wealth of oriental splendour becomes possible. The brilliant light permits colour-relationships which might be altogether too gaudy for our misty northern island. Between that equatorial exuberance and our own mild moisture (which also favours an immense range of flowering plants) there are intermediate zones where flower colour is comparatively rare and difficult to achieve without artificial irrigation, and where it must therefore be limited to tubs and pots or small areas under special control. In such countries designers have been obliged to emphasize the value of foliage (for deep-rooting trees and shrubs withstand drought better, and give more permanent effects than flowering herbs and perennials) and of light and shadow. Greens, browns and greys have provided the main colour scheme, with occasional high notes of vivid colour as special accents. These limitations have nevertheless served to bring garden design to its highest power, for where too much reliance is placed on flower colour the other aspects of garden design often seem to remain unexplored. That has happened to a great extent in England since the introduction of countless hardy flowering plants from all over the world; and as has been shown in Chapter Five, the interest in good garden design seems to have been in inverse ratio to the taste for cultivating flowers, though there is no good reason why flower colour should not take its rightful place along with the other components of good garden design. Gertrude Jekyll's planting showed the way, but there remains much opportunity for new and interesting experiment in the relationship of flower colour to design.

Every great garden style has used vegetation, related to land forms, for the main structure. The use of plants to fulfil the functions of the design can be seen in classic garden styles throughout the world. In landscape design in the wider sense, functional use rather than purely decorative use of plants is even more essential, as shown in the next chapter.

12

The Functional Use of Plant Material

In their wild condition, plants help to create soil by the addition of organic material to the mineral matter. Besides feeding the soil in this way, plants preserve the soil and keep it in place, checking erosion. In addition to these important functions, their relationship to animal life is a matter of beautifully balanced 'give and take', or symbiosis. The plants breathe into the atmosphere elements needed by animals, and absorb from it matter which, in excess, would poison the animal world, creating in return the basic foods on which those animals depend. To complete the cycle, animals fertilize the soil, returning in richer form the borrowed elements; fungi and bacteria change this and decayed vegetation into humus needed by the plants. Then, too, plants provide shelter and accommodation, serving animal life in countless ways.

In agricultural landscape this process of give and take is largely controlled by man, but the same functions are still served, and any maladjustment of the balance reacts unfavourably on soil fertility and on human health.

In man-made landscapes where agricultural produce is not the main objective, plants may fulfil, in addition to their basic life-giving functions, other requirements peculiar to civilized man. It is those which are now to be considered.

Plants, whether we are thinking of trees, grass or flowering herbs, give beauty in the surroundings of human life but they rarely give of their best unless they are serving other fundamental needs as well. On a large scale, plants must provide the very structure of the design, just as bricks, stone and timber, or steel and concrete, provide the structure of a building.

The architectural garden, developed as we have seen in England by Sir Edwin Lutyens, Sir Reginald Blomfield and others of that period, treated the garden essentially as an open-air extension of

Bodnant, Denbigh. The eye is led over the formal terraces to the view of open country beyond, and although in a garden such as this masonry and other architectural materials play an important part, their role is subsidiary or complementary to the land and plant masses. The structure responds to the underlying ground formation and the character of the countryside. This is perhaps intermediate between the walled garden which confines the eye within enclosures and the more naturalistic treatment of the classical landscape style.

the building to which it was attached—an unroofed area built of the same architectural materials as the house but furnished with growing plants. So little did this furnishing have to do with the main structure of the design that it could safely be left to other hands to fill in, and the architect scarcely needed to concern himself with its details.

The architect's extensive use of masonry and paving typified for many the 'formal garden' of that period. Even on the small scale of private gardens it was very costly, and most people found it hard and unsympathetic.

In the wider landscape the structural framework must inevitably be formed of earth and vegetation rather than of concrete and steel. The lines of the design relate to surrounding land forms except in the immediate vicinity of buildings, so the design must be expressed through the use of ground contours and plants.

We learn from a study of natural or of agricultural scenery that plants themselves, with the earth forms on which they grow, are this structural material of landscape, and that the balanced grouping of mass and void, and of surface qualities, are certainly no less important, though their relationships may be far more subtle, than in the case of masonry and other materials over which man's control is more complete.

Prevention of Erosion

In nature, vegetation stabilizes the surface soil, and under human control plants are used to prevent erosion. Hillsides are a favourite home of many forest trees whose roots are capable of holding soil on very steep slopes. Lesser slopes can be stabilized by low shrubs or turf. Even in England, which suffers comparatively little from erosion, steep slopes need protection, and are unsuitable for arable cultivation on this score alone, since ploughland is exposed precisely at the seasons of greatest erosion. Trees can be grown on almost anything short of sheer cliff, and slopes that are too steep for grazing can be protected by trees or shrubs. Massive plantings are therefore appropriate for steep escarpments, and in that position they emphasize the land forms and please the eye. On flat sandy areas hedges and tree belts protect the soil from wind erosion.

The olive groves of Italy, the vineyards of the Moselle valley and other terraced cultivations show systems of combined terracing and planting suitable for hillside cultivation in many temperate climates. In countries where climatic conditions favour erosion, contour ploughing and terracing have often been found necessary for cultivated land even on mild slopes. The surface of the intervening banks can then be held in place by trees or other vegetation.

Mass and Void

In nature, or in agricultural landscape, plants are usually massed in large groups all of one kind, or composed of a fairly limited association. The shapes of the groups are highly variable according to circumstances of function, topography and climate, and are for that very reason interesting shapes. In conscious design, groups of single species usually give the best results, and although in some cases this may limit the number of species used, it makes for more enjoyable living conditions than a mere collection of horticultural specimens of wider variety.

In the open landscape, groups of trees and shrubs and hedges provide the 'masses' of a composition in contrast to the voids which are clothed with lower plants such as turf or farm crops or dwarf shrubs and flowering plants. The same principle applies whatever the scale. Small open spaces can have proportions approaching those of the rooms in a building with the vertical-horizontal ratio more nearly equal than in land used for agriculture or recreation.

Defining the Open Spaces

The size and shape of the open spaces in park or garden are determined by factors such as use, climate, contours and others, which have already been discussed. The various divisions of space can be defined and separated by plant groups serving the same purpose as the interior walls of a building. The definition need not be by thick screen planting: a few single trees, or even a group of low

Terraced rice fields at Banaue in the Philippines prevent erosion of steep hill-sides and show a beautiful land use pattern unfamiliar to western eyes.

shrubs may sometimes be enough to mark a division of space.

In landscape design, the separation between one open space and another rarely needs to be so complete as in architectural structure, but it *is* needed to a definite extent. The divisions need to be sufficiently marked to give, within each, a sense of entity, comfort and individuality. In designs where extensive space is broken only by dots of unrelated planting, the lack of these comfortable qualities, though not always correctly analysed, is very strongly felt.

Partition walls of architectural material—brick, stone or concrete—though valuable for special uses and often well suited to small-scale designs, are unable to fulfil most of the requirements of a large-scale screen, particularly in regard to height, shelter and shade; and, above all, they are too rigid. Complete enclosure being seldom needed in the open air, it is more pleasant to emphasize a sense of free movement, with the space flowing from one area to another, in directions suggested by the design, under or between trees and shadow, in streams of varying width, offering glimpses of further delights yet to be explored.

Whatever the scale, the definition of the various spaces needs to be seen and felt clearly in logical sequence, so that changes of mood, brought about by alterations in scale, colour and general mode of treatment, may be fully appreciated as we pass from one to another.

Closely grouped plants, well massed, may serve many practical purposes beside, or instead of, being partitions. Take, for instance, their use as wind-screens, which has not yet been fully exploited in this country, though clearly shelter from wind makes for greater enjoyment of any open-air space.

Wind Shelter

Wind shelter affects health in two ways: by improving living conditions in general, and by the inducement to spend more time in the open air. Short periods of buffeting by wind may have a stimulating effect on vigorous and healthy people, but, even in small doses, high wind has a bad effect on mental activity, and prolonged exposure lowers vitality and resistance to disease. These facts, often overlooked in the case of humanity, are thoroughly appreciated in the case of agriculture and horticulture. Every farmer knows the value of wind shelter for his breeding stock, his dairy herds and for many of the farm crops, while the gardener insists on the need for shelter for any plants that are to develop their full beauty. The wind-screen is formed of hardy trees and shrubs whose development, as individuals, is sacrificed to their collective contribution to the rest of the community.

The beauty of our agricultural landscape, and of parks and

The ratios of horizontal to vertical approach those of a room in the village cricket field (*bottom*). It gives a sense of enclosure obviously lacking in the extensive recreation area (*top*) where horizontals far exceed verticals.

gardens, owes much to this need, for the wind-screens themselves, in the mass, are fine features, even though the individuals of which they are composed may be dwarfed or distorted. The landscape gardens of the eighteenth century made great use of wind-screens in the form of belts of forest trees giving shelter to farmland and game; but they provided little shelter for humanity close to the buildings, which contributed to the reaction of the following century towards those gloomy shrubberies, shrouding the house and drive in dark evergreens. These shrubberies gave seclusion, and could be used to make the site appear larger than it was in reality: by concealing the actual size and shape of the site the imagination was given play, and would, it was hoped, suppose a vast estate and further unseen glories. Heavy plantations near buildings, however, shut out light and prevent free circulation of air. The normal, calm movement of air resulting from gradual and local change in soil and atmospheric conditions is essential to health, and wind-screens should be set back far enough from the buildings or sheltered area not to interfere with that general movement. They should never completely surround a site, but be placed at right angles to the direction of prevailing winds or in such a way as to deflect or break the force of the wind without preventing the passage of air in other directions. This creates a completely different atmosphere within the shelter to the virtual stagnation which results from too close planting.

Suitable shelter contributes a very great deal to the enjoyment of garden, park or town. Any building, whether standing in its own grounds or as one of a group, will benefit by protection from strong winds and draughts: its windows will be more constantly open, its terraces in more regular and frequent use than if exposed to the full strength of the wind, and its fuel bill will be lower.

Foliage as Filter against Dust, Smoke and Noise

Plant screens may effectively bar the passage, not only of wind, but also of smoke and dust, and of sound. The foliage acts as a filter, absorbing impurities and muffling sound. An industrial country wishing to preserve its landscape beauty should be able to make far greater use of plants in this way than has been done in Britain, and planting for these purposes is now receiving further study. Shelter-planting can be of immense practical value, and becomes an important element of the design if correctly planned from the outset.

Screen planting has a part, though a smaller part, to play in the internal design of parks and gardens. A common fault in the design of parks and gardens in Britain has been the display of too much at a time—that exhibition of countless charms, of interesting plant groups and colour associations, sculptured ornament and other incidents, which, like a too rich banquet with all its courses served up, as it were, on one plate, gives the unfortunate guest at best an impossible problem of deportment, at worst a feeling of positive nausea. The rule of one thing at a time, or one set of well-blended components at a time, is fundamentally sound, and from it follows the need for arranging the sequence in which the different subjects are presented to the eye and intelligence, and for drawing attention to, and concentrating interest on, each in due order and in suitable degree.

Focus

Focusing of vision and of interest is effected by various means, of which the most obvious is the simple open vista, framed in tree stem and foliage, which leads the eye, the imagination and, it may be, the footsteps in a certain direction and towards some focal point, usually visible throughout the length of the sight line: curving walks which only reveal their objective at intervals serve equally well, and in fact the vista draws the eye whether or not a focal point is visible. All tracks, paths and waterways tend to draw the eye along to the farthest bend, any incidents on their banks or verges being noted, rather than others set back beyond the focussing influence of the open way. The other methods of focussing attention on given points are really all variants of this theme, although the framing effect may be so slight as to be scarcely recognizable. The full vista acts like a telescope, the width and length of the vista being adapted to the apparent size of the object as seen from a distance. Slighter variations of the vista theme may be the use of a single tree, or a few groups of low vegetation, very carefully placed so as to serve as pointers towards incidents on a distant skyline, which, without the use of such pointers, might easily be overlooked. In such cases the direct central line of vision must be low and unbroken, with a plain smooth surface, the pointers, like the frame of the vista, placed laterally.

Movement always tends to draw the eye, and in particular the human attention is attracted by humanity and the works of man, and in lesser degree by the activities of other animals. Plants provide nearly all the colour and texture and much of the form in any open

Bramham Park, Yorks. A garden laid out in the French style with long vistas leading the eye to sculptured groups at focal points. The high water level doubles the contrast between vertical and horizontal lines and the change from open space to the confined tunnel of avenue gives another sharp contrast.

These trees suffered severe damage in the gales of 1964.

landscape or garden scene, but much as the human mind may delight in all these, it is only in exceptional cases (as when they form part of an interesting skyline or are displaying special beauty of flower) that plants can compete with moving objects for the first flash of notice. This suggests the use, whenever possible, of human figures as the focal points of interest in the design. This happens almost inevitably in the case of public parks, where moving crowds at the path junctions are seen framed by the avenue trees.

The main climax of a design may be an important building, a lake or pool, or a distant view. Or it may be fine sculpture, or even a plant-group of special sculptural quality. The surroundings will be designed to lead the eye towards such a climax from selected points of view, and to direct attention outwards again to suggest further delights still in reserve. Trees and other plants, related to ground forms, are used in the complementary role of leading the eye in required directions.

Shade

Shade and shadow are all-important in the landscape. In agricultural areas, where short-term economy tends towards larger fields and fewer trees, the loss of incident and the enlargement of open space makes for monotony. Yet the need for shade and contrast is not merely aesthetic. Wherever stock is grazed out of doors, some shade trees are welcome, and their value as wind shelter and for stabilization of soil supports the visual intuition.

The dislike of trees may be partly due to atavistic memories of the fearful forest which our ancestors strove to keep at bay. In towns and built-up areas the objection to trees near the house diminishes with the larger windows of modern buildings. The objection to shade near the house is most voiced in the poorer districts, and we may well come to regard the possession of a fine tree as a status symbol.

Shade is needed for human enjoyment in any open air spot intended for rest and lazy enjoyment; seats in the shade, or shade where people may relax or bring their garden chairs, should be provided. Although, in our climate, there may be more days when we prefer the sun, it is precisely on the hottest days that the pleasures of the open air are most needed, so that careful placing of shade trees must never be overlooked. The quality of shade given by the foliage of trees is totally unlike the shade of an awning or even of a pavilion with open sides. Tree shade has a deeper, cooler and more even quality—probably due to the different levels, one above the other, at which the foliage meets the sun, and also to the fact that natural upward air currents are promoted by the growing tree, instead of being checked as they would be by roof or awning. Even on days cool enough for us to prefer sitting in full sun, the eye seeks shadow as a relief from glare and brilliance. The shadow patterns cast by stem, branch and foliage are a component of the design, and the choice and placing of trees should be influenced by this factor. The focusing effect of trees, referred to in an earlier paragraph, is empha-sized when their shadows, encircling the same view, form part of the frame.

Shadows form a good background for sunlit sculpture or for foliage groups of special quality. Drifts of flowers growing in full sun, or well-lit groups of tree stems, show their best against shadow.

Terrace at Rousham, Oxon. The sunlit building and urn seen against dark foliage and shadow on one hand, and a shaded urn seen against sunlit foliage and sky on the other, exemplify opposite ways of placing richly sculptured details to the best advantage.

Any neutral colour under heavy shade gives a hue nearer to black than the darkest foliage in full light, so that where a sharp contrast is needed to set off a glowing colour, the shadow of foliage may serve better than the foliage itself.

Nevertheless, foliage of fine texture and dark colour, such as yew, serves well as background and may be better for more permanent effects, since the shadow background gives full value only on bright days.

Vertical Proportion

It has been remarked in an earlier chapter that well-placed trees effectively serve to multiply the area by their height; the three-dimensional spatial volume enclosed is an important part of our enjoyment. Variations in the height of the invisible 'ceiling' supported by the vertical masses give a differing character to different sections of a design, and so to the interest of the whole—stimulating the imagination as we move through the open spaces.

Man's sense of his own structure, and of his own significance, undergoes marked changes in relation to his surroundings—a subject which might provide an interesting line of research. Japanese gardens are often made on a smaller-than-life scale, and it is said that this effect contributes comfortably to a man's sense of his own importance, whilst the vast open spaces of sea and desert reduce men to humility. This is not the time or place to pursue this enchanting subject, though it may become an essential part of landscape design.

Visual Relation of Structure to the Site

Another human need fulfilled by the trees and shrubs growing around our dwellings is to be considered. We like to have them there for the purpose of relating the buildings to the land, in a visual sense; but we disregard the biological reality of the need. How seldom an architect prepares a perspective or elevational drawing for exhibition without introducing some fanciful trees or shrubs regardless of

actual possibilities or facts! That trees and shrubs near buildings do help to relate those buildings to the land is an aspect
of planting which provides fascinating problems of design to
which all too little attention has been given. Even buildings which
by themselves may appear as intruders having no real part in their
surroundings may be reconciled to the land and become happily
incorporated into the general landscape through the mediation of
trees and shrubs.

Humphry Repton may have been the first person to notice and
to analyse the relationship between architectural forms and plant
forms. He saw that certain classes of trees were better adapted to one
architectural style than others—that there was a sort of natural
appropriateness, depending on opposite rather than on similar
qualities, between the forms of architecture and the forms of nature.
He deduced the rule that round-headed trees should be used in
association with gothic architecture, and that upright or tall, pointed
trees go better with the classic style.

Repton's rule

Repton was clearly thinking of masonry and vegetation as form-ing, together, single units of design. This mode of thought had, of course, unconsciously affected garden design earlier in the century, and was implicit in the landscape paintings from which the landscape garden derived its inspiration: but there is clear evidence that it was a comparatively new idea in conscious design. In garden design, judging from prints, drawings and plans, trees had not been used in this way before—even in the great formal gardens of the seventeenth century. They had been used to give shade and shelter, to form backgrounds, boundary and partition walls, and in many other structional and functional ways but not in this particular way.

Nevertheless, if our town-planning art is destined to develop real beauty, this synthesis of natural and architectural forms will play an important part in that development. More attention will doubtless be given to this aspect of planting; it is not merely a question of relationship of forms—colour and texture relationships are also in-volved. Extreme contrasts or delicate harmonies may both serve the designers' purpose on occasion, but a mere huddle of chance textures is often worse than useless. Just as the forms of architecture, though essentially different from any natural form, may yet be either re-flected or counter-balanced by tree shapes, so there are counterparts or opposites between the colour and texture of architectural surfaces and those of living foliage. Foliage may serve either as a foil or as a harmonious accompaniment to masonry, and the association, if well balanced and well grouped, emphasizes and accentuates the indi-vidual qualities of both partners in the group.

Under suitable circumstances, buildings may become a part of the landscape—an organic component of the surroundings—without the mediation of plant forms. Where the lines of a large building or group of buildings are exceptionally well related to the ground forms of both near surroundings and of the skyline, and if the buildings are of such a type that the austerity of unrelieved masonry is not over-whelming, then trees and shrubs may be unnecessary. But the great majority of architectural compositions benefit from an accompaniment of natural forms which brings them down to earth and gives them an

Sizewell nuclear power station, Suffolk. In this bleak coastal situation, it is appropriate to relate the buildings and land forms without extensive tree masses. By setting the building back from the sea, as recommended by the landscape architect Peter Youngman, the composition suggests a response between the power of the tides and that of nuclear energy. The low planting on the left conceals clutter and transport without attempting to dominate the structure.

appearance of stability and of belonging to their surroundings. These effects can be achieved, firstly, by trees in the background, whose outline blends with those of the elevation and roofs to form the skyline as seen from various points; and, secondly, by low shrubs, whose mass gives weight at the base of a composition, dovetailing with the lines of architecture on the one hand and those of the land on the other. Austere simple lines in a building seem to call for a freer treatment of plant material than buildings having rich ornamental features or any elaboration of design.

An exciting field of experiment and study lies open to young architects and landscape architects of the future in the use of natural plant forms in relation to modern architectural lines, whether asymmetrical topiary or free growing forms are used. Plants clipped into architectural or sculptured forms may yet play a part in design.

Plants grown in their characteristic habit contrast with architectural material in form, colour and texture. Special emphasis may be thrown on to either form, or colour, or texture by reducing the degree of contrast in the other two: or emphasis may be put on to any two of these by introducing harmony between the foliage and architectural material in the third aspect. The use of hedges or clipped shapes reflecting architectural lines brings the contrast of colour and texture into greater evidence, and, in the same way, differences of colour are brought into a different kind of relationship when the texture of the two materials is closely matched.

The Sculpture of Landscape

These thoughts lead on to the subject of the next chapter. Before proceeding, let us pause and look back at the subject in perspective. The functions in regard to design of plant material which have been under discussion in this chapter are those in which plants form a part of the main structure. The use of plants as 'interior decoration' is a separate subject. The beauty of plants themselves, their flowers, foliage and fruit in detail, has not been overlooked or underrated, but those more detailed beauties cannot be fully appreciated unless they are given their proper place in relation to the whole. The designer visualizes the design in a sculptural unity, thinking of his material as malleable stuff which he can mould to contain spaces of suitable proportions. Apart from certain limitations such as that of tree height, the choice of individual plants can be left to a later stage: thoughts of particular items need not influence problems of fundamental structure. The designer knows that when he comes to the stage of making detailed planting plans for that structure, and to the yet more detailed stage of planting plans for ornamental planting within, there will be no lack of plants to fulfil his conceptions and to play the parts he has imagined.

More than one of the uses under discussion in this chapter may be served by the same tree or group of trees. The wind shelter may form part of the skyline, linking roofs and chimneys to the ground. It may also give shade or a valuable shadow, and may be, in addition, a part of the background, setting off nearer features or more brightly coloured plant groups. The more uses any one group can serve, the greater its value and the more satisfaction we may feel with regard to its position in the general scheme. On the other hand it often happens that conflicting needs arise, such as when the prevailing wind blows from the direction of the most interesting view-point—a very common difficulty, particularly on coastal sites, usually to be over-

Sidmouth, Devon. A town linked to its context by old hedgerow groups which give shelter and entity to various sections of the built-up area. Individual specimen trees, as seen in the upper centre, do not meet these needs: the compact groups are not only more functional but also make a better visual composition with the buildings and open space.

come by devices such as slight changes in the direction of approach and of the shelter belts.

Plants which are introduced for the sake of their own beauty alone must be regarded as part of the interior furnishings—a certain amount of which is usually needed and must then be provided. But it is all too easy to ruin the simplicity of the whole and to clutter up the open spaces with too much ornament. Special features in addition to the structural material can be introduced where necessary, but they should be used with restraint.

Wild Life Habitats

The provision of homes and subsistence for wild life may fairly be regarded as a function of plants in landscape design. Ecological balance is threatened by development over much of the country. The extermination of animal and plant species may start a chain reaction of whose long-term results we are ignorant. Landscape planners can do much to aid conservation by preserving or creating suitable habitats in the design of new projects. Every such area, however small, can contribute something to over-all balance, in addition to the interest of each individual site.

13

Form, Colour and Texture

The form of the landscape is shaped by earth and vegetation in conjunction. In our climate nearly all the horizontal land forms are clothed by vegetation except in the case of arable land, where the colour of ploughed earth makes a sharp contrast with the surrounding vegetation for a short period. Nature herself never fails to cover soil and rock with greenery, except on steep vertical planes such as cliff-sides, quarries and chalk-pits, giving, in these cases, sharp changes of form to reinforce the interesting change of colour. Human buildings, well sited and designed, may fit into their surroundings equally well, on the same principle.

It was seen in the last chapter that plants may be the means of relating architectural outlines to the land forms—but too seldom is this triple relationship fully brought into play.

Every one of the structural uses of vegetation discussed in the last chapter can be augmented by suitable modelling of the ground or by making use of existing contours in such a way that plant and land forms combine to produce the effect. To design in terms of plants alone, even on flat or nearly flat ground, is to lose the advantages of relationship between the two materials, earth and vegetation.

A river flowing between its banks draws the eye unfailingly along the reach. Even without the charm of water, similar contours have the same effect—as in the case of a shallow dry riverbed. Plants grouped on or near the bank serve to emphasize the ground forms, endowing them with a richer and more variable interest than the land alone could hold.

The distinctive elements of the composition, made up of 'mass' and 'void' are emphasized and brought into greater contrast when plant masses and land forms are combined, and their separate functions are thus often better served. In the case of shelter or screen planting in particular, the value of planting on the highest available ground is self-evident. Any slight rise of the ground itself tends to give some shelter, even without planting: with trees and shrubs it adds to the total height of the screen, and a few feet of land lends the equivalent of some years of tree growth in the early stages.

Skylines are often spoilt, however, by straggly thin trees of unsuitable type; and the sweep of upland hill may in many instances give finer lines than tree-clad horizons. But the association of open down and beech hanger on the southern chalk is entirely satisfying, and gives the benefit of contrasting forms. The occasional clumps of emphatic outline have been planted or preserved, as landmarks, shelter, or purely as landscape features: and on the sandy uplands pines have been used in the same way. In either case, the close-grouped trees, standing on the crest of sweeping curves, accent the heights in a vivid and unexpected way, adding untold wealth to the scene. It is difficult to imagine how much beauty would be lost to the surrounding districts if such tree-groups were to disappear.

Colour, form and texture in plants and in landscape generally are interdependent. It is in the appreciation of these relationships that the designer's knowledge of plants differs from that of the botanist or horticulturist. He realizes that the emphasis to be gained by the use, say, of a group of cypress depends on its dark colour and smooth 'mat' surface as well as on its form. Its effect, and therefore its use, would be quite different if its colour were pale green and its texture composed of large shiny leaves of elaborate outline. He knows that if he wishes to use foliage alone or several flowers of one colour in a group, he must choose plants whose form and texture will be in striking contrast with each other, or the group would be dull.

Texture in landscape, even more than colour, depends on the quality of light, and on the distance, or depth of atmosphere, between the eye and the object. In the hand, a laurel leaf has a smooth and shiny surface. Seen across the lawn on a sunny day, the laurel tree (or hedge) presents a broken rough surface, the large leaves reflecting much light on their upper sides and casting heavy shadows beneath. The highlights appear paler in tone than those of the leaf held in the hand indoors. Seen at a greater distance, the texture no longer

Orange trees and cypresses in Italy. Contrasts of colour and texture reinforce the contrast of form between the tubs of citrus plants and the cypress trees behind.

depends on the size of individual leaves but on the general outline of whole plants and on their spacing; and at still greater distances—on the skyline of a distant mountain, for instance—individual plants cease to have any significance, and the sense of texture is in the outline of the group or of the land forms themselves, and depends on the geological structure. In Britain our horizon is never so distant that the type of forest tree forming it cannot be distinguished by the naked eye. A forest of conifers makes a spiky skyline as compared with the smooth, rounded hardwoods. The strong green of pines tends to reduce the apparent depth of atmosphere between the eye and the skyline, making it in effect seem closer.

In natural scenery, a fairly consistent scale of texture can be distinguished, rising from that of still water on a windless day, more smooth than anything else imaginable, yet reflecting all the colour and forms of the surroundings, to the texture of a mountain range— the roughest in our experience. And although the interest of a landscape (as in music) lies in the rearrangement and variations of the scale and the intrusion of accidentals, yet the sequence itself is suffi-

ciently marked, in both wild and agricultural scenery, to be noticeable. The two extremes of water and mountain range form respectively the lowest and the highest limits of the scale, and between
those extremes various causes give rise to a general sequence of
intermediate stages. The best grazing and the best soil for farm
crops lie in the valleys near the lakes or rivers; marsh and swamp
check the tree growth in the wettest parts near the water's edge. On
the steeper ground, trees grow more easily than crops, and there is
more need for shelter or for forest to check erosion. In alpine
scenery, the change occurring at a given height, from deciduous
forest to pine-wood, marks another stage, and above the tree-line
comes the rocky pasture and finally the peaks and crests themselves.
In much-eroded uplands, such as we have in this country, the heather
moors and rough grassland above the tree-line seem more like a
return to the lower parts of the scale, as do the chalk and limestone
ranges which are largely given up to sheep-grazing and other agricultural uses. But even these, in many cases, are so much broken up
by clumps of scrub or woodland as to be included in the general
series.

Fin Lough, Delphi, Co. Mayo. In the near foreground individual plants and even
the size of leaf and twig determine texture. In the middle distance tree groups
and the size and shape of plantations are seen in contrast to smooth pasture or,
as in this case, a water surface. In the distance the land forms themselves and the
quality of the horizon are the elements giving the sense of texture.

From the river in the valley the texture scale seems to rise through the rougher effect of cultivation to woodland. In the upper levels the groups of trees or scrub, broken by open pasture, give the coarsest texture in sharpest contrast to the water surface below. Accidental variations through the scale add change and variety. Symonds Yat (p. 118) shows a similar progression.

On the small scale of park or garden, foliage of elaborate pattern giving a sculptural effect is invaluable. It is best provided by plants such as figs, vines, *funkias*, *acanthus*, *bocconia cordata* and certain trees having large well-spaced leaves of interesting outline. Such plants give a very coarse texture in contrast to plain wall surfaces or smooth lawn. Flower colour may or may not have a place in such groups, which in themselves provide enough interest for the eye.

Elaborate texture obtrudes itself into the foreground, whereas plants of fine texture melt easily into the distance and may even suggest a sense of distance—that is why laurel and other large-leaved plants make such bad backgrounds for colour groups or any smaller-leaved plants in the foreground. Their broken surface competes for the eye's attention, to the disadvantage of the foreground group.

The common practice of placing obtrusive colour groups in

gardens between the view-point and the view is ill-judged. Both call for attention, but they appeal to different modes of appreciation: the mind cannot deal with both simultaneously, so that they are in direct competition for attention—causing an unrestful conflict. And although the eye may be greedy for both, taken together they are, so to speak, indigestible. Obtrusive textures on the other hand—say, of foliage of a single hue deep in tone—may be perfect as a frame or setting for a view where distance has smoothed out the vegetation textures, and where soft colour predominates. To equalize the colour and texture of foreground and distance is to cancel out much of the separate values of each.

As in the case of texture, colour values vary under different lighting conditions and at different distances. Depth of atmosphere, depending on distance and on atmospheric pressure, reduces the strength of the actual colours and interposes tones of blue, grey or

River walk at Buscot Old Parsonage, Berks. Coarse sculptured texture in the near right-hand group is graded through finer foliage and turf to the smooth water of the Thames on the left. The gradation from the first view at the entrance, where the photograph was taken, to the pale poplars along the path echoes the effect and increases the impact of the vista.

violet—giving that effect of separate layers of varying tones (usually of blue) over each visible land outline. Wherever the possibility exists of seeing this effect, it is a source of constant pleasure and should be given full consideration in the design.

Owing to this familiar blueness of the distance, blues of smooth texture easily serve to give an impression of distance, unlike the warm reds and orange colours which obtrude themselves into the foreground. It was remarked by Gertrude Jekyll that by planting warm colours nearest the main viewpoint, and cool blues and violet further away, an impression of distance is gained: also, that the eye enjoys that arrangement of colour as being in harmony with nature's own system.

Frank Dark, the architect of Drakelow 'C' Power Station near Burton on Trent, chose a warm red colouring for two of the cooling towers, in order to bring them forward, visually, from the four grey towers. On clear days the idea is effective, but the Burton climate too often clouds all in a grey dimness.

Other colour effects depend on mental associations rather than on what is seen. There is, for instance, a seasonal colour scale—or rhythm—which, though not rigid, is sufficiently constant and well-marked to cause mental associations which the designer should always bear in mind.

Snow and snowdrops are the first marked changes from winter browns and greys, and then appear the pale-yellow aconites with their green frills; the earliest crocuses are pale mauve and yellow, then come the primroses and the daffodils, with the unbelievable, phantom green of bursting tree-buds. Gorse and blackthorn come early in the year too, though gorse is said to be never out of bloom. Yellow, white and green are the colours of early spring. They are followed by fruit blossom, hawthorn and bluebells, and more, much more, of that vernal green; but in June the green takes on a deeper tone and a whole tide of other colour rises—the pale pinks and blues of May giving way to deeper-toned flowers such as foxgloves, roses and willow herb. In July and August the whole force of plant colour reaches a climax—fields of yellow corn, blue flax, pink clover and other colourful crops (and their enemy the scarlet poppy), are matched in gardens by the greatest variety of the year. The greens of deciduous trees have by now become heavy and dull, and the conifers seem at their gloomiest. Then the autumn, though it may be even richer in colour, spreads a brownish tinge over all the strong reds, orange and purple, and as the season goes on, that brownness becomes dominant with touches of flame and scarlet, until the leaves have fallen. There is a late moment of pale gold marked by dying bracken fern and by the elms and birches, the last leaves to fall; and then the quieter tones prevail—soft silver greys and browns, the colour of ploughed earth and winter stems, relieved only by the black-green of conifers and broad-leaved evergreens.

Trees whose foliage is normally copper-coloured, such as copper-beech and some prunus and maple species, often give an autumnal effect too early in the year, and the same may be said of early-flowering dahlias and zinnias whose colours 'belong' to the end of the season. In gardens this is usually a disadvantage: but there is the alternative possibility of choosing plants of spring-like colours before and after the period with which we associate them, in order to extend the idea of spring.

Light and Shadow

In the case of groups intended to attract the eye in landscape or garden, much depends on their placing. The daylight is not in our control, but we can place our plant-groups (or other ornamental features) according to our knowledge of the sun's position at any season and at any hour of the day. Objects in full sunlight or at focal points draw attention, but the focal point is not necessarily the right place for a 'blaze of colour', for reasons stated earlier. It more often happens that brilliant colour groups should form a subsidiary attraction and take therefore a secondary or lateral position: but wherever they come, they must be well-lit at the hour and season for which they are intended, and are seen at their best against a background of shadow or of dark smooth foliage. Only in the case of detailed planting to be seen at a distance of a few yards is there the possibility of planning colour monotones or close harmonies in order to lay the whole stress of contrast on form and texture. This is done, for example, when green plants of bold foliage pattern are grouped on a lawn, or against a smooth-clipped hedge: or when white flowers with pale grey foliage are seen against a plain wall surface of white or grey.

Moonlight gives a different view of familiar schemes, eliminating variations of hue and so bringing out the full value of form depending on light and shadow. To design a patio garden mainly for its moonlight hours would be a valuable exercise for any student of landscape design, forcing him to value form before colour, and to think of it in relation to light and shadow. White or very pale-coloured flowers and silver leaves provide the highlights in moonlit scenes, and many of the white flowers are night-scented, since their appeal is to moths and other night-flying insects.

Floodlighting on dark nights provides very different opportunities. Unless great care is exercised, its effects can be tawdry and un-suited to the calm of the garden and open air: but floodlighting, sensitively used, has revealed new beauty in the landscape. It can bring to view aspects no less beautiful than, though dramatically different from, those of daylight. Sunlight, moving through the upper arc of a circle, brings different aspects of a scene into full play at different hours of the day, and moonlight shows us those same aspects under a different quality of light. But artificial light can explore a different set of aspects from the lower angles. Moreover, the beam of light can be directed to pick out one object or a group at a time, showing it up against the blackness of all beyond. A single group of trees, the underside of the foliage lit and the shadows rising instead of falling, is a new delight to the eye. And some small pattern of leaf or bark which passes almost unnoticed in the daytime can be picked out and shown on its own merits, free from the competition of its surroundings. The placing of the lamps to give the precise effects wanted, and their removal or concealment by day, are part of the designer's problem. Floodlighting can well be used in parks, outdoor theatres, and gardens attached to large buildings, where steps and other architectural features could serve the double purpose, being wired for night lighting in addition to their normal use. Lamps

Night lighting at Chenonceaux, France. Son et Lumière has taught us much about the dramatic use of night lighting. Lighting from below reveals a new and different aspect of scenes usually lit from above. The lights need to be sunken or screened, in order not to intrude in the ordinary daylight scene.

set below ground level, under a grille screened by low plants or rough grass are effective in more open areas. There is no need for obtrusive lamps spoiling the daylight scene.

Selective lighting, picking out special groups of plants shows up very clearly any faults of composition in the group, especially any haphazard relationships of form and texture between the plants concerned. Only groups which are really satisfactory in this respect are worthy of special emphasis.

Floodlighting of the over-colourful and tawdry type has prejudiced its exploration and better use, but with more sensitive use, night lighting will give the night landscape a new and exciting quality.

Plant Grouping

The growth of individual plants in association with others is quite different from their untrammelled development. The beech tree growing alone in a favourable open position may spread its lower branches over an area nearly a hundred feet in diameter, while grown in a wood in competition with other beeches it will develop instead a straight tall stem with no lower branches and a small rounded top of about fifteen feet in diameter—a different shape altogether. Yet the outline of a beechwood seen against the sky is essentially an outline of typical beech, recognizable as such even at a considerable distance. The group retains the character of the species even though each individual has lost its typical outline. Plants grown in close association with other plants have their shape and character modified in endless degree, and it is necessary to know something of those modifications and to be able to foresee their effects in order to design successful planting groups.

Individual trees, grown to their full natural beauty, are a great feature of British landscape. A single tree may dominate and give character to a meadow or lawn, but to repeat the single specimen too often within an area may quite spoil the effect. If we wish to get broader effects it is usually best to group several trees of the same species close enough to form a single unit. In this case no single tree develops the full spread of which it is capable, but the outline of the group retains the character of the species. This collective treatment of one species tends to throw the emphasis on the stems, making a rhythmic pattern by repetition of similar forms. This pattern is brought out to the full when the lower boughs are removed and the ground underneath kept free of undergrowth, by grazing or cultivation, so that the stems are seen rising clean and emphatic from the earth.

Mixed groups, having no strong contrasts or marked likeness of form, but a general dissimilarity of character, are restless in outline and do not give the rhythmic stem pattern. These mixed groups tend to be dull and meaningless in design; but groups of different species selected for strong contrasts of form or other special relationship are of great value and could be planted more frequently.

These sculptural groups of two or more species of markedly different outline, planted so as to build up into a unity which one alone could not provide, can be full of interest. The spacing may be

Beech stems on Edgehill, Warwicks. The repetition of stems of one species gives a rhythm to the composition. Each is a different individual shape, yet they share a common character. The curve, following the footpath line, invites further exploration and anticipation.

Weeping willow and Lombardy poplar, Compton Beauchamp, Berks. Another system of grouping using contrasting shapes to form sculptural groups instead of the rhythmic pattern from repetition of a single species.

even closer than in the group of one species, but instead of a rhythmic stem theme, the group usually requires to be well clothed with foliage to the ground, with additional low shrubs massed at the base to give a sense of balance and stability. The characteristic outline of any one member of the group is of importance only in so far as it contributes to the whole. Seasonal variations and contrasts of foliage colour and texture play an important part in such groups.

Massed trees and shrubs forming shelter belts should be considered as unities. If for functional reasons they are to be built up of sub-groups, each sub-group should contribute visually, no less than usefully, to the whole. The collective effect seen from a distance may be improved by a tall group forming a climax to the general outline, but restless outlines are unimpressive. Spacing of plants in wind-screens is usually so close that individual shapes are lost; but any group of a single species will show the outline characteristic of its species.

Whether the dominating theme of the whole group is some harmonious colour scheme for special seasonal effect, or whether it is the permanent form values of the outline, contrasts of texture and other foliage qualities will emphasize the individuality of each sub-group and give character to the whole.

Symbolism

Plant-grouping may be a science, or an art or both. In the Far East it is regarded as an art based on underlying spiritual principles. Certain forms and associations convey symbolic ideas, as do the individual plants themselves, and without such symbolism garden art, flower decoration and much else besides lose, for the Eastern mind, all sense and meaning.

Although such symbolism may be unimportant or incomprehensible to the uninitiated Westerner, its aesthetic results are of universal application. We enjoy the sculptural group referred to earlier, without knowing that to other intelligences it may embody the fundamental symbolism on which all Japanese plant arrangements are based, in which the tall upreaching form—the climax of a group—represents divine aspirations and the spiritual relationship of the creature with the Source of Life. The second element, usually of contrasting form on an inclined axis somewhere between the horizontal and the vertical, represents humanity and all that has life: and the low horizontal line or base stands for the earth and the soil supporting life.

Individual plants composing such groups may bear other symbolic meanings. For example, there is the time-honoured association of cypress and almond which recurs so often in Persian designs; in which the tall evergreen cypress, unchanging through the seasons, stands for solemn thoughts of death and eternity, and the almond, flowering on leafless boughs in an outburst of vernal frivolity, evokes the opposite ideas of youth, fertility and the renewal of life. Whether or not we attach such significance to the group, its contrasts of shape, colour, texture and seasonal change are profoundly satisfying to anyone with an eye for beauty.

Plant-grouping based only on æsthetic principles has its critics, particularly among botanists and ecologists: and it is clear that in

Spanish chestnuts. Although introduced to Britain by human agency, the Spanish chestnut grows well on light soils and suits our landscape. It has become so well integrated that the eye accepts it as a native tree.

some situations exotic groups or plants not adapted to their context may strike a very inharmonious note. The cypress and almond group, which may be at home in a Persian scene and which may translate well into a formal garden setting of any country, would come as an irrelevance seen among the marsh marigolds of an English water-meadow. And although that sense of shock or inappropriateness may, in itself, have a certain appeal for some, the group could never have the quality of 'belonging' to the landscape. It could never have that innate and essential fitness which is felt when native plants form a pleasing group.

Symbolic plant-grouping in the East tends to follow ecological laws for the reasons that it is easier to grow things in the conditions which suit them, and that an ancient and traditional art is not easily adapted to new material and introduced species.

In Britain, however, as we saw earlier, the term 'native' plant may be ambiguous and can be differently construed. In a strictly botanical sense the sycamore is not a native, having been introduced to Britain by man. The Romans imported the sweet chestnut, yet both these trees are common features of our countryside and could scarcely be termed 'exotic', since they can survive permanently in native plant communities without human aid. If we go back far enough, to the period of the Ice Age, Britain possessed very few plants of any sort, and everything that now grows here has come as an intruder at some period since then. In the botanical sense the natives are those which established themselves without human intervention.

Leaving the exact definition of the words 'native' and 'indigenous' to the botanist, it remains necessary for the landscape architect to make some distinction between those plants able to hold their own in open competition with other wild vegetation, and those which will survive only if competition is eliminated in their favour by man. The appearance of being at home in the landscape is another factor of vital importance to him; in general, the two go together—those trees and shrubs which can reproduce themselves and hold their own with the rest of the vegetation having already become a familiar part of our landscape. It will generally be found that plants combining these two qualities of survival-power and of 'looking native' are those which have been able to establish themselves in one or other of the plant associations—those ecological groups—referred to in an earlier chapter. *Rhododendron ponticum*, for instance the pale magenta one that grows so freely from self-sown seeds on light acid soils, has found a place along with heather and gorse, pine and birch, on many a common. In certain districts of Ireland it has displaced arbutus and even holly in light woodland. Sycamore, which has been growing in Britain for several centuries, can hold its own against many of our native trees, even becoming locally dominant in mixed woodland. It is so prolific and quick-growing that if

Setchy, Norfolk. Under controlled conditions in small areas, plants not normally found together in nature can be combined for special contrasts of colour and texture. *Rodgersia* can be supplied with a moist root run in a dry area if its broad leaves are required as a foil to neighbours.

left to itself it would soon form forest on many a stretch of gravel and river silt.

On London's bombed rubble after the air raids of World War II, thickets of sycamore sprang up, interspersed with cherry and plum seedlings, and drifts of purple buddlea. With a little imagination one might visualize a London left to nature's healing hand after all mankind was doomed, and see, in the mind's eye, a lost and broken city hidden under a great forest of sycamore, with a sprinkling of wild cherry, plum, and other garden plants on the fringe of glades, and a 'field layer' of coltsfoot and willow herb covering remnants of floor and fallen masonry.

Any plant which can propagate itself, hold its own, and take its place as a member of a natural plant association is for the purpose of the landscape designer the equal of one which is truly indigenous.

It is not suggested that ecological considerations need over-rule other principles of planting design, nor that we should apply them to all planting schemes. There are many sites, such as parks and gardens in towns or related to human habitation of any sort, where purely visual and æsthetic standards unhampered by ecology are appropriate. Let us suppose that a group of the sculptural type, referred to earlier in the chapter, is required for reasons connected with its architectural setting, to give dark-green vertical lines as its main feature, with a silvery-grey base of varying height and texture. Choosing freely among the available material hardy in this country (regardless of country of origin), the species chosen might be the American 'Red Cedar', or upright juniper (*Juniperus virginiana*), white Spanish broom (*Cytisus albus*), and *Senecio greyii*, a grey-leaved New Zealander, whose broad, round leaves will harmonize in colour with the foliage of the broom, but provide a sharp contrast of texture, and whose low, rounded form will be good against the taller spiky broom and the dark-green upright lines of juniper. Such a group would do well in an open position on light loam in any of our southern counties; though drawn from widely separated countries, all the three members of it would be quite happy growing together here.

Should we wish to group plants whose natural habitat is not only different parts of the globe but on different types of soil with different degrees of moisture, we can do so with care by providing the necessary conditions, either in an apparently natural manner—as, for instance, by arranging a moist spot at the base of a dry wall—or in a frankly artificial manner by growing the plants in tubs, boxes, pots or built-up beds where drainage and irrigation are under complete control. The first treatment, which would enable us to grow plants of widely different habitat in association for the sake of some pleasing effect of colour, form and texture (for example, *Saxifraga peltata*, or one of the *rodgersias*, growing in the damp spot at the base of a dry wall, would provide an interesting contrast to the mossy green of *Arenaria balerica*, starred with white flowers, covering the vertical wall face) is the general treatment in rock gardens and other naturalistic types of gardening. The provision of artificially controlled conditions is especially suitable for courtyards, loggias and roof gardens or terraces in very close association with architecture: it makes possible the use of almost any kind of foliage in any position where it may be required.

Where the surroundings are entirely the work of human hands, art dominating definitely over nature, such plant groupings, selected from the widest possible range of material and governed by visual considerations regardless of ecology, are felt to be appropriate and pleasing. There are, however, many positions in the wider and more open landscape—beside main roads for instance, or in connection with national parks, camping sites and other places—where natural landscape is the dominating consideration, and where far more satisfactory results can be achieved by following the indications of ecology and by limiting our new planting to the native plant association of the site. The principles of good æsthetic design can be still applied—we can appreciate our native plants far better if their beauties of form, colour and texture are brought out by good grouping and placing. But our range of choice is limited very considerably, tying us down in such cases to comparatively few species. Such restraint, correctly applied in suitable surroundings, brings its own reward in the resulting sense of unity and of harmony: that 'oneness' with nature itself, giving simplicity which is calm, enduring and full of deep repose.

PART THREE

Design in Practice

Wasdale, Cumberland. There is a clear demarcation here between the cultivated farm land of the valley floor and the wilder mountain scenery into which it fingers its way. We see two contrasting landscape types resulting from land use differing according to its potential. Soil eroded from the slopes has brought the little settlements up the valley: the road connects them to more advanced communities and more complicated land use patterns in the broader lands below.

14

A Pattern of Contrasting Types

Our landscape is of three main types—wild, agricultural and urban —and each type can be subdivided into other categories according to position and use. Linking the three types is the network of communication—railways, roads, canals, farm tracks and footpaths. Geographically the three main types are not clean-cut, separate entities, but make an interlocking pattern over most of the country, the open country extending into the towns in the shape of parks and gardens, and the towns being situated in agricultural or wilder districts according to their industries and the sources of raw material. Parks and recreation areas vary in character according to their urban or rural siting.

The integration of the different types, provided it is really integration and not a haphazard mixture, and so long as each type preserves its own distinct character, adds interest to the whole and gives our country that 'well-lived-in' look which is one of its outstanding charms.

We like the character of each to be strongly marked. The general blurring of outline and loss of individuality that result when a town spreads indeterminately over open country, or when open space invades a town till the widely spaced houses have no effect of grouping or cohesion, debases the quality of any landscape.

The distinction between wild and cultivated land is usually clearly marked in this country, if we take rough pasture as belonging to the 'wild' (and without it what could we indeed call wild?). The clear definition between these two is a lovely attribute of many country districts. In districts where the two types are more mixed, as in parts of Ireland, the 'wild' usually predominates, and the little homesteads and tiny patches of cultivation do not detract from the wildness, but add accents of special interest.

If these three types are to remain distinct, separate, undiluted yet harmoniously balanced as they should be, over the face of Britain there is need for very broad-scale planning, embracing the whole country. A national view of the whole is essential, no less than the realization of the value of each distinct type. New or growing industries affecting, as they must, the position of other developments such as transport, housing, and the towns themselves, affect also the character of the countryside surrounding them; and no balanced judgment of the reasons for or against choosing certain sites for new factories, works, aerodromes and other undertakings is possible from sectional or local interests alone. The view-point of a single industry, or of a local population, even where the two are reconciled, may leave out of account wider view-points affecting the country at large. Certain districts possess special conditions giving landscape and wild life unique in Britain; others may be, by comparison with neighbouring districts, of comparatively common type, more easily spared for new use from a national standpoint. Local planning without strong central direction can scarcely assess the full national implications of local changes and must act in accordance with immediate local indications even if these differ from wider interests.

An over-riding recognition of the importance of preserving the full range of landscape types, of maintaining beautiful clean-cut landscape, calls for general agreement between the various authorities concerned with different types of land use. Otherwise, how can the inevitable changes of the future come about without 'messing up' our landscape, blurring the distinction of existing types, and sacrificing the national heritage of natural beauty?

The Call of the Wild

In Britain we have no great reserve of virgin landscape left, and for this reason even the relative wildness of our highland and coastal districts has a heightened and far greater value than it would in more spacious lands: the preservation and beauty of these areas are a subject of vital concern to every one of the inhabitants of the islands, present and future.

Box Hill, Surrey. The chalk slopes have a rich range of plants which enjoy alkaline conditions, from the small orchids in the turf to the yew and beech of the forest climax. All the stages of reversion to woodland can be seen where the absence of grazing animals permits natural regeneration of native species.

The land under consideration in this chapter is the relatively or nearly wild country such as we have in the highland districts, certain coastal stretches, sandy commons and marsh lands where erosion, steep slopes, cliffs, poor soil, bad climatic or drainage conditions have prevented arable farming. There is also some land preserved as nature reserves or on account of its special landscape beauty (much of which has been presented to, or acquired by, the National Trust) and land at present used only for purposes of sport.

In considering such areas, we should bear in mind to what extent their present appearance depends on their present use (which means knowing what human uses they do, in fact, serve) and what alterations in their appearance would result from different uses or from no productive use at all. This is a subject on which ecology can enlighten us: in spite of the vast field this opens up some elementary knowledge of it should be implanted in the minds of all who have to deal with country planning, since it forms a background essential to the proper understanding of all problems of land use in the countryside.

If left to itself, any land rich enough to support mixed farming is liable to revert to dense forest, the type depending on climate and soil conditions. Above the 1500-feet contour line, conditions in Britain do not at present favour scrub or tree growth, and the existing vegetation of rough grass or heather would probably hold sway with little change. Many coastal areas would suffer more rapid erosion than at present if deprived of the protection of groins, sea-walls and special planting, but their familiar appearance would be preserved by sea-spray and wind. In other places the building-up processes due to lack of drainage and other natural causes might be speeded up. Slow-moving rivers in wide valleys would be constantly altering course as their flow became checked by reeds, raised bogs and developing scrub. In highland districts, tree growth, wherever conditions favour it, would be scrubby woodland—much of it dominated by small sessile oaks; though in parts of Northern Ireland and Scotland, pine and birch might again become established. Dry, sandy districts would also favour pine and birch with heather and gorse in the open spaces. On chalk downs beech would become the dominant forest, with ash, yew, whitebeam and cherry in the more open glades, and all the rest of the typical chalk scrub clinging to the steeper slopes and the forest fringes.

We too readily assume that the highest landscape beauty results from complete and utter 'wildness'—from the absence, that is, of any human use whatever. Yet paths and tracks enabling such beauty to be appreciated in themselves reduce, in some degree, the wildness of the scene, while surely adding to its beauty: so that clearly the first assumption is incorrect at the outset. Open spaces amongst the forest, kept free from trees by grazing or other human use, give far greater beauty than endless stretches of unbroken forest. Open rolling country with few trees is a pleasant contrast to thick forest. At every stage it can be shown that human use in itself is not incompatible with landscape beauty in the case of 'wild' scenery, but it is perhaps true that the emotional impact of wild scenery is lessened by visible signs of human existence. The experience of truly being alone becomes even more rare and difficult to know. Certain it is that over-use by man destroys the landscape for man's own needs.

Now that land of low productivity can be brought to higher fertility by new methods of agriculture and forestry, the risk of losing the last remnants of the wild should raise its scarcity value. Forests planted on a large scale to protect the upper slopes from wind, may increase the height of the 'tree line', now about 1500 feet, and give better protection for grazing and cultivation beyond that height.

In 1943 the Forestry Commission argued that timber production on the mountainous districts of Britain gives better returns than sheep-grazing. But the point has not been proved. If agriculture in such areas is aided by loans and bonuses, rapid changes occur.

The Forestry Commission continues to stress the need for more home-grown timber both for normal use and as a reserve against emergencies such as war or other causes which might check imports. The 1943 report proposed new planting in highland districts of three million acres of woodland (mostly conifers) in addition to the renovation and replanting of two million acres in other parts of Britain, mostly of hardwoods; and this total was estimated to produce only one-third of our peace-time needs.

The huge demands on the present estimated land surface in low-land districts (for industry, airfields, roads, housing and public open space) will lead to the necessity of raising the agricultural yield of highland districts.[1]

These two great 'priorities' are therefore already in competition for a changed use of much of our wilder country. A third and growing interest involved is the recreational value of these highlands to the population in general—an interest which is bound up with the question of attracting foreign visitors to Britain, and so adding a tourist value to land of 'low production'.[2]

For the ordinary citizen having an interest in the landscape, the

---

[1] See R. G. Stapledon, *The Land Now and To-morrow*, Faber, 1944.
[2] See J. Dower, *National Parks in England and Wales*, HMSO, 1945.

urgent question is: 'How far would these proposed uses add to or detract from the beauty of the scenery as we know it?'

The answer, surely, is that good design, balancing these three interests (and also certain other long-term considerations showing less obvious immediate benefits which will be referred to in due course), should be capable of finding a happy solution to the problems involved without destroying the scenery, provided the regions concerned can be dealt with as a whole—the different interests and areas being correlated in regional schemes. If, on the other hand, the areas should be allotted piecemeal for the different purposes to be dealt with by each concern, without an over-all scheme, the wild landscape may be lost.

Variety is the source of much pleasure, in landscape as in other aspects of beauty, and this is particularly true of Britain—a small land with a large population. The more different types of landscape in a region, the richer its variety and the more pleasure it gives. To allow all the existing wild scenery to be changed through new land uses would mean a very serious loss. Some of it should be preserved in its present condition, and there is strong argument for allowing certain areas to revert to a completely wild state, having no productive use at all and serving man only as a 'refreshment of the spirit'. These need not be large areas, since variety is the objective. They should become conservation areas in the widest sense, to serve as nature reserves of great scientific value, though other types of nature reserve would also be needed. Even areas primarily devoted to economic human uses may serve in some instances as nature reserves.

In the low-production areas, land preserved in a completely wild state need not involve serious economic loss and could easily be compensated for by higher yields of other areas whose changed use and appearance would contribute to the landscape variety of the whole. There are, at present, extensive uplands, where nothing grows but coarse grasses giving very poor pasture, whose appearance would be positively and decisively improved by the growth of forest related to a higher state of cultivation. Related they must be, in the sense that forest plantations should be sited to shelter farms and

Djurgarden Park, Sweden. Informal tracks through natural woodland are ideal for recreation. The dappled shade of mature woods with open glades is better for this purpose than woodland whose sole value is economic timber production.

stock, and to prevent soil erosion, if the landscape is to be satisfying. This functional relationship of farm and forest may make a beautiful pattern, whereas if the two are unrelated, the square intractable plantations of trees appear as intruders in the scene.

If the use of land for holiday-making and for visitors from far afield is taken into consideration also, in addition to its use for farm and forest, the possibility of landscape beauty becomes yet greater, and the need for it more marked. Rights of way, tracks, rides and open spaces within the forest would not only add to the beauty and interest of the scene as the result of appropriate siting, but would be planned and planted for their visual effect. This problem was discussed by Sylvia Crowe in an admirable paper addressed to the Institute of Landscape Architects at Alexandra Palace on April 28th, 1966, in connection with the *Observer* Nature Week exhibition.

Landscape of a distinctly wilder type than that of lowland agricultural lands will still be characteristic of the uplands. This different type should be stressed, and its psychological importance fully recognized.

It would be possible to allow landscape considerations the place of first priority in the planning of these wilder districts, without even short-term economic loss and with immeasurable long-term gain—assuming the values to be administered by a single all-embracing authority; since fine and dignified landscape attracts visitors and could reconcile them to the discipline and good manners which its proper maintenance requires.

Besides the three interests already referred to (agriculture, forestry, and recreation) there are others no less important in the long run, but which, because they may not be assessable in terms of economic value within the period of a generation, can be given due importance only by a far-seeing and widely comprehensive authority such as the State or a Regional Commission. These include conservation of water-supply, the maintenance of soil fertility—or the creation of fertile soils in districts now poor in this respect, and the maintenance of biological balance.

It has been shown earlier in this book that any site or area destined to fulfil more than one specific use calls for integrated design. Above all, in the case of the wider national planning, the better the co-ordination of all the purposes a given area is to serve, the greater the possibilities of a fine landscape in that area, provided all those purposes are recognised and related from the start.

This statement will be examined in greater detail, but before doing so, let us remind ourselves that sooner or later all these functions of the land must be taken into consideration, and that if they are left until circumstances drive us to deal with them, and are then imposed separately one by one on a landscape which has been developed on piecemeal principles, that landscape, instead of being grand and lovely, will become a mass of unrelated bits and pieces, losing its old character and gaining nothing by the change.

Water

A better water-supply than we have at present is urgently needed in many parts of the country, and the demand is constantly growing. In the south and east of England the water table supplying the ordinary wells is sinking, and new artesian wells bored to meet the need only aggravate the general condition. The chalk districts in dry spells become, by modern standards of living, almost uninhabitable, and throughout the lowland parts of Britain farms need a more regular supply for stock, dairy and other purposes than was formerly thought necessary.

Rainfall in these districts is low in any case, and a high proportion of it is carried into the rivers, before it has had time to percolate the sub-soil, by drainage operations of every kind which have been so greatly developed in the last two centuries. Throughout the built-up areas little or no rainwater reaches the sub-soil, and in agricultural districts deep drainage of retentive soils, though improving surface fertility, reduces the water reserves below. Local measures may reduce this tendency to some extent, but the problem is clearly national rather than local.

Ultimately the country as a whole must be largely dependent for a better water-supply on the high-rainfall districts—those highlands of the north and west which also give us our finest natural landscape. Urban requirements for water constantly increase, and have to be supplied from distant hill areas, causing disputes between town and country. The conflict may be one of the worst threats to landscape in future decades. The problem is too intricate to be briefly discussed in these pages and the reader is referred to recent publications dealing with this special subject, such as the Year Book of the Association of River Authorities, the reports and publications of the Water Resources Board, and HMSO publications on Water Resources and Conservation.

Rainwater is conserved either in the form of sub-soil reserves in the rock beneath, or by catchment schemes and dams designed to collect and distribute surface water before it percolates through to the deeper layers. In either case the landscape is profoundly affected.

The first is nature's method; it depends on a surface covered with vegetation, with matted roots holding the top-soil together, and preventing it from being washed away. The roots also provide downward channels through the soil, through which the rainwater percolates till it reaches some impervious layer. Soil exposed to the action of rainwater without the protecting covering of plants, particularly on sloping ground, is liable to rapid erosion, and this creates channels which, instead of leading the water downward to form subsoil reserves, carry it over the surface in the form of streams, torrents and rivers till it leaves the land to join the sea.

The planting of forest on land liable to erosion is therefore of value for this purpose alone. No other vegetation serves this purpose better than deep-rooting trees, though grass and other low, close-growing plants have to a lesser extent the same effect. Trees will grow well on steep land which, if ploughed, would lose soil through erosion, or on hillsides too steep for the plough or too poor to be worth ploughing. They will even grow on slopes so steep as to discourage lesser vegetation whose shallow roots give less anchorage and cannot grip the soil so widely or with such strength as tree roots.

Reservoirs, dams and catchment schemes, will be discussed in Chapter Seventeen. In this country some of these schemes have had lamentable effects on the landscape. But why should they be hideous disfigurements of natural scenery when they might instead become beautiful features? The ugliness of older reservoirs was usually the result of their having been designed with a single purpose, and limited to strictly economic efficiency from the point of view of that purpose alone. But since recently the advice of landscape consultants such as Colwyn Foulkes and Frederick Gibberd has been sought,

Water conservation in the Ruhr area, Verse reservoir. The secondary dam retains the high water level in the upper reservoir while the water level in the lower reservoir falls. The roads wind through forest with open views at chosen points. The forest cover is dense for economic reasons. In Britain a more open treatment might be indicated, and from the landscape angle the tree nursery and fields in the upper right corner could be more happily shaped and placed for visual effect.

some reservoirs have become fine landscape features.

Modern methods of water treatment have greatly reduced the need to exclude the public from reservoirs, and access for fishing and sailing can usually now be permitted. This necessitates planning for 'multiple use'; and fine landscape is not the least of the resources to be conserved.

Conservation of Soil

To return to those other functions of forest and the wilder landscape referred to earlier in this chapter, let us consider nature's method of turning the earth's rocky crust into cultivable land. Agricultural soils throughout the world are a legacy of ancient forest and especially of those having a high percentage of hardwood trees. Deep roots draw up minerals in minute but constant quantities from the rocks beneath, and these, after undergoing elaborate chemical processes in the leaf, are returned in organic compounds to the ground surface. Further intricate biological processes take place in the forest floor, in which tree roots, bacteria and other forms of life all play important roles[1]. Until man can produce equivalent results in other ways, he should regard forest not merely as a timber crop but also as a soil factory. Much is still being learnt about how to maintain soil fertility in existing soils: the question of soil production is being studied in relation to polluted or derelict land and to industrial waste materials, and this will be referred to again in Chapter Seventeen.

Timber can be produced on the poorest land; but if, through ignorance and greed for immediate profit, it leaves that land no richer than before, the generation responsible for such practice is robbing future generations of a birthright. Research into the effect of conifers on the ultimate quality of soil may settle this debatable question. Many believe that pure coniferous stands impoverish the soil: mixed conifers and deciduous woods seem to be coming into favour, and this produces a more balanced soil and a richer variety of bird and animal life.

The generation which allows a deterioration or loss of soil fertility and of wild life also loses landscape beauty which could be enjoyed in its own lifetime. Our sense of beauty could, and should, be a sure guide to the proper treatment of the land, if we allow it to play its due part.

Nature Conservation

The Nature Conservancy with the International Union for the Conservation of Nature and the Wild Life Trusts are doing excellent work to educate the public in the appreciation of our natural heritage. Nature conservation and fine landscape go together, and nature reserves, wherever they occur, involve the preservation of special types of interesting landscape: the same sort of widespread education of the public is needed for both purposes if the general population is

[1] See Appendix B.

to become aware of their significance. Biological interests are very easily aroused, even if largely dormant, and, through these, people can be given a sense of their own relationship to the balance of the whole. The negative 'don'ts' applied to litter, gates left open, damage to crops, and fires started, mean little to people in whose minds a positive interest in nature and country life has not already been aroused. Once aroused, that interest leads us on to cherish and revere, rather than to destroy, the country we love.

The inclusion of every stage between the truly wild and the fully cultivated is an enrichment of the landscape. Let us consider in closer detail those intermediate stages, particularly that farm-forest pattern which may well, in the future, assume a larger place in highland scenery than it has held in the past. With these we can consider also those changes of the pattern which result if an area is to be used for recreational or holiday purposes as well as for productive use.

Upland Forest

Closely planted forest plots of rigid geometrical outline, imposed on the hillside without regard to contours and other existing features, look 'wrong' in the landscape no matter what trees are grown. The outline or boundary shape of the whole plantation is, in this sense, of far greater importance than the treatment within the plantation. From a distance the rigid rows in which the trees are planted are not evident, and it is not those rows, but the outline of the whole, and the straight fire-breaks dividing the compartments which are seen. It has been suggested that pure stands of conifers may be camouflaged by an outer fringe of deciduous trees, but this in itself, though it might serve a good purpose in flat country, is useless in hilly country where the plantations are usually seen from a far hillside, the observer looking into the pattern from above. From such a position the device of the contrasting border is ridiculous, and merely serves to emphasize the incongruity of the shape and the underlying contours; just as the appearance of a badly fitting garment is made worse by the addition of borders and fringes of contrasting colours.

If plantations serve also as shelter to farm land, they must be

Beddgelert Forest, North Wales. Rectangular plantations unrelated to land form have caused much of the prejudice against forestry in upland areas. The Forestry Commission's recent plantations are sited with greater sympathy for other land uses and for visual effects.

designed to fit the general topography and adapted to the contours in relation to wind direction. Their outline and shape would then be quite different—non-geometric—and would appear as the logical outcome of, and therefore 'belonging to', the rest of the landscape.

Square blocks are convenient for working, and economical in fencing. It is true that plantations 'fitted' to contours and serving uses such as shelter for farms would give shapes and outlines less economical in fencing, road-construction, and haulage, if timber values alone are considered. But in an inclusive economy other factors, such as improved values of the agricultural land and the greater attraction offered to tourists and visitors, would compensate for the loss involved.

Rabbit-wire fencing—whose high cost is one of the main reasons for rectangular plantations—could be dispensed with alto-

gether if the control of the rabbit population became a regional concern. It is useless to exterminate rabbits in the forests while they breed
on the farms. But a high population of rabbits leads to soil erosion
as well as to the destruction of saplings, and a more effective control
is needed all round. Myxomatosis has reduced but has not ended the
rabbit menace.

Ordinary fencing could probably be reduced to some extent if
the farmers' needs were closely studied. One of the objections raised
by sheep-farmers to Lakeland afforestation schemes was that whereas
sheep recognize the summits of hills as a natural boundary, and themselves prevent the intrusion of strange sheep across those ridges,
eliminating the need for fencing at those points, it became necessary
to fence on both sides when the ridges were planted with trees. The
farmers also pointed out that in cases where the ridges and hill-tops
above the planting-line were isolated by forest belts from the main
farmlands, these 'islands' of open ground became useless and sterile
for lack of suitable communication with the farmsteads and lower
land—another example of the need for thorough co-ordination of
the various land uses of a whole area.

Other objections to the Lakeland afforestation schemes are often
raised by residents and visitors on æsthetic grounds, particularly
when the planting affects the ridges of the hills and hence the skyline.
The familiar open clean lines become blurred and made jagged by
pointed coniferous trees. These objections will be far less vociferous
if hardwoods rather than conifers are concerned. Conifers are felt
to be out of keeping with the British scenery and to introduce a
foreign element. Ecologically, however, the objection to conifers is
not quite soundly based, though as we have seen there may be a
strong case against too extensive a use of pure conifers. It should be
remembered that in all our high-rainfall districts the soils are those
usually associated with conifers, in which only softwood timber
develops to full perfection, and that parts of the British Isles still lie
within the conifer belt.

The demand for softwood largely governs forestry practice, as
pulpwood seems likely to remain all-important in the foreseeable
future. But for other purposes future needs may change and other

Dense conifer planting. This Welsh farmland is cut off from the upland pasture above the conifer planting on the slopes of the hill. The upland becomes an island, isolated from the valley and less profitable for any use. The unbroken extent of conifer forest is visually heavy and monotonous and adds substance to the public prejudice against conifer planting.

timbers may be called for. The timber planted in response to naval needs in the seventeenth and eighteenth centuries was never used for shipbuilding; and in the same way, at the ever-increasing rate of changing needs, the present day planting may live on into a future where landscape qualities are of far greater importance than the value of the timber.

Unfortunately, although the Forestry Commission is doing much to improve the landscape in its areas, recent changes in the Forestry Commission's organization suggest an even greater emphasis on commercial timber-production in future. The terms of reference do not give promise of the 'multiple use' of forest land which would so greatly benefit the national landscape. The other land uses which could be so happily integrated with forestry, such as conservation of soil, water and wild life, wind shelter for agriculture, and recreation for holiday visitors from home and overseas, have not been related to the work of the Forestry Commission, except in the

National Forest Parks. Excellent as these are, the Forestry Commission's main terms of reference concern only the production and industrial use of timber.

Nevertheless, among the members and personnel of the Forestry Commission and foresters generally in this country, there is a growing interest and awareness of this wider aspect of their work, which may lead to further changes in the future. The appointment of Miss Crowe as Landscape Consultant to the Forestry Commission is a hopeful sign.

Public dislike of conifer plantations in this country will not diminish if pulp production is the main objective. Conifer forests can be beautiful if trees of all ages, including really mature specimens, are mixed, and the visual effect is improved by the inclusion of some hardwoods. But whole blocks of trees all of one age, clear-felled before full maturity, are increasing the prejudice against conifers, especially spruce plantations.

If such blocks could be divided by open rides or generous bridle

Picnic site in a National Forest Park. An informal picnic site provided by the Forestry Commission in a forest park. The use of simple local materials and natural surfaces is in keeping with the site, though from the design point of view the rustic woodwork and the exotic conifer saplings may be criticised. The notice board seems unduly obtrusive.

Highmeadow, Forest of Dean. Selective felling of mature hardwoods ensures continuity of forest cover. In this instance the mature oak is underplanted with Douglas fir, so there will be a change from deciduous woodland to conifer forest. The reverse process is to be seen in other Forestry Commission plantations.

paths irregularly planted with mixed trees reaching maturity and even old age: if the extent of dark 'gloomy' spruce could be relieved by open areas devoted to camping and other recreational sites, or farm units divided by tree belts of mixed species, the prejudice against conifers would be much less. We need to be made aware of how beautiful conifer forest can be, and to see the wonderful contrasts between conifer and deciduous foliage. The preservation in critical positions of some aged trees must make any sensitive observer more tolerant towards the younger gawky growths.

The rides and open spaces could serve not only to provide relief and contrast from conifer plantations and to delight the eye by a view of some more mature and natural beauty, but would also serve as fire-breaks and would check the spread of tree diseases. They would have to be designed in relation to contours and ecological conditions, and this would ensure that the general effect seen from afar would be as good as the internal views. The arbitrary grid derived from the drawing-board and imposed on hilly ground has created a bad impression of forestry practice.

Clear-felling. Provided the areas of clearances are not too large, clear-felling creates open glades amongst standing timber. In the period following felling a variety of ground flora develops, which can add interest to the character of the forest. Over larger areas, where no surrounding woodland is retained, clear-felling creates a sense of devastation until the next rotation nears maturity.

Clear-felling of timber in forest land is often condemned on æsthetic grounds in favour of a system of selective felling, by which only the mature trees are taken, leaving younger ones to take their place. Selective felling means that the ground is never completely cleared, and that it retains the same general appearance permanently. On steep slopes, or wherever there is risk of erosion, it is preferable to clear-felling. Yet to advocate selective felling in every case is to overlook the value of the open spaces in the general pattern. Provided that the areas of clear-felling are not too vast, and so long as the scale is such as to give the appearance, not of the removal of the forest but only of clearings within the forest (leaving belts of standing timber at suitable intervals), clear-felling can give interest greater than that of selective felling, and it provides far more variety. It is progressive, and gives a constantly changing scene. After the heavy shade of the trees is removed, a carpet of flowering things springs up from dormant seeds, and new sheets of colour are seen against the standing timber of the background. That in turn gives way to a nursery plantation, to a sapling growth, to a thinned wood-land approaching maturity and finally to high forest again. The open space with the carpet of woodland flowers moves onward, revealing new aspects of the countryside each season and each year. Clear-felling and replanting in the clearings makes possible the introduc-tion of improved 'clones' bred from selected trees. This improvement does not occur in natural regeneration areas.

Rotational changes must be better for soil fertility; and provided always that the felled areas give the effect of clearings within the forest retaining some surrounding shelter, they would enrich the wild life of the whole area, contributing much towards a good biological balance. All this probably calls for a policy of wider responsibility and a new assessment of economic returns taking into account values (less easily estimated than those of commercial forestry) such as recreation, and conservation of natural resources for the inhabitants of the future.

Those who prefer open hillside at all costs might not easily be reconciled to integrated or 'multiple land use patterns' in highland areas, but changing circumstances and population trends may make these inevitable, and the treatment suggested above could meet much of the usual opposition to forest development. If forestry plantations should come to be associated with new landscape beauty instead of loss of landscape, the prejudice in favour of open country would lose much of its force.

Further research into ecological and biological aspects of land use is likely to support these views, and may lead to methods more closely related to nature's plan. Tree slums are probably as unhealthy for trees and soil as human slums are for men: in each case the visual appearance is a warning, in advance, that something is wrong with our system.

Forest on Flatter Land

A high proportion of conifers is being planted, not only in high-land forest schemes, but also in thin sandy soils of the south and east, too poor for high agricultural production. In these districts the same principles would apply; for although it is true that on flat land distant observers on the ground see only the outside of the plantations (making the problem simpler in some respects), we should still consider the appearance inside the plantations wherever public access or through-ways exist, and also the view from the air. Both these viewpoints call for the same sort of treatment as has been already discussed.

On sandy soils, dark masses of pine in compact, but not too large, plantations are usually welcome incidents: the flatter the district, the more dominating is the landscape importance of any tree groups or timber stands. They provide much-needed vertical emphasis, and they form the skyline and background for a wide extent of surrounding land.

On the richer soils, and on the limestone formations of the south and east, any forest areas would of necessity be small in extent and devoted mainly to hardwood trees. They could only add grace and beauty to a landscape predominantly agricultural. Objections to the use of conifers on these soils are often ill-founded; young plantations intended eventually to be of beech or other hardwoods need the help in the early stages of coniferous 'nurse trees' to give shade and shelter. These conifers are more visible especially in winter: thus many plantations which appear now to be evergreen will, after the removal by thinning of the conifers, become mainly deciduous. These smaller woodlands are referred to in the following chapter on agricultural landscape where they commonly occur.

Commons

Some common land in lowland areas is preserved in a 'semi-wild' condition and may well be considered under the heading of wild landscape. The public is usually ignorant about the meaning of the term common, and of the uses to which common land may be put. It would be well if all those who wish to wander over the commons, to park cars, and picnic on them would read the leaflets published by

Midhurst Common, Sussex. This is typical of the scenery we like to think of as being free and open to all—our natural heritage—though in fact all common land is owned by individuals or groups. The thin acid soil of this area is reflected by the vegetation of heather and birch: such soils are easily eroded by over-use where the public has free access. It would be sad for all of us if the paths had to be metalled and defined.

The Commons, Open Spaces and Footpaths Preservation Society, and join as members in order to help in the work of protection and registration of commons. Under the Commons Act of 1965, all land not registered as common will cease to be common. The Association advises on how best to ascertain the status and laws governing areas thought to be 'common land.' The term is loosely used and is applied to many different categories. Commons are in fact all owned by individuals or groups, though certain neighbours may have limited grazing or other strictly defined rights.

Commons have usually become established on land of poor agricultural quality: this is the main reason why many are still available to public access and remain almost unchanged from their primitive condition. Nevertheless, care and maintenance is needed to preserve this situation; and like any other land they can easily be damaged by over-use—whether the use be by human visitors or by domestic animals.

Commons used mainly for recreation, such as Box Common, Burnham Beeches and parts of the New Forest, do contribute a special landscape character. Good management can preserve their almost primitive character, exhibiting all the phases occurring in nature from open pasture to high woodland. In contrast with commercial woodlands, the trees on common land can be allowed to grow old instead of being felled at maturity. Old trees improve in appearance with age, and they may live to delight us for centuries, though the timber deteriorates after the period of young vigour when its commercial value is greatest.

In order to maintain the continuity and survival of the natural type, and the succession and rotation of open space, scrub and woodland, in despite of public access, careful maintenance is needed— where too much is left to chance common land soon becomes dull and uninteresting waste. Compare any familiar over-used heathland with Wimbledon Common which, being so near London, would

A path on Wimbledon Common. Although so popular and well used, Wimbledon Common has preserved a rural character. The simple country atmosphere undisturbed by intrusion of suburban horticulture is for many city workers a calmer haven than the more elaborate parks. Its character is largely due to the work of Miss Madeline Agar, whose advice was sought by the Conservators after the damage it sustained during the First World War.

have suffered serious damage had it not received careful planning and maintenance.

In the case of Wimbledon Common, the Board of Conservators employed a small staff, acting (from the year 1923 to 1934) under the direction of Miss Madeline Agar, an experienced landscape architect, whose objective was to preserve the existing view-points and the finest timber, to open up other view-points and new rides through the woods, and to control the undergrowth so as to leave ample space for public use and to show the trees at their best. The dominant species of different areas were favoured in order to give variety between parts and to emphasize the special character of each, and a good deal of thinning of other species was carried out to increase this effect. Some planting was done where necessary, but the main work consisted in regulating the existing growth and controlling natural regeneration. The results of this system are very evident on the common at the present day.

Hertford Bridge Flats is an example of an area which for many years deteriorated through lack of proper management. Natural regeneration was prevented by persistent deliberate burning of heather and gorse, whether by commoners or others, in order to ensure open grassland for grazing animals. The appearance of the common was ruined without any real improvement of the grazing. A balanced plan and strictly controlled grazing could have created a landscape like that of the New Forest. Now most of it has been taken over by the Forestry Commission and planted with conifers, and an aerodrome occupies much of the remainder.

The conflict now developing between advanced agriculture and common rights threatens to reduce the commons. The arguments for cultivating them are that their value and their appearance can be improved by modern systems of farming but a tragic loss of interest and variety would result if this happens on too great a scale. The Commons, Open Spaces and Footpaths Preservation Society, which saved Epping Forest, Wimbledon Common and Hampstead Heath for public enjoyment, deserve public support in the continued struggle.

National Parks and the Countryside Commission

The excellent report on National Parks prepared by John Dower (HMSO, May 1945) defined a national park (in application to Great Britain) as follows: 'an extensive area of beautiful and relatively wild country in which, for the nation's benefit and by appropriate national decision and action, (a) the characteristic landscape beauty is strictly preserved, (b) access and facilities for public open-air enjoyment are amply provided, (c) wild life and buildings and places of architectural and historic interest are suitably protected, while (d) established farming use is effectively maintained.' Forestry use was, curiously, omitted from this definition.

The Scott Report (1942) had urged that a National Parks Authority should be able to co-ordinate land use at least within the National Parks, but the powers of the National Parks Commission when set up seemed very limited. Now the Countryside Commission will have far wider terms of reference which may perhaps bode well for the future.

A full-scale multiple-use pattern has not yet been attempted in Britain, and it remains to be seen if the Countryside Commission will be able to tackle such a problem. Can farming and forestry both prosper when allied to recreational facilities? Is this not a case where good landscape design should help to ensure the correct balance between the various uses? The full possibilities of forest planting on the poorer soils would be better seen and appreciated if recreation and landscape considerations were to be taken into account: agriculture, together with these other uses should be part of the alliance.

The more widely spread are the facilities for touring and holiday recreation, the less risk would there be of congestion in the national parks; but to encourage roads, car parks, camps and all the other tourist attractions everywhere, would incur the loss of the wilder solitudes. Some of these should be preserved in their wild uncluttered condition.

In this small country, no *large* areas can be devoted purely to virgin landscape—we cannot have a Yellowstone Park or a Kruger Nature Reserve. The behaviour of holiday-makers enjoying the available national park space in this country must be tempered with respect for agriculture and forestry. Holiday visitors cannot be confined to National Parks, but their rights of access and car-parking facilities will have to be restricted wherever they go in the interests of other essential land use, and not only for the sake of those whose livelihood is immediately concerned, but equally for tourists themselves and for the population of the future. The respective rights and responsibilities of both the inhabitants and the visitors must be fully recognised, a process which calls for education in countryside appreciation, such as the Wild Life Trusts are now fostering with some success.

Recreation

Variety of landscape types is all the more valuable in a small country like Britain, and the different priorities accorded in various areas of multiple use add so much to the quality of the whole. For instance in the National Parks, holiday visitors have priority over forestry, while the reverse priority creates a different type of landscape in National Forest Parks. In the Forest of Dean, Argyll and North Wales the interests of forestry are supreme, though the public is admitted and given wide facilities on land not immediately required or unsuitable for planting.

Tourism is now seen as a means of repopulating the more distant countryside whose inhabitants have been drifting to the towns, but unless the visitors accept essential controls they can easily destroy the landscape they come to seek. The inhabitants living by the soil and rooted, so to speak, in the land, instinctively protected it for the future. Hordes of visitors from other places have no traditional knowledge of the damage they can do, so that rules and controls, however irksome, become essential. Cars will have to be confined to certain roads and definite parking areas; dogs must be kept to heel, if walkers are to be allowed to enjoy the general countryside; and camping must be limited to authorized sites, located and designed to form a pleasing landscape.

Bad siting and design have, in the past, caused much hostility towards holiday camps, youth hostels, caravans and tents—just as

Malhamdale, Derby. A few tents staying for short periods in an uncrowded valley such as this have little impact on the scene. But as numbers increase the organized and regulated camps become essential. In the few places where this ideal camping is possible, much depends on the good manners of the campers, who know the need for leaving the site as nice as it was before they came.

ugly plantations cause hostility to afforestation. Bad manners and ignorance on the part of visitors have also much to do with the resentment caused by their presence, but if we can overcome that, then the advent of new life into country districts becomes a benefit to the inhabitants, bringing a market for their produce to their doors, as well as the interest of new faces and fresh ideas.

Where possible, it is clearly best for hostels and other necessary buildings to be grouped with existing villages or farms; but even where they are needed in isolated spots they can, by careful planning and design, become a pleasing part of the landscape—as has been seen in some of the best recent examples here and abroad.

Isolated groups of buildings—youth hostels for instance—should be merged into their surroundings. Unlike a building in a town or on an esplanade, they have no justification for blatant self-assertion, and should be simple and unobtrusive. Being essentially there to provide indoor shelter at night or on wet days, they do not need an elaborate garden—part of their charm lies in their wild surroundings. A small area of turf for seats is probably the most that is needed. Shelter trees, which might also serve to screen a view of the group from other points or to unite it with the land, would be an important feature, but they should be chosen and grouped for their native quality, and should not strike an incongruous exotic note. The buildings should not be too closely surrounded by trees, however; even those in wooded districts should be on a spacious open site, the effect being that of low buildings standing back from an open glade and seen against trees behind. Above the tree-line the relationship of roof and outline to the surrounding contours becomes of the greatest importance—on hilly ground it is possible to relate the lines of buildings and land forms without the use of tall trees. Shelter, too, may depend on ground contours and low shrubs.

Sites for camping under canvas can be dealt with on the same general principles, though the question of wind shelter and screening is of even greater importance in this case. Camp sites within reach of farms are always the most popular—for reasons of food and water-supply—and farmers usually welcome summer visitors who show a proper respect for crops and stock. Friendly relationships between inhabitants and visitors are worth encouraging by every means.

The planning of sites for tents is no less important than that of more permanent camps, both for the comfort of the users and for their landscape appearance. A level, sheltered, but open area, larger than would be actually needed for the number of tents to be accommodated, should be allowed, so that the tents may be pleasingly

Yellowcraig caravan park, East Lothian. Many stretches of coastline, especially in the south and west of England are disfigured by huge caravan parks blatantly obtruding in the natural scene. Careful siting and planning, as seen in this example, points the way to a better approach. The park is sited well back from the sea and screened by planting on banks, and its scale is broken down by forming 'enclaves'. A car park for day visitors is unobtrusively sited with a grass floor. A footpath and nature trail through the coastal area beyond the site gives it additional interest and value.

grouped round the margins, near the encircling trees. There is no reason why they should look unsightly, so arranged, but they should not be visible from every direction or else they will appear obtrusive and would give no sense of seclusion for the camper. In the larger camps some permanent buildings for cooking and sanitation are needed, and even in small family camps some form of permanent hearth reduces the risk of fires.

Accommodation for parties of various sizes is essential, from the large scout or youth organization to the small groups and families who want quiet and seclusion. Such individual holidays appeal to more discriminating tastes and to the true nature-lovers, who should be encouraged by every means. Sites for three or four tents are

Mepal Fen, Cambs. A superb moment when the wind and the light emphasize the rich variety of form and texture in sky, land, water and vegetation.

Gravel excavations in wet areas leave extensive lakes which can be hideous or beautiful according to the way they are worked, and the condition they are left in by the industry. This flat fenland seems an appropriate place for wild life and nature conservation. A chain of wet pits can be planned to accommodate various holiday activities as well as a quiet lake for birds and beasts.

easily found on any farm, and they should be numerous and small, so that each party can have one to itself for a short time. They can be attractive features of the landscape.

Caravan holidays are more limited as to siting than the tents. They must be accessible by car from a road, yet not too exposed to view or to passing traffic. The large site for numerous caravans is the terror of most discriminating caravaners, and those who want to be alone in pleasant surroundings should not be discouraged. A short visit need leave no traces, and such parties will of their own wish choose places which are not too conspicuous, first seeking the permission and goodwill of the farmer or landlord.

The sea is the greatest attraction for the majority of summer holiday-makers, mainly on account of the bathing. The tendency to overcrowd the coastline and to neglect inland districts can be remedied to a certain extent by better provision for fresh-water bathing inland. Wherever possible camps should be sited within reach of a river or lake where bathing can be allowed; in other cases small pools can be made.

Wet gravel pits—their area increasing constantly through the excavation of gravel for development purposes—can be used for bathing, boating and fishing, and can be happily merged into the valley landscapes where they occur. These are often within easy reach of towns and built-up areas, and so tend to attract large numbers of day visitors. Their development for recreation concentrates large numbers conveniently, and so reduces pressure on the more vulnerable and far off solitudes. The main conflicting interest in these cases is that of wild life preservation. Some part of any chain of waterways formed in gravel areas should be set aside for nature reserves and wild life studies, so that conservation and education can both play their part for the benefit of the future.

There are also conflicting interests between different kinds of recreational use. Sailing craft and motor boats do not mix well. Anglers resent boats and bathers. A chain of lakes can be purpose-designed to accommodate all tastes in separated waters.

The shaping of the margins, with varying depths, and the planting of tree belts to provide shelter, setting and screens is no less important than the provision of access, car parks, club buildings and other facilities. A unified setting should be designed to give landscape beauty as one of the main attractions.

Coast

Coastal scenery has suffered more in the past from uncontrolled development and individual egotism than almost any other landscape: the existing controls have come too late to save much of it, making it all the more urgent to save what remains in its natural conditions for the benefit of all. It is intolerable that private rights and enclosures extending to the very cliff edge should not only prevent access and

Saltdean, Sussex. Much of Britain's coastal landscape has been destroyed by ill-considered development. Compare this scene with Sidmouth (p. 204) where the buildings seem to nestle among trees and hedgerows. A narrow strip above the cliffs is preserved—just enough for us to see how much, by comparison, is lost.

break the continuity of the coastal footpaths, but also alter the character and beauty of the coastline as seen from elsewhere. Some of the worst examples of 'urban sprawl', ribbon development, and general untidiness through lack of planning have occurred along the coast, ruining what we prize most.

Seaside towns must break the continuity of natural scenery where they occur, but provided they do so only within narrow limits, being sited according to the indications of the land forms, and if only they are compactly planned, they can, without loss of accommodation, appear as an interesting contrast to their surroundings. The sharp contrast between seascape and landscape is a main charm of the coast. A small fishing village or town introducing a third element of contrast in suitable proportion may add to that charm, but excessive contrast may overwhelm it.

Seaside camps are notoriously ugly. They could be improved by belts of planting and better screening, but they should not be permitted where they ruin the general view of the coast.

The same is true of car parks, and although many would wish for parking places where the public can view the sea without getting out of their cars, to use open country cliffs and shores in this way seems a very selfish indulgence. This question invariably raises the cry of 'Why shouldn't poor Grandma enjoy the scene?' Surely if she ever visited such places in her youth she will wish to ensure equal pleasures for new generations of the future.

Wartime experience in the camouflage of parked vehicles showed how cars can be parked unobtrusively under trees. But this is not good for woodland in the long run. Wooded car parks should be specially planted to ensure that the roots do not suffer from compression, oil and drought, and provision should be made for regeneration of the trees either by natural means or by planting to insure against damage or deaths due to old age.

The sense of distance, open space and loneliness which we associate with the sea requires long stretches of cliff, beach or marsh unmarked—or almost unmarked—by man, for its enjoyment; though an occasional human structure, such as a lighthouse, a jetty, a windmill or other building, may well add an accent of dramatic interest. For this reason, suitable landscape treatment may be to screen certain objects from view, say, by planting, and to reveal others. It should be remembered that where no trees grow naturally, introduced trees may look unnatural even if they can be grown. On the other hand, almost any group of trees will unite with the landscape more easily than any human structure, and it is for the planners to weigh up the relative advantages or disadvantages of planting in such cases, according to the context and local conditions, not excluding the possibility of 'tying in' certain structures to the land, without the necessity for complete screening, by means of low ground cover and modelling of the existing contours.

Where planting is indicated to screen off undesirable views from very open flat country, such as we get on salt marshes and estuaries, much can be done by subtle contour-modelling on a small scale, combined with the plants native to the district, but the banks or new shapes must conform closely to the general lie of the land. A casual hummock appearing on the horizontal undulations caused by age-old sedimentation is inharmonious—but a determined convex curve,

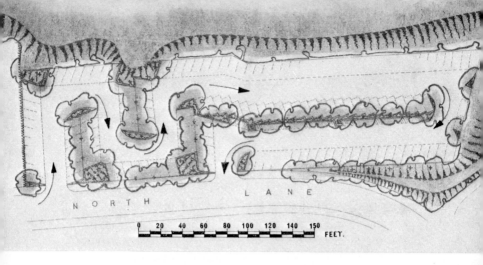

N O R T H   L A N E

0 20 40 60 80 100 120 140 150 FEET.

A small car park cut into a rising hillside is screened from the road by banks formed from the excavated soil. Trees planted on the banks and between the rows of cars extend a canopy of foliage and provide welcome shade for the cars on sunny days.

leading up easily to another sharply defined horizontal line, such as might have been formed by the receding tide or a change of course in the riverbed, may give the required height without incongruity. The landscape architect must study the geological processes which have formed the land.

Reclamation

The prevention of coastal erosion and the possibility of reclamation of submerged coastal land are aspects of landscape design. Engineers, ecologists and other experts are primarily involved, but reclamation depends much on land shaping and planting, and these create new landscape. Reclamation may involve the creation of new coastlines. Nature's own methods must be studied and followed, though they can be accelerated by scientific methods such as the building of sea groins and planting of species which, though suitable, may not be found growing in that particular area.

At Holkham in Norfolk thousands of acres have been reclaimed by the gradual planting of pines on sand dunes, and the value of much inland agricultural land now sheltered from sea gales and salt spray has increased to an unforeseen extent. Wind erosion has been

checked, though on similar sandy districts of the east coast not protected in this way erosion has increased in recent years to a point of
real danger.

Reclamation methods vary according to local conditions, and
especially with the material which is to form the new land. In some
areas this may be shingle thrown up by the incoming tides and
normally withdrawn by retreating tides; much of this can be held on
the beaches by means of groins. When the level of the accumulated
shingle is sufficiently high, vegetation such as *Suæda fruticosa*
(shrubby sea-blite) may colonize it under natural conditions, or may
be deliberately planted according to a well-considered plan. *Suæda
fruticosa* grows up through the accumulating shingle, spreading
laterally at the same time until a compact network of roots throughout the mass holds the shingle in place. Humus is formed on the
surface, and eventually higher plants can gain a foothold to complete
the process of reclamation.

In other places blown sand may be the material of the deposit.
Shifting sand dunes, changing their contours and positions in

Holkham, Norfolk. Self-sown pines grow on the windy side of dunes once the
sand is fixed by the growth of marram grass. A thin soil forms and a woodland
develops, killing the marram grass but creating conditions suitable for deciduous
shrubs and trees. Younger dunes are forming near the sea.

every gale, are a menace in inland sandy areas such as Breckland. Dunes can be fixed in the first instance only by colonization of marram grass, but once fixed by this means pine trees can be planted in the rough turf created by the marram grass, and the blown sand can be checked and induced to form new dunes to windward by fresh planting of marram grass or by rows of pine branches placed upright in the sand to provide slight shelter. At Holkham the pines have become established to the point where natural regeneration takes place and ensures the permanent maintenance of the woods. *Pinus sylvestris, maritima, laricio* and *laricio nigra* have been used, and many hybrids especially adapted to the district have arisen from self-sown seed. The dunes are growing out seawards, so land reclamation takes place by natural means.

Sand dunes fixed by marram grass alone are only moderately secure; the roots of pines form a far stronger defence against erosion by wind and water, besides giving additional shelter to the landward. In course of time, deciduous species and undergrowth, if encouraged, improve the soil of the older landward part to the point where it can be put to higher agricultural use.

In the case of shallow submerged ground, or of salt marshes and mud flats lying between high- and low-tide levels, the quickest colonizing plant, if such areas are to be reclaimed for dry land, may be the astonishing hybrid *Spartina townsendii*, or 'rice grass', which appeared in Southampton Water in 1870 and has since spread very rapidly, raising much of Poole Harbour and other submerged shallows to above water-level. Open channels and anchorage free of vegetation depend in such cases on the depth of water being greater than the height of *Spartina* and other halophytes.

The possibility of using industrial wastes or city refuse as the material of reclamation is referred to in Chapter Seventeen. In most cases a colonizing plant would probably hasten the process and be an essential stage in the formation of fertile soil on the surface.

A vast opportunity for future development opens out, and in every case the need for conscious planning of the new contours and for fixation of the material by vegetation makes possible

Wells-next-the-sea, Norfolk. To the right, where there is no shelter planting, dunes and marshland extend right up to the little town. On the left, the pine plantations on the Holkham estate have made possible a belt of agricultural fields. New dunes grow on the shallow coast beyond the old dunes now fixed by the pines, and self-sown pines are growing on these younger dunes. In the older plantations deciduous trees are becoming established among the pines. This mixed woodland improves soil fertility.

the creation of fine landscape once it has been recognized that a good appearance is not the least of the values to be reclaimed.

Low-lying coast, with its sand dunes, shingle spits, beaches and salt marshes and the dykes that accompany them, is the home of interesting groups of birds and plants, and its scenery has a fascination unlike that of any inland landscape. It is essential for the wealth of British landscape as a whole that a high proportion of such scenery be preserved intact. But the power of control which can be exercised over coastal erosion, and the possibilities which exist of increasing the land area of the island, are often underestimated, and much is still left to chance. The coastline is constantly undergoing changes: the time will doubtless come when the power of hastening or slowing down these changes, according to the needs of the people and the possibilities of the district, will be more actively pursued. Unless the real importance of maintaining and creating fine landscape is fully realized at the outset these developments might bring a sad loss of beauty to the English coast; on the other hand, if the work should be done with due appreciation of landscape factors there could be immense variety, interest and beauty in the new coastline, and new land could be reclaimed without any loss of the typical charm of the low-lying coastal districts.

Projects such as the reclamation of the Wash, or Morecambe Bay could produce wonderful new landscapes. Alternatively they could be just dull areas or positively ugly, ruining the charm of the existing coast. The new Dutch polders planned in consultation with R. J. Bentham[1] show one excellent way of dealing with such land, and while the British method would probably be different, it could well draw on experience from the Low Countries.

[1] Bentham's 'Management of Agricultural Landscape' in *Landscape*, 2, 1956, is a mine of valuable experience.

Noord-Oost Polder, Holland. One of the settlements on land retrieved from the Zuyder Zee. It is laid out with typical Dutch precision, perhaps the logical treatment for this flat area, though an informal treatment would make for more pleasing landscape. Broad shelter belts round the settlements and tree-lined roads are sound conservation features.

15

Agriculture and Landscape

The agricultural landscape of Britain has a character of its own, a character more individual and unique to this country than has our wilder landscape. It has become domesticated without losing its beauty, and has attained a highly evolved maturity without losing the simplicity of natural landscape. The great richness of detail never distracts, and the wealth and variation of colour, beautifully modulated, are constantly interesting.

This humanized, well-lived-in landscape has an organic beauty, and the more we study it the more we grow to love it. It is closer to the lives of the people and is more constantly seen than our wilder landscape, and has been the very foundation of the nation's life—a point which, even for those who do not regard it in that light, has deep psychological importance. When the British traveller abroad thinks of his homeland, he is more likely to be visualizing a scene of fields, orchards and hedges than a wilder landscape; and the average foreign visitor coming here probably sees—apart from the towns— more of the homely agricultural country than of mountain, moor and fell.

This agricultural land is more liable to change than the wild or semi-wild areas—it is essentially an evolving type, and it can be altered and even lost, almost before we have time to realize it, by changes of policy, use and custom. 'Suburban spread', new roads and ribbon development swallow up miles of land, and transform its appearance in a very short space of time. Changes of agricultural system and even of ownership alter in a few seasons land whose nature we have carelessly taken for granted as something timeless and immutable.

If we are concerned about the beauty of the countryside, it is essential to recognize its changing quality and to be actively aware of the causes and effects of such changes, appreciating the relationship

between the underlying causes and the superficial effects. It is necessary to be on the watch for the existing trends and the direction of
present events in regard to the changes they may bring about. Changes
are essential—inevitable—but, in this age, they should add beauty
to this growing landscape and not be allowed to damage it.

When landscape beauty is destroyed and no new beauty created
to take its place, we may feel sure that other evil results are in the
offing. It is a warning appealing directly to our senses and instincts,
often before it becomes evident in practical terms that all is not well
—a sign of 'imbalance' which must, if the trend is not checked,
eventually have bad results on the humanity whose environment is
concerned.

Apart from the major changes which may take place during a
period of complete re-orientation of agriculture—such as occurred
in the eighteenth and early nineteenth centuries—or of industry in
recent times, country landscape is constantly fluctuating as the result of varying economic conditions and the general evolution of
agricultural method. When agriculture is prospering, the countryside reflects the general trend in a cared-for and highly cultivated
appearance, with a high percentage of arable land: in times of depression it shows a tendency to revert to a more primitive type. In such
periods, only the best land remains under the plough, much former
arable becomes pasture, and much of the pasture reverts to rough
grazing, moor or scrub; farm buildings fall derelict, drains become
choked, hedges left untended grow into thorny thickets; life in the
villages ebbs low and the population is drawn to the towns. This is
what was happening between the two wars, 1918-1938, and it is
hard to estimate how far the process might have gone had it continued unchecked.

In *The Land Now and To-morrow*, R. G. Stapledon showed in
1935 the rate at which land was then being lost through urban encroachment on the one hand, and through deterioration or wastage
on the other: 'If the present rate of wastage continues . . . the end of
farming in England is already in sight. . . . No more than two hundred years hence may see the farm lands of England reduced to one
half.' Stapledon showed too that the facts were even worse than the

figures indicated, because unless agriculture continues as a whole, important and flourishing industry, the rate of deterioration increases and the remaining farms become helpless anachronisms.

Since he wrote, the rate of encroachments on agricultural land has increased beyond anything contemplated in his figures, and this rate will continue to grow to meet the needs of housing and industry. But the wastage of agricultural land through neglect and deterioration has stopped and a reverse movement has taken place.

World War II brought home the lesson of Britain's need for healthy agriculture, and since then technological advances have revolutionized farming in Britain. This island remains all too dependent on imports which may cease or at least shrink due to causes beyond our control: not only wartime blockade, but famines abroad, shipping difficulties, and changes of agricultural systems overseas, reflected in rising prices, may throw us on to our own resources. A more balanced system of farming in the wheat-growing areas of the New World might necessitate higher production in Britain. The Food and Agriculture Organization of UNESCO is constantly giving warnings of coming disaster if world population continues to outgrow the rate of food production. Farming in Britain must build up the soil's fertility, and store it in the land against such emergencies.

The land has always been the reserve and origin also of healthy human stock: the solid base of the population contributing to sturdy heredity through the interchange between town and country populations, and to health through the provision of good fresh food.

The idea that Britain can afford to become a purely industrial country, depending on imported food and using her land merely as a playground for the industrial population, which has sometimes been advanced as a logical proposition, has lost any force it may have had. But it is interesting to speculate what might become of British landscape if this theory gained ground either as a result of letting things continue to drift, or of a planned policy, if we fail to appreciate its danger. In the former case—that of drift—we can imagine England becoming one vast Suburbia, interspersed with a few golf links and national parks. Under a planned policy, forestry (which is less dependent than agriculture on a general country-wide distribution) might be greatly increased along with the industrial playground scheme, in order to provide some healthy outdoor occupation, to improve the landscape and to prevent the wastage and reversion of land previously farmed. In either case the transformation would be complete, and the country, as we know it, lost: perhaps not in our lifetime, but within a foreseeable future.

A modernized efficient agriculture involves very drastic changes too, many of which we see transforming the countryside now. Cultivation of the chalk downs and other hill areas formerly un-touched by the plough; the erection of new barns and other buildings of a scale beyond those of the past; clearing of hedges and hedgerow trees to make larger fields: all this creates a new pattern.

A conflict arises between the farmers who would advance at the fastest possible rate, for the sake of immediate increased produc-tion, and those who would first ensure the conservation of the soil and the well-being of domestic animals even at the cost of slower advances.

Technological skill advances faster than true knowledge of its ultimate effects on soil fertility or on human health, and until we understand more about the powers now in our hands, we should be wise to err on the side of conservation, which we understand. Up to the present, research has been under suspicion of bias on one side or the other. Research that is above such suspicions is urgently needed. In the meantime landscape indications would be a safer guide than quick profits.[1]

We need to know what population could be supported by Britain by our own efforts in event of emergency—not only for a few years. The *permanence* of soil fertility and the maintenance of health (both of humans and of the animals which support us) through succeeding generations needs to be ensured. The alternative, of surviving on seaweed or synthetic pills or protein derived from oil, can scarcely be acceptable to a generation used to present standards of living:

---

[1] Books on this aspect: R. G. Stapledon, *The Land Now and Tomorrow;* Rachel Carson, *Silent Spring* and G. P. Pollitt, *Britain can feed herself.*

Pea-vining in a Scandinavian field. This shows what industrialized farming can do to the landscape. It is a vast factory in the countryside. This and any urban industrial plant are as like as two peas. Compare it with pp. 5 and 282.

emigration would then perhaps restore a better balance of population both in Britain and in countries having land not yet developed.

Sir Joseph Hutchinson, F.R.S., in his presidential address to the British Association for the Advancement of Science in Nottingham in September 1966, stated that this country had not yet accepted that population pressure is an immediate concern of our own and not a vague distant menace. He referred to William Allan's concept of 'Critical Population Density' (the maximum population that can be supported by a given agricultural system without progressive deterioration of the land),[2] and pointed out that the concept should be applied not only to undeveloped countries but also to our own situation, if we are to avoid long-term detriment of the system through over-exploitation of resources.

Landscape is perhaps the most vulnerable of our resources—the first to suffer destruction. We can see great areas lost already through over-exploitation by industry and housing. If the process should spread through agricultural areas, we risk the loss of much that makes life, as we know it now, worth living.

[2] W. Allan, *The African Husbandman*, Oliver & Boyd, 1965.

Near Freiston, Lincs. Arable fields in wind-swept areas, open to sea gales and unbroken by tree or hedge, lead to erosion of the soil and loss of crops. The monotony of the scene points to the danger of the system. It is the taxpayer rather than the farmer who deserves compensation in such cases.

The industrial farming towards which present tendencies seem to point involves a much more intensive use of the land: machinery and stock housed in huge buildings surrounded by concrete floors; less grazing in the open; less of the varied scenery typical of 'ley farming' where grass formed a part of the rotation; fewer trees and hedgerows. Some 'farms' seem to consist only of buildings and concrete; in other areas miles of one crop are seen stretching to the horizon—and in spring gales, the soil off these latter fields blows across the country forming an impenetrable fog, and settling as thick dust on the furniture in adjoining houses. These are the visible danger signs in the landscape.

At best, however, British farms are lovelier than ever, and they go to show that a good living is obtainable from a balanced agriculture where modern methods are applied without over-exploitation. So long as these predominate, so long as farming does not become over-industrialized, British agricultural landscape stands supreme. Conservation of fertility is reflected in the visual scene.

The need for new equipment, new types of farm buildings, the re-arrangement of housing for farm workers, and of the size and shape of farm units is being met. Transport facilities, water-supplies and other services for homes and farmland can be provided in a decent landscape setting. The allowance of land needed for a reasonable proportion of trees and woodland, and the careful siting of the new buildings in relation to these, is a matter of pride for the agriculturalist looking to the long-term values of his land. In many cases the sporting values are sufficiently important from the economic aspect to justify the maintenance of woods, spinneys and hedges, and with all deference to those who object to blood sports, this contribution to landscape and conservation should be acknowledged.

The need for wind shelter by well sited trees and hedges has been stated by the Ministry of Agriculture, the Forestry Commission and many other authorities. J. M. Caborn's excellent book *Shelter Belts and Windbreaks* gives figures to support the practical advantages of shelter planting, and invaluable information on the siting and establishment of wind shelter.

When the main field enclosures were carried out in the eighteenth century, other motives besides that of profit entered into the distribution and treatment of the land. But for that leavening of other motives and considerations, we should have had a very different landscape today. There was the motive of planting trees for the future—slow-growing hardwoods for the country's protection. Owners may have thought of these as a legacy for their heirs, but certainly not for their own personal profit. For profit alone, those trees need not have been planted, since arable and grazing land produced better returns; regarded as profitable heirlooms they would, in most cases, have been differently sited and designed. They were planted, however, in positions where they also served the purpose of wind shelter, and where, while maturing, they could contribute most to the beauty of the countryside. They were grouped about on almost every owner's land and not planted in large forest areas, and, as they were not eventually wanted for shipbuilding, there, in many cases, they remain today still serving well their other functions. These motives of planning for multiple use, for posterity and for beauty, are not lightly to be overlooked in assessing the work of the past. They applied, in lesser degree, not only to the tree planting, but to other features of the general lay-out. However grave the faults in the system of land distribution, selfish motives were tempered by these wider motives which mingled with them.

Planning at the present time is actuated by motives of efficiency and of the needs of the future. But does it allow sufficiently for landscape beauty among those needs? And is the relationship between efficiency and landscape beauty fully appreciated?

We too readily discount as 'sentimental nonsense' any arguments based on the appearance of the landscape, still reacting to the idea of use versus beauty. If it could once be realized that in landscape they are fundamentally complementary, we should suspect, profoundly, any line of action which clearly tends to destroy either.

The charm of the existing agricultural landscape depends much on the variety of pattern made by the distribution of hedges, hedgerow trees and shelter belts or spinneys. A common criticism brought against English agriculture is that too much space is 'wasted' on these trees and hedges, and that a larger area of arable or pasture would become available if they were removed. Yet under the existing system the production per acre is higher in England than in any other country; and the production per man compares favourably even with countries where farm machinery is most highly developed.

Mixed farming systems which have produced much of our landscape require enclosed fields with shelter and shade for grazing stock. The sizes and shapes of fields are in many instances still small in western districts, and changes could improve the pattern. A higher degree of mechanization and general efficiency may call for larger fields even where mixed farming is practised. The field pattern has changed in response to the tractor: it has always been influenced by the character of the plough, and further changes might well be

Shelter belt in Cotswold hill country. The massive tree belts planted to protect the crops and the fertility of the land give the scenery form and character. Without them these high plateaux would present a cold monotony.

expected. We might find that a hexagonal cellular system would be more easily worked, and could provide positions for trees and barns in the angles. On sloping ground the need for ploughing along the contour to reduce erosion is even greater in the case of the tractor than it was for horse cultivation: in many countries this is leading to a new and very pleasing pattern related to the shape of the land surface. (See photograph on p. 279.)

An outstanding characteristic of our landscape, distinguishing it from other highly developed systems, is the pattern produced by hedgerows enclosing fields, with their hedgerow trees which may originally have been planted to provide shade and timber in small quantities, but which now spring up as seedlings or suckers from the parent trees. Another characteristic is the distribution of small woods and spinneys which give strong accents of contrasting colour and form to almost every country view. Most other European countries show a different pattern even where balanced agriculture and woodland prevail. In mid-European countries a greater extent of unbroken

Hedgerow trees. Much fine timber grows in the hedgerows. Elm can only develop its full quality in open situations, and as saplings develop naturally from the roots of old trees, farmers can easily arrange for a succession and ensure visual continuity without foregoing the value of the timber. Mechanized hedge clipping threatens the future of all hedgerow trees.

forest, surrounding large agricultural areas without visible enclosures, is probably not unlike our rural scene before the enclosures.

Well-trimmed hedges need more maintenance labour than do wire fences, but the space they occupy need not be grudged if they are well 'laid' and narrow, and if the fields they enclose are large enough for economic working. They contribute to biological balance on the farm by accommodating insect-eating birds, and they help to check erosion on wind-swept or sloping sites, besides providing shelter for the stock. It is good to see that the art of hedge laying is still being practised for these reasons on many private estates in the midlands and south even though fewer hedges are retained.

Hedges help to check wind erosion, and by providing wind shelter at frequent intervals the ground temperature of the fields between is moderated. They are a haven for the ever-dwindling wild life of our countryside, and many species survive only in that habitat. Leaf fall from hedges and hedgerow trees supplies humus containing nutrient drawn from deep levels of the soil, whose value should be balanced against the amount taken up by hedge and tree from the surface.

The Ministry of Agriculture has advised that small groups of trees should be planted at odd field corners to replace unwanted hedgerow trees. Where this advice is followed the effect is pleasing: the groups provide shade and cover for wild life, and are more economically managed than single trees. But special planting and fencing is required, whereas the self-sown 'hedglings' look after themselves, needing protection only from the automatic hedge cutter. This can be provided by hand cutting a short length on either side of any sapling to be preserved, as a clear warning to the operators that the tree is required and is to be preserved.

Small Woodlands

Our typical agricultural landscape depends largely on the small areas of woodland, mostly privately owned, distributed throughout the countryside. If these were to disappear through changes of use and ownership no amount of massed national forest in poorer uplands or sandy breck would compensate for their loss, for their value lies in their distribution—it is rare in Britain to find any view without

Mixed woodland. The association of hardwoods and conifers enriches both the soil and the landscape. Together they support a more varied flora and fauna than woodlands composed of a single species.

the incident of spinney, wood or windbreak to enrich the scene. Present day changes tend to destroy many of these, and any reasons for adding to their number deserve appreciation. On however small a scale this may be possible, the landscape value is great. New plantations being made by industry around new installations, factories and surface mineral workings, and by governmental authorities for new towns and housing developments, roads etc., are making a valuable contribution to the future landscape. But one could wish for far more generous planting of small spinneys and woods. Quite apart from all the large areas of derelict land crying out for restoration, of which more will be said in Chapter Seventeen, there are many small disused areas in and around country villages and farms which are neglected and unsightly, but which, if planted with indigenous trees, would immeasurably raise the quality of the general scene. The lack of funds or organization for maintenance of these until the trees are established is often the main difficulty in such cases, as public-spirited individuals sometimes discover when they offer to supply and plant trees: in many cases however, where parent trees exist, the self-sown saplings need only the protection of a fence while growing. The 'ornamental' cherries and flowering trees are, in any case, unsuitable for these positions, both visually and for practical reasons.

Woods and spinneys which in many cases have been preserved mainly as coverts for foxes or pheasants also serve as wind-screens and are the home of insectivorous birds useful to the farmer. They have often been allowed to become derelict and valueless from the timber point of view, but, properly managed, they may yield much that is needed in village and farm, such as hurdles, stakes, fencing timber, tool handles, kindling wood and the materials for toy-making and other village industries. It would be a serious loss to landscape and to the community in general if they were to be swept away for the sake of increasing the cultivable area.

Such spinneys and tree belts should be (existing ones usually are) planted on the least productive land and designed to give the maximum shelter for the open farm land from the wind or frost, as the case may be, and in positions where they best protect the soil from

Scots pine on eroded site at West Stow, Suffolk. The soil has been eroded around this tree and is now $4\frac{1}{2}$ feet lower than the original level. Although in many places ground levels tend to build up around old structures, this effect of erosion in light soils is not uncommon, and indicates the need for protection against wind or water according to circumstances.

erosion. Sloping land, where the soil is shallow and liable to wash down in heavy rain, is the natural position for trees: grown on rising ground they shelter a larger area on the leeward side than if on flat or concave sites. These slopes and rises are usually precisely the position where they give the eye æsthetic satisfaction, their massive forms and darker colour emphasizing the land masses in contrast to the paler tones of cultivation on the flatter land.

Soil Erosion

The risk of erosion may seem small in this country, but there are signs that it is already a real risk against which we must be on our guard. On the light, rich soils of the eastern counties, where flat land and low rainfall favour arable farming, and where there are consequently the largest open areas unbroken by hedge and spinney, the soil has been blown by recent gales to an extent amounting to a serious warning. Some of these soils were so rich in humus when first cultivated that the tendency was not apparent—the humus, as long as it remained dominant and active, holding moisture through

dry summers. But the balance has been upset by continuous cultivation—the humus content has diminished, and the clearing of trees
and shelter has allowed the wind too much space in which to gather
strength. The effect can be remedied at this stage, by building up the
humus content through more balanced farming including grazing
leys, and by making smaller divisions of space, planting trees and
hedges to break the wind at suitable intervals. At the more advanced
stages of erosion seen in America, Africa and Australia, far more
drastic measures scarcely serve to check the rate of increase of an
eroded area, which itself becomes uninhabitable. It is not surprising
that all the anti-erosion methods adopted in various parts of the
world, such as contour ploughing, planting of forest belts, terracing
and irrigation, tend to produce an interesting and civilized landscape,
in opposition to the devasted appearance of eroded land.

The old open field system produced a pattern closely related to
the contours, but different from that of the present day. When the
open fields were developing, the problem was one of surface drainage
in a rain-soaked and marshy land: the furrows and the narrow-strip
fields therefore ran up and down the slopes in order to get rid of
surface water as quickly as possible. Once we adopt underground
drainage, however, and a higher population makes heavier calls on
the land, ridges running parallel to contours become necessary to
keep the soil in place. Contour ploughing is in that sense a symptom
of a higher civilization.

Besides holding the soil and providing shelter and timber, trees,
especially deep-rooted species, bring up from deep layers of the soil
mineral foods otherwise inaccessible to surface crops. These materials, in minute but potent quantity, after serving the purpose of the
trees, fall with the dead leaves and are distributed in the neighbouring
top-soil by worms and other animals. It has been suggested that the
famous experimental wheat plot at Rothamsted, where wheat has
been grown for over seventy consecutive years without any
fertilizers and with no apparent deterioration, maintains its
fertility by this process, through the help of its neighbouring
spinney.

Contour ploughing. Following land shapes with the plough to reduce the risk of erosion creates exciting patterns like modern abstract painting, though founded on practical biological facts. This example from Preston, Minnesota shows trees planted only on steep slopes or near farmsteads. The large extent of open ground might call for more wind shelter.

Shelter planting

Shelter planting should always be designed in relation to the land forms, remembering that these influence the direction of air currents according to their speed—just as the design of the barrel of a gun influences the curve of a projectile. Fast-travelling gales can be lifted off the ground like a ski-jumper by an obstacle with a stream-lined approach on the windward side, but not by a narrow wall of equal height. A wall gives little or no shelter in a gale, the wind curving inwards again almost immediately after the obstacle. A streamlined shelter belt of some width, low on the windward side and rising to whatever height is required, leaves a wide area of shelter to leeward. Slight rises in the ground often do this even without planting, but by combining plant and ground forms the effect is multiplied accordingly. Nature herself produces these streamlined effects on coast and moorland, and the angle of the wind-swept vegetation is a good guide in such districts as to the degree of stream-lining required in a new plantation. It would not be possible, in very

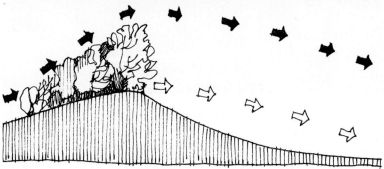

Windbreaks. A wind-carved hedgerow may demonstrate how to shape our windbreaks to shelter land from constant gales. The current can be raised by planting low on the windward side and rising at the angle indicated by local vegetation to the required height to leeward.

Ground contours may be shaped to combine with planting. The width of the belt is determined by the height required.

windy districts, to get the taller plants established without this 'defence in depth'. The low windward planting protects the tall main defences to leeward.

In inland districts, or in places where it is only necessary to break the force of the wind and not to deflect it, a narrow belt of trees of a single species, even without evergreen foliage or dense 'twiggery', may serve the purpose, but whatever shelter from a given direction is required, foliage on the windward side should be continuous from ground level to the upper height of the plantation. In the majority of cases planting on the north and east gives the best general protection against cold, though there are districts where a prevailing south-west wind is the most serious consideration to be guarded against.

Protection from late spring frosts is a matter of aspect and contour rather than of wind direction. The cold air flows slowly down-hill, resting in hollows on still days, where it does more damage than whilst on the move. The cold stream may often be deflected by plant-ing above the site; at the lower end any obstruction which dams up the outlet is to be avoided—rapid drainage away of cold air is essential.

Shelter plantations need to be closely and compactly planted: the material composing them, whether trees or shrubs or both together, becomes part of a whole unit, and the plants are not to be thought of as separate individuals. Many of the most suitable species give finer effects when seen in the mass than as single specimens, and simplicity of grouping should be the keynote. Strong contrast of foliage colour and texture can be effectively introduced, but a meaningless collec-tion of different species tends to spoil the general appearance. Restraint in the number of species used, and simple grouping, give magnificent landscape features, their beauty being largely the out-come of the relationship between their purpose and the configuration of the site.

The average group of farm buildings in England, keyed into the field pattern and to the land itself by its hedges and trees, is a familiar and charming example of a happy association. However much the architecture of the individual buildings alters to meet modern needs, the groups could still have this characteristic. Farmsteads built for modern standards of health and efficiency still require for conven-ience to be compactly grouped round spacious yards, and the need for shelter remains. There is always a delightful variation in the height and bulk of farm buildings according to their function, and this variation within each group is likely to increase rather than decrease with modern methods. Specialized buildings for machinery and new processes such as grass-drying become increasingly necessary.

When silage-making was in an experimental stage, architects visualized tall silage cylinders towering above the barns: like oast-houses, windmills and other special-purpose buildings they would have a distinct beauty. Since then, much silage has been made in pits, but the tall tower may yet become a feature of farm groups. Dutch barns have doubtless come to stay and, contrary to all expectations,

A farm group near Amersham, Bucks. Brought up to date for present requirements, it keeps the local character and makes an interesting feature. White paint
unites the buildings and contrasts cheerfully with the beechwoods on the hill.

the landscape has accepted them readily. By all preconceived ideas
they should have been hideous with their semi-circular corrugated-
iron roofs perched high on iron girders. But their very bulk often
saves them—they contribute a new proportion to the farm group.
Even out in the fields they fit happily into the landscape. Let anyone
with a critical, but unprejudiced, eye observe them in a rolling landscape with trees and hedges, and it must be admitted that they
'belong' happily when well sited.

This cannot be said of modern poultry houses and pig 'palaces'.
Whether the system is that of 'factory farming' with huge buildings
of no character, or scattered mobile sheds spread out over the fields,
they need the help of trees and hedges to relate them to the general
pattern. Remembering that their ancestors were woodland creatures,
one wonders how pigs and hens endure the circumstances of their
lives today. Elspeth Huxley's comments in her book *Brave New
Victuals* are of interest in this connection. She suggests that human
judgements are prejudiced by the ugly appearance of factory farms.
It may be argued, however, that just as the sense of taste is nature's
guide to good food, so the sense of vision is a natural guide to sound
agriculture. Quick profits are for a greedy generation, often at the
cost of enduring fertility and the health of future generations. We
must hope that science will find better means than this of meeting the
problem of over-population.

Wherever farming has produced a man-made (but unplanned) landscape, it is clear that mixed holdings give more interesting visual results than single-purpose regions. Variation in the scale of the components—whether these are open fields or buildings—give better compositions than extensive repetitions of equal units. A general pattern made up of farms of different sizes, grouped with woodlands and gardens, is typical of much of our best country scenery. The records of land-settlement schemes seem to prove that where a number of small-holdings of equal size intended to form a community have been confined to that single occupation, and to people of equal income, the occupants have not, in fact, remained settled. They do not strike root, but drift away to surroundings of a more mixed and congenial type, where diverse interests stimulate a fuller life.

Farm near Bradfield, Berks. Even when the various buildings are, in themselves, undistinguished, farm groups usually look pleasing in their setting because of the compact functional grouping of differing shapes and sizes around the farm yard, and the rational scale relationship between open space and built-up area. Trees and hedgerows link the groups to the land.

Historic Buildings and Estates

A great many of the larger private estates whose existence seemed threatened between the world wars are now again thriving owing to the revival of agriculture generally, and these still contribute immensely to the quality of landscape, when their owners follow the tradition of caring for the appearance of their estates; but where land is too poor in quality or insufficient in extent to support the home as in the past, inevitable changes threaten the landscape. When sold for industrial or housing development its visual impoverishment could be mitigated to some extent by careful landscape planning. In the case of industrial development, planning consent conditions, well considered and applied, may prevent serious debasement of the area, but in too many cases, especially those of housing areas, nothing is done to compensate for loss of former quality.

The loss of fine landscape which occurs when beautiful old estates are sold and broken up for housing or other development is serious, not only for the owners and immediate neighbourhood, but also for the nation. Our great country houses and their parks and gardens, world-famous for their beauty and historic interest, draw visitors to Britain and are as much a part of the national heritage as any other forms of art. To allow treasures of this order to be squandered seems folly of the worst significance. Their character depends on their unity, and any breaking up into lots spoils the whole.

The surest way of preserving the character of fine estates is to continue their present use. Farming and forestry are the use to which the majority of such land is put, and provided that the public has ample opportunity for visiting the estates, the owners are, in fact, acting as the nation's trustees. But if through high taxation, death duties and other causes the survival of a beautiful old estate is threatened, it becomes a national interest to prevent its break-up.

For the work of the National Trust in this connection, no praise is too high, and all who care for landscape and the countryside should support it. The Trust depends entirely on public support and gifts of property and funds, without any government assistance. The land is managed productively as in the past, so far as possible.

Ham House, Richmond, Surrey. Built originally in 1610 by Sir Thomas Vavasour, it was enlarged during the reign of Charles II. The lavish interior decorations are of that period, but the gardens which were also greatly altered at that time have reverted to a simplicity better adapted to its present use as a museum. The house is open to the public under the care of the Victoria and Albert Museum.

Much landscape is also preserved by various governmental and other authorities. There is the long list of properties owned or controlled by the Ministry of Public Building and Works, (six volumes published by Her Majesty's Stationery Office).

Local authorities find new uses for many fine buildings in their areas, and this is usually a means of preserving the grounds as well as the buildings. Various educational and charitable organisations putting country properties to new uses also maintain the grounds and so make a contribution to the local landscape. Schools and hospitals housed on new land or on former fine estates can do much to preserve former landscape quality for the benefit of the neighbourhood and for the fame of Britain's countryside. In many cases however, there is much room for improvement and a keener recognition of the responsibilities of ownership.

Country clubs, hostels and holiday camps can sometimes be established on existing estates without damage to the original character of the house or grounds, but in most cases new buildings and grounds especially laid out for their purpose meet the needs of a club more satifactorily. In either case the part played by such a site in the landscape as a whole can be much the same as that of a private estate, adding that suggestion of richer treatment in contrast to the general agricultural pattern. The need for such clubs, hostels and holiday camps grows ever greater, and must be met in agricultural as well as in distant semi-wild areas.

There is scope for good landscape design in the treatment of all such sites. Every type of individual is to be considered—not merely the wealthy whose expensive sporting tastes have usually been catered for by country clubs and hotels, but also people with simpler tastes, needing a country retreat in pleasant surroundings, whose search for rest and a change of scene is not met by an ordinary hotel; also people of low-income groups who may need family holidays providing for a number of different tastes and activities. Each case calls for entirely different treatment and design, and the interest should be in the possibility of fostering real individuality of character in each separate undertaking. A particular section of the community has to be catered for, but that should induce a special quality unique to each one arising from the circumstances of the site. In the treatment of the grounds no less than the buildings this quality can be emphasized, so much of the character of a place depending on the treatment of the landscape.

Commercial holiday camps, hospitals, hotels, no less than universities, schools and a host of other community groups all need grounds to meet special needs of the users—some providing restful calm, others catering for activity and colour, but all should be contained within the wider landscape rather than aggressively obtruding their character on the surroundings. Well-designed individual buildings grouped in a good setting about a main central building, can be delightful if the cohesion and relationship of the parts in the group are evident.

Coxwold, Yorks. The charm of the English village, here typified, depends on the fellowship of cottage and fine house, which congregate to form a natural community, as if agreeing that it takes all types to make a world. The church and the great tree hold the group together with quiet civility.

Villages

The principle of compact grouping of various-sized units round a central nucleus is characteristic of many of the most beautiful English villages. The nucleus may be the church or a large house, or the village green itself. Often a well-used open space, with a pond or some other feature (unique of its kind in that particular group), seems to mark satisfactorily the centre of gravity of the group, as at Finchingfield in Essex. Each cottage, house, pub, shop or forge is clearly an individual, yet its individuality is marked not by separation or aloofness, but by its own power of contributing appropriately to the whole. The architecture of the individual houses counts for less in the general effect than the method of grouping. These groups imply, and often reflect, a sense of community typical of village life.

The buildings do not overcrowd their space like pigs at the trough, nor do they stand like suspicious and self-centred misers. Rather, they arrange themselves around a central space like a group of friends intelligently debating a subject of mutual interest.

Where there is a village green, the gardens belonging to each

Village school. The influence of the setting on the memories and mentality of the children has been given little thought. This grim tarmac enclosed by prison-like railings can scarcely foster any appreciation of beauty at the impressionable stages of childhood.

house are usually at the back, where they enjoy some privacy. Front gardens, where they exist in a village, are usually open to full inspection by passers-by, though nominally enclosed.

Ruthless road widening, and garages smothered in blatant advertisements, are spoiling many of the old villages. With the increasing number of cars, adaptations of the old layout are inevitable, but good manners and neighbourliness should be able to make these adaptations with the least possible damage to the character of the village scene. Perhaps the garages fail to realize that some motorists are repelled by hideous signs and advertisements and seek for petrol and service at calmer places.

The village school and playgrounds are too often ugly relics of insensitive design. We still see buildings of grim Victorian Gothic, whose playgrounds, instead of being places of invitation and delight, are stark stretches of tarmac surrounded by iron fences. Even if tarmac is necessary, why cannot its surroundings be made at least as pleasant as those of some of the gardens round about? Such an appearance in one of the most important buildings in the village is uncivilized. It must surely shock visitors to this country, infuriate any inhabitants who are sensitive to such things, and numb the thinking powers of the rest. It certainly makes no contribution to the children's cultural education. The idea of learning, associated in the earliest years with all that is most drab in the child's surroundings, can cause a barrier or defensive attitude against culture in general which must be difficult to overcome in later years, and it surely represents a mistaken attitude on the part of education authorities that so little is done to improve the appearance and atmosphere of the village school and its grounds.

It is a relief to turn to the cricket ground, which in most villages is charming enough to make cricket endurable even to a baseball fan. Whether on the village green itself, or beyond the village in parklike surroundings, village cricket nearly always finds a pleasant setting.

Compare these with the grounds of the average athletic club belonging to an urban industry—which, as in the case of the school-yard, has been laid out for the game alone with no regard for setting. The difference of atmosphere between a gaunt treeless waste, and a playing-field against a natural setting, must influence the enjoyment of players and onlookers and, above all, those memories which are

Impington Country College, Cambridge. A modern building with fine surroundings capable of educating not merely by the organized teaching but by raising standards of visual perception and good taste, even though these standards may be absorbed subconsciously.

Brockham Green, Surrey. Village cricket, when set in fine surroundings, carries happier memories for players and onlookers than the flat treeless expanses often considered adequate for industrial recreation clubs on city outskirts.

carried on throughout life, subconsciously working on the future. Industrial playing-fields and athletic clubs are often on the outskirts of towns, but sometimes in rural areas. It is surely false economy which limits the area purchased to the bare amount needed for games, allowing no space for the setting. Too often they are bare, open sites having no relationship to their context. If they are to tie happily into the landscape, and to provide for something beyond mere physical exertion, some provision of space in addition to that needed for the games themselves is essential. They need only a little extra ground for planting to make them places of pleasant memories with a gracious setting of fine trees and green foliage: the space under the trees would give room for friends and relatives watching the games, and for players themselves to relax in comfort between games. The contrast between the surroundings of leisure hours and those of the working day is of psychological value to the worker and the work itself—a fact which is not allowed sufficient weight. Trees must not, of course, be so close or so spreading as to overhang courts and playing-fields, nor must they be placed where they interfere with the game by their shade or root-spread. Tree species require to be carefully chosen and sited with these points in mind, and the growth of their branches controlled as they develop. But the argument so often put forward, that trees are unsuitable in the surroundings of playing-fields and games, is refuted by the fact that those made for public school grounds, perhaps by wealthy private owners, have never had this denuded and poverty-stricken appearance even where space was a major consideration.

A fine setting to each site can contribute much to the appearance of the whole neighbourhood, making the country more inviting and attractive to visitors. Too many individual concerns, however, consider the appearance only from inside the site. The two points of view are easily reconcilable, and only in rare cases does it happen that individual tree plantings mar the view from other positions; yet this outside aspect requires more attention than it generally receives, particularly in relation to placing of trees and other major plantings. Minor details of the interior treatment count for little beyond the site itself.

Whittenham Clumps, Berks. Outcrops of the Chiltern chalk extend into the Thames valley. The beech clumps create a lovely skyline by emphasizing the land form. Many such clumps are old and their vital contribution to the land-scape can only be preserved by intelligent and very careful renovation.

Horizons are Important

Certain hilltop sites and high ground form the skyline for a very wide area of surrounding country, and the outlines of woods, spinneys or small groups of trees become the background and give the shape of the horizon for a population far larger than that of the site itself. During the last war, a member of the C.P.R.E., asked to provide timber for pit props from his estate on a high sandy ridge, prepared a felling programme based on the principle of preserving the existing skyline formed by his woods, whatever else had to be sacrificed. Such public-spirited action earns no medals, but deserves the gratitude of all who live or travel within the sight of that ridge; and they are many.

In the past, clumps of trees on high ground were preserved or planted as landmarks for the surrounding district. In the eighteenth century such clumps were often planted for their landscape value alone. In an earlier chapter the special importance of the skyline has been discussed: it was doubtless a recognition of deep-seated psychological processes which led landowners to plant those hilltop groups which we still enjoy today. The South and the West Country, particularly, owe much to the considered placing of tree groups, small or large, on outstanding escarpments and on domed hills; beeches on the chalk downs, pines on sand, and oak on the clay, each emphasizing the character of the soil and district as a kind of hall-mark.

Today they are little valued and it is a sad loss for a locality when they go. There was 'Ogden's clump'—a group of ten or twelve pines on a high common east of the road between Ringwood and Fordingbridge, whose very name was forgotten as the trees succumbed, one by one, to old age. The last survivor was known to a film-fed generation as 'The Lone Pine'; now he is gone, and that road has suffered immeasurable loss. Whittenham Clumps near Abingdon are in a bad way. Can we afford to lose such landmarks? They have now been replanted only just in time to save them. In the opinion of many they have as great an importance in the national heritage as the white horses cut in the chalk, and the ancient buildings and trackways which we have gradually learnt to treasure. Trees need more than mere preservation—they need maintenance and occasional replanting; but these distinctive clumps, whose siting was so often a stroke of unconscious genius, would well repay the small outlay required. It should surely be a matter of pride for local authorities to preserve such magnificent landmarks.

Local pride and appreciation of the rural scenery might be one of the most powerful means of maintaining a well-balanced rural population, in opposition to the cities' magnetism. Satisfactory living conditions in the villages, and quick and easy means to travel between town and village must of course be assured. But whereas in the matter of social convenience the country district must at best be at some disadvantage when compared with the town, it should stand supreme so far as its landscape is concerned. In England the countryside suffered far less than the towns during the industrial period, and in the towns the changes of landscape to be effected, if beauty is to return, can only be effected gradually and by degrees.

16

Landscape in Towns

Many villages and towns small enough to be seen lying compactly within a wider landscape have an endearing charm which larger towns could scarcely achieve unless they were divided into 'neighbourhood groups' or in some other way built up of parts separated by green belts. Bath, of course, is an outstanding example, and in some degree Cheltenham, Burford and hundreds of others show the same characteristic, whereby much of the charm at first view is the result of the obvious relationship, and the clear definition, between town and surrounding country. The evident dependence of a town on the earth, the hills and rivers of the site—the way such a town lies cupped in the hollow, sheltering under the lee of a hill, or stretching out along the line of a valley or river—explains much of its character at a glance: an impulse of kinship and sympathy is communicated to the newcomer, and a feeling of homecoming felt by the native, viewing it in the distance.

Many scenes in large cities and towns depend entirely on architectural composition, without any natural setting. The principles of composition apply equally whether or not land form and trees enter into the picture. Where, however, there is the possibility of combining the man-made and the natural setting, as in Edinburgh or Bath, a dramatic opportunity is presented to enhance the urban quality. A single tree in a street can contribute a subtle quality to the urban setting as in the case of the sycamore in Oxford High Street, or the one in Winchester (See p. 320).

This sense of close relationship between a town and its surroundings, arising most readily in places which have grown slowly and not too large, adapting their growth to their circumstances by degrees, follows all the indications of the site intimately known through experience. Buildings were compactly grouped because no one wanted

Burnsall, Yorkshire Dales. The impression of a small town contained within its landscape is lost on the larger scale. But much can be done by breaking up the areas of a larger town and allowing space for massive tree planting to give each area its own 'territory' distinct from the built-up mass.

to be too far from road, river, spring, or whatever feature originally caused the site to be selected: footpaths taking naturally the easiest levels and most convenient directions became the basis for new roads: wind screens, planted as their need was felt, linked buildings to contours in an even closer embrace.

New towns or housing development, built without that accumulated experience of living on the site, and at a rate precluding such influences from making themselves felt, often lack homeliness, intimacy and comfort in spite of all the other advantages they may possess.

In order to win mature charm, towns need that clear relationship with their natural surroundings. Previous landscape analysis of the site, together with the exercise of imagination on the part of the town-planners, can compensate for gradual experience of the place: sensitivity to the indications of the land forms and the local climate is called for.

In general, the position which provides the best shelter and convenience is the position in which the landscape will most readily accept new building—where, that is to say, the new shapes will most readily blend into existing land forms; and in other cases, new planting to provide shelter will help to reconcile building and land forms even where the position is not ideal. But if tree-grouping is to serve this purpose, it must be bold and massive and its position must be a preliminary, not a final, consideration in the plan since it will influence the siting of buildings.

Where a town lies below the crest of a hill rather than on the skyline, so that roofs and chimneys are seen against higher ground, and where the horizontal lines and vertical faces are simple and dignified, it can take its place in the scene as naturally as a quarry or cliff-face. In the case of roof-lines which are to be seen against the sky, the evenly serrated outline is the most uncomfortable of all. Just as, in the case of trees, most of us prefer the smooth curved lines of hardwood trees on the English skyline to the toothy effect of conifers, so the skyline formed by a single massive building or long group of simple outline is preferable to a series of oft-repeated forms and countless chimneys. It follows that in the case of town outlines where there is little variation of scale and much repetition of equal forms, the need for tree outlines to lift the skyline is greatest; but large buildings and groups of simple form, particularly if these have pleasing variations of level along the roof-lines, may in themselves give satisfactory skylines without the mediation of trees.

Present-day planning strives on one hand to make a clean-cut, sharp distinction between town and country, so that inhabitants may enjoy the best of both in undiluted form; and on the other hand it sees the necessity for providing towns with a larger share of open space and natural vegetation, and country districts with a richer social and cultural life and a standard of living nearer that of the towns. These two tendencies, far from being incompatible, are interdependent, and would draw town and country into closer sympathy, improving the relations between the two populations. The only alternative under present conditions is a continuation of increase of already huge suburbs and of slow decay of rural life. Thomas Sharp has put the case for clear demarcation between real country and real

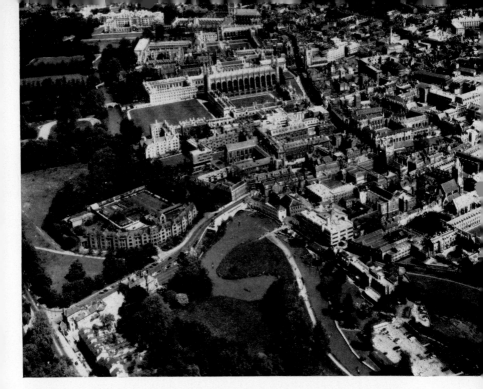

Cambridge. The excellence of the composition results not only from the quality of the architecture and the consistency of the scale throughout, but also from the compact siting of buildings with widely differing shapes and functions, and the relationship of open spaces to the building groups.

town in his book, *English Panorama.* The difference, if strongly marked, and not blurred by many miles of intervening half-and-half hybrid, gives one of those large-scale landscape contrasts which contribute so much to the enjoyment of both types.

A town without gardens and vegetation, in which the open-space element of the pattern consists only of roads, courtyards and paving, soon becomes monotonous: only the smallest country town can make a success of this treatment, and the larger the town the greater the need for green open spaces and tree forms as a foil to the buildings, and as additional elements in the design—æsthetic indications again corresponding with the biological foundations of sound health and social structure.

The principles of grouping, to give satisfactory visual effect, seem to be fairly constant for large or small groups, though there are undoubtedly upper limits for the size of satisfactory groups. Those broad characteristics of grouping already noticed in the case of farm and village still seem to hold good on the larger scale of town. Compactly grouped buildings, differing widely in form and bulk but functionally related to broad open spaces containing trees and other vegetation, make up a far more beautiful and interesting unity than scattered, separate buildings of nearly uniform size distributed evenly over an equal area. In towns compact grouping of buildings makes possible a high population density in good surroundings and in a form which need not be irksome. Shorter distances between home and work, or between town and country are not the least advantages of compact building.

The satisfactory results of this closer type of grouping in towns depends very largely on the relationship of building groups and green space. A closely interlocking ground plan giving a keyed-in pattern of building and open green space is needed if the two elements are to be complementary in both function and appearance. The health value of the open spaces is reinforced by their other uses, so that their real value can be judged by the amount of use they actually receive— whether for leisure or recreation. In a densely populated town, open spaces serving only to provide buildings with a green setting, or to separate them spatially, but which do not invite constant use, strike an incongruous note by their aloof emptiness, and they are, in a sense, wasted space. On the other hand over-use spoils the quality of open space.

An interlocking arrangement of open spaces and buildings—the building groups enfolding the gardens, and presenting their main doors and windows towards them—invites full use of the open air; whereas when open space and buildings are treated as separate enti- ties, each withdrawn in its own confines, it often happens that the open space receives little use. Being in a lateral or rearward position, without important and inevitable connections with the buildings, it can be by-passed and almost forgotten. This can happen in the case of a park sited away from main traffic and important buildings; of gardens separated by road and railings from the buildings to which they belong, or placed behind large blocks of flats whose main entrances open direct on to a road; or in the case of those odd corners in towns, and strips of garden space in housing groups, whose shape was not determined by any thought of their own specific use, but happened as a chance by-product of the building plan. 'SLOAP' (space left over after planning) is the appropriate term of abuse for such waste of land.

In large towns, tree belts or parkways with ample planting may serve to divide the different sections, separating the industrial area from the residential districts and the main civic centre from the various neighbourhood groups, giving each greater individuality, a pleasant setting, and checking the spread of smoke, dust and noise. Wherever it is possible to site important tree groups on rising ground, they help to relate the town to its topography by emphasizing existing land forms, and trees on high contours give maximum shelter and background for the buildings. In some cases, however, the ground forms may have special interest in themselves, and if kept free of trees or buildings can be better seen against sky or woodland beyond; a grassy knoll in urban surroundings can strike a delightful note of contrast if the grass can be kept in good condition, and not trodden to death. Lawns in towns must be properly maintained and protected in some way from too much trampling underfoot.

Streams, canals and rivers provide wonderful opportunities for interesting treatment of the town: they should serve as an inspiration, and a point of focus for the whole layout. Too often they are hidden away, and even, in the case of small streams, covered over by streets and buildings. Yet how much the whole town may gain from their full use. Compare Henley, which takes advantage of its riverside position, with Newbury, which hitherto has turned its back on the Kennet and Avon Canal. One has to go to Holland to see what lovely features of a town canals can be.

Wherever there is a steady flow of water, however small, the canal effect or some variation of the riverfront theme could be brought into play, adding to the town's attractions. How sad that London's smaller streams should have been turned into sewers.

Other attractive natural features may suggest an appropriate site

Amsterdam canal. Flanked by fine buildings and tree-lined streets, the waterways of Holland contribute to the beauty of the towns through which they pass. The canals with their bridges are a central feature of many of the loveliest streets.

for open treatment. Old quarries and gravel pits, instead of being filled up and flattened out, might serve as children's playgrounds: anything which keeps the town in contact with the country beyond may be worth preservation, just as ancient monuments, or traces of forgotten history keeping us in touch with the past, can be preserved and valued for the interest they bring to the present, and for the sense of continuity, in spite of change, which they give. Wherever possible, such features ought to be well displayed in the park system.

Open Spaces in Towns

The open spaces in a town may be considered under three general categories—firstly, public open space including parks, parkways, squares and gardens open to all and maintained by public authorities. Secondly there are community gardens maintained and used by the community owning them, and thirdly there is all the space related to individual homes, privately owned gardens of varying size maintained by individual families. Their functions are inter-related because the amenities available in one category have some bearing on what should be provided in another. Large public parks are needed most in densely built-up areas where there is little privately owned or community garden space.

Parks have been called the lungs of the city. If we think of all the parks and open spaces of a whole area as being part of one system, linked by wide avenues and distributed in such a way as to bring fresh air and natural beauty within reach of the whole population— serving literally as the lungs of an organism—we arrive at the idea of the 'Park System' as it has been developed in America; the parks in all the towns of a whole region being directly connected by parkways —or highways which are treated as extensions of the parks. With such a system the open spaces become central features of each town, or the green belt separating different sections of a city, providing the main wheeled-traffic communications. This brings them into more constant use than would be the case if the parks were sited as island oases in a desert of buildings and streets. It also makes possible the interlocking of buildings and green space throughout the built-up areas.

The park as a central feature of towns linked by parkways is a fine idea, uniting a region in a continuous system. However, it is perhaps less well suited to Britain than to less heavily populated lands. In our long established cities the town centre is usually a built-up area of strongly urban character, while the parks are sited on the outskirts or in lateral positions. But where important new development takes place, opportunities can be seized of linking the various open places where people congregate by some 'parkway' treatment, as in the case of Bristol, where space related to new road junctions

Green Park, London. One of the 'lungs' of the metropolis. Groups of people moving or resting in the parks are a constant feature to be taken into account in the design—they are the living sculpture for which the park provides a setting.

and fly-over roads has become a part of the park system, following Sylvia Crowe's designs.

At Dusseldorf in Germany a fly-over road sails overhead across a charming park, with little disturbance of the ground plan. These developments create an excellent welcoming impression. Their proximity to fast traffic routes, however, is not ideal for quiet family parties, whose need for a day in the open is perhaps better met by enclosed parks near their dwellings.

Each of several main parks in an area can possess individuality, offering different attractions and catering for different needs, if, taken together, the services they provide are suitably distributed and well balanced to serve the needs of the population. Provision for odd leisure hours in the form of lawns, trees, walks and seats for those who want to saunter along or to rest, watching the ducks, is a general need, common to all; but special features such as playing-fields, boating-lakes, swimming-pools, children's gardens and allotments may depend largely on the character of the neighbourhood and the amount of space available, and it is more interesting if each park develops a special character. A park near educational centres or in a factory area may devote a high proportion of space to athletics and games grounds for active young people, whereas another, surrounded chiefly by residential buildings, may cater primarily for old people, children, and housewives whose open-air leisure time may be burdened with the perambulator. Grown-up people will readily go farther afield for games than they would go for a casual stroll, but children's playgrounds are worth little unless sited very close to their homes. They are needed at far more frequent intervals than the larger sports grounds. Each park, therefore, requires to be planned in relation to other parks in the neighbourhood and to the character of its immediate surroundings.

Variations in the purpose of the different parks can be underlined or stressed by the details of the design and planting, and this helps to make each more interesting. For instance, the 'domestic' park providing for a residential neighbourhood can stress the character of a garden, richly planted with flowering trees and shrubs, bulbs, annuals and bedding plants, with comparatively small divisions of space; whereas the play park, with its larger open spaces and more active pursuits, calls for quieter tones in the plants which define the various parts. Here foliage effects could show to their full advantage in the absence of rich flower colour.

Whatever the special character of the park, the people using it will be a constant component of the visual scenes it presents. An experienced designer will think of the crowd as part of the whole pattern, ever moving, ever changing groups and masses—dark in colour for the most part, but flecked with pale and brilliant dresses here and there, providing the focal interest for each separate scene in his project. Movement, and especially the movement of other human figures, draws the eye and the interest unfailingly, and the effect can be enhanced by the focusing devices referred to earlier in Chapter Twelve.

In the great classic gardens, sculpture was used at focal points to attract the eye; but those were gardens which might be seen only by a privileged few, and in which for long periods no human figures might appear at the significant points. But in public grounds, designed to attract a constant flow of visitors, one of the functions of garden sculpture vanishes, and consequently its placing and relationship to the rest of the design calls for a change. If used in the parks to commemorate individuals or events it may stimulate the thoughts and imagination and artistic appreciation of those seeing it, and it may still serve to draw people to the focal points. But, seen from a distance, sculptured form and human figures should not compete for our attention. The living crowd, moving in low, sinuous and changing groups along the paths, meeting at their junctions, pausing to examine sculpture perhaps, or pool, or flowers, itself supplies the motif the eye seeks: and the immediate object of interest, whether pool, flowers or sculpture, can be reserved for close-at-hand examination by being placed, not centrally, but close to the focal point, as in the case of Epstein's Rima in Hyde Park.

Roads and footpaths form the main skeleton of the park design, and though these are governed in general by the direction of the main flow of through traffic, and access to important buildings such as civic centre or community buildings connected with the park, they must also be disposed to suit the required sizes of playing-fields or other divisions of space to be enclosed in the park. Wheeled-traffic

Villa d'Este, Tivoli, Italy. Fountains in light and shadow add their movement and sound to enrich the motionless carvings.

Open-air restaurant in a Stuttgart park, W. Germany. Sited near the boundary, this serves a hotel and appears as part of the park—linked to the town on the outer side and to footpaths in the park where no wheeled traffic enters. The ever changing groups of people become the focal points of interest.

routes should be as direct and short as these considerations allow, but the footpath system may have, in addition to direct routes, some tracks deliberately planned to pass the time and to increase the apparent size of the park. Large buildings, whether for social and amenity use, or administrative offices for park maintenance, are more conveniently placed on its boundary rather than within the park, together with their parking spaces.

Smaller buildings such as games pavilions, cafés and cloakrooms, auxiliary to some particular section of a park can, if suitably designed, be fitted in with the general scheme where wanted. They ought always to appear in that close relationship to their particular section, neither dropped, as it might seem by chance, in a large open space like many of the cafés and bandstands in the London parks, nor hidden away discreetly among the evergreens. There is no reason why a building serving the purpose of garden shelter as well as cloak-room should not be a nice-looking building in a good setting,

Stuttgart park. A feature of these parks is the large number of *sitzplatz*, each having a separate identity and sense of seclusion, so that any feeling of over-crowding is avoided in spite of the many groups using them. All are connected in the general plan by walks or hard-surface paths.

contributing to the general appearance of the park. This has been done far more successfully in other European parks than in our British ones. There are some particularly good examples in the parks of Stuttgart.

Other problems of park design have been very beautifully solved in the Stuttgart park system, in particular that of providing accommodation for large numbers without losing the sense of intimacy. A great many centres of interest are provided in the form of paved areas with seats, fountains and planting, allowing for innumerable small family groups to spend an hour or so in beautiful surroundings—the scale of each adjusted so that separate groups can enjoy a sense of seclusion without any firm enclosure. These paved areas are linked throughout the parks to footpaths designed to prevent over-use of the wide lawns through which they wander. Fountains grouped in fascinating diversity give movement and sparkle to the scene, and the sound of water splashing from various heights or falling smoothly over low weirs, combines with the bird song to lend enchantment to the scene. The encouragement of bird life in the parks adds enormously to human enjoyment, a point which we in Britain have often neglected.

Firm boundaries with railings and gates which can be locked are usually necessary, and in this case, broad plantations of trees and shrubs inside the boundaries can be designed to reduce the sense of enclosure, besides absorbing the noise of outside traffic and providing shelter from wind, dust and smoke. But there are cases where an open boundary is to be preferred, with perhaps some internal enclosed areas for special purposes. The appearance of an unfenced park, with lawns reaching to the road curb, is a pleasant change and gives more sense of spaciousness. The risk of vandalism is, however, greatly increased, and the design of such open areas must be tough and very simple: the treatment is best suited to outlying areas of low population density. A small public garden in Salisbury, lying between the river Avon and a side street, is unenclosed and available as a play park at all times. Perhaps the fact that it is overlooked by houses across the street may help to check vandalism. Because of the need for simplicity there, the design depends on ground formation, trees and grass rather than more vulnerable features. A water course crossing the grounds was brought into view from the road by lowering the contours on the central sight line, and raising lateral mounds on which tree groups serve to frame the open vista across the water to the Cathedral spire.

In a large park the various sections fall into natural groups, according to their use and upkeep. Lawn and lake are mutually complementary in function and appearance, both providing restful, leisurely occupation in a naturalistic setting. Playing-fields, more formal in appearance, are conveniently grouped together for ease of maintenance, and the 'garden' area of more elaborate design and richer treatment than either of the two others must necessarily be all together in a compact space on its own where it can be given the supervision and special maintenance it needs. In most large parks a section of this type is railed off separately from the rest and is subject to special restrictions, dogs not being allowed in except on a lead. In some cases, greenhouses, sheds and storage space may be needed in connection with the garden section, or one large service and nursery garden on the outskirts of the town may serve a number of parks. The flower garden attracts in particular old people and mothers with prams, or very young children; so that it needs ample provision of

wide paths and dry ground, good seating accommodation and complete wind shelter. Small divisions of space, with a good deal of
incident and biological interest in the flower garden, contrast well
with the free and open treatment of lawn and lake and with the more
severe lines of the sports-ground area.

There is still a tendency to design such an area in formal style and
to call it 'The Old English Garden'. If closely related to a building of
some importance and of traditional architecture, such formal treatment may be in pleasing contrast to the rest of the park. But a formal
garden unrelated to a building of suitable type, enclosed at random
within a more naturalistic setting, seems ridiculous. The freer treatment adopted in the Stuttgart parks described previously, meets the
same requirement for enrichment and special features at specific
points, in strong contrast to the open character of the main park, and
meets present-day needs far better than the firmly defined 'old
English garden' whose harsh rectangular shape usually conflicts with
the context. The flower garden now becomes the 'sitting about place'
(*sitzplatz* in German) and should clearly belong to, and share, the
general character of the rest of the park in its general lines, though
its proportions (more planted-up space and smaller open planes) and
its detailed planting and incidentals are in marked contrast to the
rest.

Playing-Fields and Recreation Grounds

Subdivisions within the park need to be defined and given a
sense of entity also by means of planting, which need not necessarily
be dense or amounting to enclosure, but sufficient to mark the
distinction between one expanse and another and to give pleasing
scale proportion in each. Interest flags if the open spaces are too
large: in the case of a playing-field area this easily happens unless
ample space is allowed for tree-planting over and above that
actually needed for the games. A football ground is, in itself, a
large space, and to have several side by side, without a break,
makes a seeming desert of the site. Trees must not be allowed to
overhang and spoil the turf, so a generous provision of space is

needed. If this is not available, narrow species or tall shrubs may serve the purpose.

A building group of pavilions, cloak-rooms and toolsheds may serve several sports grounds, and since these need a setting of trees, the width they occupy may well be extended on either hand for tree-planting and to accommodate onlookers.

Swimming-pools, open-air theatres, concert stages, allotments, children's gardens and other special attractions are welcome in the large parks, though they may equally well provide the main theme of some of the smaller open spaces in the park system. An open-air theatre is an attraction which, like the swimming-pool, accommodates large numbers of people in a comparatively small space, and is therefore suitable for quite small parks, giving them a distinctive character. It can be used for meetings and other public functions besides the theatre, and should be designed for day as well as night use. Stage and auditorium can, if so planned, be thrown open to the rest of the park in winter or whenever not serving their special

Open-air theatre, Copenhagen. The classic grandeur of the design is reminiscent of Delphi or Epidauros. Its curves relate it to the context, and to the contemporary world it serves.

purpose, in order to make the fullest use of the space, or for free concerts and functions where no gate money is taken. In the uncertain English climate it is usually necessary to consider the open-air theatre only as an alternative to an indoor hall or marquee nearby. When its use runs on into the hours of darkness, it seems by far the most appropriate place for floodlit garden scenes which might seem too artificial—too theatrical—elsewhere.

Children's Playgrounds

Special playgrounds for children are now being set aside in every park, but this does not necessarily provide fully for the needs of all the children. Others may be needed at closer intervals, especially near the homes and schools. Generally speaking, separate playgrounds for different age-groups give best results.

Children of about eleven to fourteen years old, perhaps more than any other age-group, need imaginative and adventurous play: they need larger spaces than can conveniently be spared within the housing group, but can go farther afield to find it. At this age they are rapidly developing individuality and expanding their range of thought. Observation of their play under natural conditions shows that in addition to physical exercise they need games calling for some mental activity—games in which they can act a part derived from stories of adventure and which involve a good deal of 'make-believe' as well as action. It is an age when the child really needs to roam over larger and wider areas than the made playground can provide, but even when such roaming is possible a small spot is often selected for group games. For town children the made playground should, so far as possible, fulfil that particular place. A flat, bare space enclosed by railings, however magnificent its special play equipment of slides and swings, fails utterly in this respect.

The games invented and played by children themselves in natural country or in odd neglected corners of old towns develop the imagination and character better than those they can play on flat enclosed tarmac. The fun and excitement that children got during the Second World War, playing Red Indians in bomb craters and

Children's playground, Cardiff. The swings, climbing equipment, slides etc. are popular, but trees, sloping ground, water and all the more natural features make for more creative play and better looking sites. Hard surfaces are essential for the areas of constant use, and these need not be unsympathetic if related to turf and foliage.

tank traps indicated the kind of play space they like: in new orderly housing estates and town parks this kind of play can be made possible by imaginative design.

A great improvement in the treatment of children's play areas has begun in many countries; further new and interesting developments will doubtless follow as the idea gains ground. Imaginative play, freely indulged in, is an art of no mean value—a means of expression to be encouraged by all possible methods. The iron railing and the flat tarmac tend to stifle the powers of make-believe, reducing play to a stereotyped conventional level. The effect of the play hours in the development of the future citizens is probably no less important than the school classes.

There is a spot on the open downs near Luton where children from workers' homes congregate—apparently spontaneously—for play. They have selected only a small space on the available downland, but it is a very beautiful spot and it has characteristics which mark it as the ideal playground. There are no bomb craters, but there is a stretch of steep chalk escarpment, perhaps twenty feet high and twice as long, whose slope is held together by the gnarled roots of trees growing on the bank itself and along its upper fringe. Ropes and swings hang from their branches, and the children have made slides on the bank below—all much more inspiring than any manufactured play equipment. At the bottom of the slope there is a flat, grassy area, bounded on the opposite side by thorn trees and shrubby plants. Though within easy reach of the houses below, the place has an aloofness—a feeling of being away from the real grown-up world —providing a haven for childish imagination. Such conditions can be difficult to reproduce in other places, but a study of self-chosen playgrounds of this sort, many of which exist on the outskirts of industrial towns, would probably enable us to provide, in made playgrounds within the parks, something nearer the heart's desire than flat tarmac and iron railings. The magnetic attraction of the area should keep the children inside rather than prison-like bars surrounding a vacuum.

The ideal rules for the 'made' playground for these ages are that the contours of some part of it at least should be extremely irregular, providing steep slopes and the unevenness conducive to stalking games: that it should contain trees suitable for climbing and swinging, and also trees or shrubs which can become 'houses'. The surface of the ground should be rough grass or consolidated soil, and the surroundings, so far as is physically possible, should suggest woodland or forest. Water is always a great attraction.

In addition to playground space there is in towns a great need for children's gardens, and although up to the present parks in Britain have made little provision for these, they would be a very popular and valuable addition to many. There is a real need for some practical garden training for the children of the cities, a need which cannot always be satisfactorily met in the school or community garden.

Community Gardens and Individual Gardens in Housing Groups

Community gardens can play a very important part in the life of the city. Their value in connection with factory and industrial undertakings has been shown at Bournville and elsewhere; but the possibilities of gardens attached to a housing group have not made much headway. There is still a tendency to devote the whole of the available open space to individual gardens attached to each separate house, whether the houses are grouped in the form of terraces or separated as detached or semi-detached villas.

The advantages required in the private garden are seclusion, quiet, freedom from interruption or interference from neighbours. There is also the national love of gardening and other hobbies which cannot be indulged in the community garden, and the need for an enclosed open-air space under the mother's eye for prams and very young children.

The need for private garden space is most strongly felt by families with young children, but is by no means confined to them. On the other hand, there are many people, particularly young single workers, students and some elderly people, who would rather not be bothered with the maintenance of a garden, however small, preferring to live in a flat or hostel provided good community or public gardens are available near at hand.

If, however, these two groups are housed in separate places, the one having a community garden only, and the other only private gardens, some of the private gardens may become neglected through being too large for the needs of individual owners, and none will be

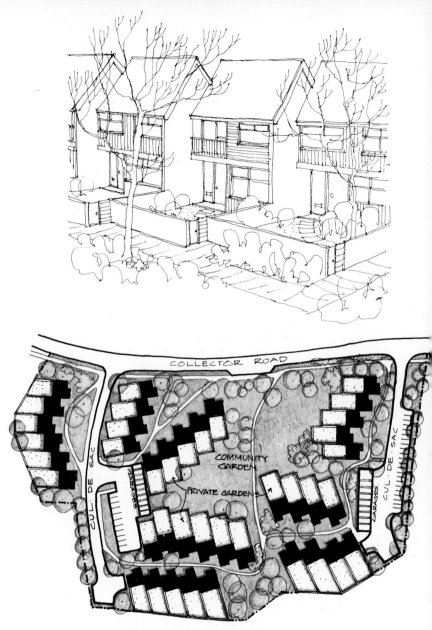

Individually enclosed gardens for each house give a space small enough to be looked after by busy owners. Each 'patio' space has access to a community garden where older children can play. The communal space can be maintained either by the landowner or by a club to which occupants contribute. The drawing above is an imaginary group, the plan is of an actual estate to be developed.

A small courtyard in London. Interesting grouping of plants in a very small courtyard, where raised beds retain the soil. Varied foliage catching the sun against a dark wall draws the play of light and shadow down to ground level.

The brick paving is just enough to accommodate a few chairs normally kept under cover and a small weather-proof table in the position from which the photograph was taken.

large enough to provide adequate playing-space for children over seven. The appearance of the community garden may be very nice, but it will rarely be in full use if the inmates are mainly students or young single workers out all day.

If possible, therefore, the grouping should be such that houses, flats and hostels share the benefits of a community garden, the houses having, in addition, small gardens not all of equal size. If the community garden is closely related to the houses it can compensate to a great extent for smaller individual gardens, especially in the case of children of seven to eleven years old.

For the family not wanting to spend much time on maintenance, a small 'outdoor room' designed as an extension of the ground-floor plan is sufficient. In a space less than that of the ground floor of the house the family can entertain a few friends, have meals in the open and find room for a small flower border, a sand pit, and dry ground for the youngest children's play. It is essential, especially in the case of low-income groups, that this outdoor room should be designed and constructed with the houses, leaving only the cost of minor planting for the occupants to bear: otherwise there is a risk of its becoming an unsightly backyard.

Those who want a larger garden will need more than double the space of the outdoor room, since it will then be required to give a small lawn and perhaps a few fruit trees. Some may need, in addition, a vegetable plot of five or ten rods. Several different sized gardens are needed even in the case of houses intended for people of equal income, but differences of income should not be stressed by segregation of the houses.

Compare the appearance and social atmosphere of the average country village having a well-mixed community with those of a modern housing estate composed of all one type of house and garden, or with segregated types of dwelling. Monotony seems to make for squalor or genteel snobbery according to the class of house, while a mixture of different types and classes redeems both squalor and gentility, just as, in the case of soil structure, mixed texture is essential for fertility and aeration. The village system produces a living and happy community in the country, and something of the same sort should be possible in towns, particularly in the case of industries where workers and managerial staff want to live within easy reach of their work.

Community gardens, even more than community hall and buildings, may, if suitably designed, foster the social unity of a group. To this end they should be centrally placed, forming the natural meeting-place on the direct route from homes to the outer world. This central area should not be the games ground, but should be designed for quiet and rest, and to form a civilized setting for the buildings, with a simple treatment of grass, trees and benches.

Existing gardens related to a particular group of dwellings such as we have in many of the London squares are, in a sense, community gardens. But when such gardens are separated from the life of the community they serve, either by road and railings or by severe restrictions on their use, they fail in their main purpose and are

New housing, Cambridge. This view in a modern urban housing group retains something of the intimate village character because buildings of various shapes and sizes appear as part of the group, connected by the paved walk between walls softened by planting. New and old combined give a sense of community. The grouping of different identities can still add interest, as it has done in the past.

usually empty and forlorn-looking. During the war we saw the railings removed and the squares thrown open to the public for a short period, but since the design was left unchanged, with paths relating to non-existent gates, and since these squares lie in the path of the general public as well as that of their own community, the public walked across the grass and destroyed it. Community gardens should be directly accessible from the dwellings they serve, and not easily accessible to the public. Where, as in the case of so many London squares, public roads, carrying through traffic, intervene between

Gillingham, Norfolk. R.D.C. housing designed by Tayler & Green. Modern dwellings arranged in a pleasing terrace layout respond to the local tradition and landscape with sensitive courtesy. Existing trees have been carefully preserved. Link walls and low white-painted railings unite the building groups.

the homes and the garden, the sense of community ownership is weakened, and the garden, if open, is used by a far larger public than that for which it was designed, making the maintenance of turf exceedingly difficult.

The risk of too much hard wear on turf is greater in cities than in country places, but it exists wherever numbers of people walk on the grass. It is better to plan extensive hard surface areas and to permit turf only where light use is assured or where it is not to be walked over. Turf panels raised some inches above the level of paths and hard surface areas have in some cases made it possible to use grass between walks designed to suit pedestrians' needs in highly populated area.

Oxford and Cambridge quadrangles, and those of palaces such as Hampton Court, provide a fine tradition for this country: the tendency to follow that in modern idiom is to be warmly welcomed, as the grounds within and around such groups can be logically designed to fit the needs of the various users besides giving shelter and a suitable setting for the architecture. A great advantage of the quadrangle system, as opposed to endless streets lined with dwellings on both sides, is that it fosters a community sense. Occupants of a block have something in common and are naturally more in touch with each other than is possible in open-ended lines.

Visually the semi-detached repetitive pattern has ruined vast areas of suburb which could have housed equal or greater numbers in more pleasing settings. If the need for individual gardens necessitates this kind of development, the area devoted to it should be limited, and it should be broken up by flats or other more massive building so that the groups can be of interesting and varied outline. The principle of mixed 'texture' seems to be no less valid for community dwelling than it is for soils, or for cultivated crops. 'Monoculture' has been proved unhealthy in forestry and agriculture. The charm of the old towns and villages lies largely in the mixture of sizes resulting from mixed-income groups, with all the variety of their different gardens, side by side, creating a sense of community and friendly relationship which can never arise where all is monotonous repetition.

Full Use of Space and of Plant Material

The use of the garden space should be a governing factor in the lay-out of housing sites, no less important than the number and size of the houses to be accommodated. Odd corners resulting as a chance by-product of the lay-out are usually too small for any specific use, and are a waste of space no less than a walled-up windowless space inside the building. The value of the garden space does not lie merely in its acreage, it depends on its proper disposition in relation to the buildings and roadways, and on the functions it may serve. In some instances, small spaces *are* needed for trees having a definite function.

All the plant material, and especially the trees, should also be used to full effect, as shown in Chapter Twelve. In housing groups, the central lawn, or 'green' should be spacious enough to accommoate a few trees of the largest size without blocking any light from the windows, because in that position they unite with the roofs of the

buildings to form part of the skyline of the whole group from where-
ever it may be seen. A single group of really tall trees in this position
serves to relate all the surrounding façades to the land in a way which
cannot be achieved by planting smaller trees along the road
frontage.

The planting of trees in towns too often seems to take the form
of avenue planting which, as has already been shown, tends to be out
of scale with the speed of modern traffic, even within built-up areas,
except on very wide roads. A single large tree, or an important group
suitably sited with some space around it, may compose far better
with a town street than an avenue.

The space allowed for tree planting beside urban roads permits
only small species, which, evenly spaced along every road, become
monotonous and do not give the houses the necessary setting. Their
scale is too near to that of the houses themselves, and they fail to
provide that majesty in the skyline forms which is given by full-size
forest trees.

Where new housing is sited on land already possessing fine
groups of noble trees, sensitive planners are alive to the chance of

Great Munster Street, Winchester, Hants. A single tree contributes much to the
charm and urbanity of this little street.

Stevenage, Herts. A pedestrian precinct—paved space surrounded by compact buildings. Trees preserved from a former hedgerow lend maturity to the new town, and their stems contrast with the horizontal lines of the raised walk-way.

borrowing their beauty for the new lay-out, and many site-plans have been designed to retain and make the most of existing trees. But the idea seems to end there and it is seldom realized that small avenue trees will never give the same effect. If it is worth adapting a plan to include full-size existing trees, it is equally worth while making space available for such important trees for the future, and hence the site-plan should allow for their needs.

The variation in the street-line to allow the necessary width is a welcome feature in itself. The life of the trees may be longer than that of the buildings, but that thought need not distress the designer. They may influence a new design in a later century.

Quick-growing trees can be used with slower species for temporary effect; or, in cases where immediate effect is required, large 'semi-mature' trees can be obtained and planted with present-day machinery. Transplanting of 'semi-mature' trees should not, however, be regarded as a completely satisfactory substitute for traditional planting: young nursery trees of large size grown especially for transplanting will in most cases give better results at maturity. Quick-growing species, to be removed as the slower ones come to maturity, can give the effect required in a very few years.

The fault common to so much modern planning—that of treating planting purely as applied ornament—is at its worst in the matter of street planting and housing schemes. Chapter Twelve deals in detail with the structural use of trees and other plants. These principles are applicable in the case of housing estates, and if applied might alter present tendencies considerably. But it cannot be done if the whole question of tree planting is ignored until after the housing site-plan is prepared.

Countless existing housing schemes have trees dotted about in ones and twos, aimlessly—their only relationship to the site-plan being that of occupying empty space. They seem to serve no specific function—though all, of course, serve the general purposes of health and ornament. Most of the positive functions to be served by trees call for groups rather than for single specimens. Above all, wind shelter requires bold groups, and this factor, if given due consideration, inevitably influences the siting of buildings. Meaningful relationships of this kind will produce a far more dignified and beautiful landscape than will ever result from the system of making site-plans without reference to tree planting (unless old trees already exist) and adding new trees as an afterthought where space permits. This 'spotting in' of odd, unrelated trees wherever there happens to be room for them produces, on the plan, something like a bad attack of measles, and gives a restless and unsatisfying effect which tends to be attributed by uninformed critics, not to the designer, but to the trees themselves.

Champs Elysées, Paris. The avenues and boulevards forming the main axes of the layout of Paris were originally planned by Lenotre as extensions to his design for the Tuileries gardens. Later the town plan was developed along the lines of this open space conception.

Avenues

Avenues are characteristic of classical town planning. They go with wide streets and imposing façades framing long vistas. They enhance the geometric symmetry of the design, and in sunny climates their shade is a welcome relief from the glare of light: by close planting of full-sized forest trees a continuous canopy is not too much. This we see in many continental towns and even as far north as Paris, where the Champs-Elysées and many of the boulevards give this effect. In the Mall, in London, the equivalent, adapted to a greyer climate, is obtained by wider spacing and by very careful pruning and thinning of the branches of the plane—a species whose growth is rarely dense in any case.

The finer and more interesting the building and the wider the boulevard, the greater the opportunity for relating the spacing and form of the trees to plan and elevation. The trees themselves, and their shadows, serve to emphasize and to underline the character of the architecture, never screening it too much from view nor sealing the light from its windows.

In avenue planting the relationship of the trees to the rest of the road construction needs even more care and forethought than for groups or single specimens. The need to allow space for tree roots without interfering with services (drains, water, telephones, etc., etc.) and street furniture, is obvious in every case.

For all street trees ample width and depth of good topsoil suitably drained and irrigated is essential for healthy growth. The wide unpaved strip of ground which provides the best biological conditions also gives the most pleasing appearance, displaying the junction of stem and root—wood and earth—which is no insignificant part of a tree's beauty. If conditions determine that the trees *must* grow out of the pavement, then a grill should be provided round the roots to admit as much air and water as possible, and the fall of the paving arranged to drain into the tree roots.

The extensive drainage in towns and the huge proportion of non-permeable surface cause excessively dry conditions in the topsoil. Old trees can sometimes establish connections with deep supplies, but for the young stages and for all shallow-rooted species irrigation must be provided—underground perforated pipes being probably the best method. Losses among newly planted trees in towns are usually attributed to smoke and atmospheric conditions, but drought, if not the actual cause of death, is often a contributory factor.

Trees throughout the Town

Where smoke nuisance and atmospheric pollution have to be considered, the choice of trees is limited. The list recommended for such sites by W. J. Bean in *Trees and Shrubs Hardy in the British Isles* is a safe guide. But as smoke nuisance becomes less, a far wider choice of tree species could be used in our towns, unless traffic fumes in the future pollute the air more seriously.

Small public gardens, sited off the main traffic routes but close to shops and office buildings, are especially valuable in a heavily populated city. Parkways or boulevards with wide sidewalks and open-air cafés fulfil the need in towns such as Paris and Prague, whose basic design is spacious; but in London the little city gardens, such as those on the embankment near Charing Cross, or 'precincts' such as Lincoln's Inn Fields, Red Lion Square and some of those laid out by the Metropolitan Public Gardens Association, are in huge demand by city workers. In London the number of such places is pitifully small compared with the need, as can be seen by visiting them during a summer lunch-hour. We have all too few open-air cafés and restaurants in Britain, and much as we blame our climate, it does not deter people from eating in the open wherever facilities are provided. Buildings catering for al fresco meals should have sliding screens, awnings or other devices making some portion of the space available whatever the weather.

Parisian restaurants on the wide boulevards, with the open-air portion separated from the street by boxes of neat evergreen shrubs (giving a sense of privacy without shutting out the view of the avenue), enable the city workers to spend much of their leisure in the open air, and contribute in no small degree to the traditional gaiety of Paris, as well as to the general charm of its appearance.

The amount of time spent by the townspeople in the open air depends to an incredible extent on the design, not of the open spaces alone but of the whole town; and the full use of the open space influences in turn the health and happiness of the people. A recognition of these facts is leading town-planners to place more emphasis on landscape aspects of their problem.

Allotments

During the two World Wars and in the period of food rationing following the Second War, allotment gardens were in great demand. At the present time this need is scarcely felt, and allotment grounds are becoming derelict or being put to new uses. Pressure of population, with increasing food prices, may renew the demand in spite of competition from the 'telly'. For this reason, if not for present amenity, these areas should be preserved as open spaces. To use them as building sites is a very short-sighted policy. Lady Allen's booklet on the design of allotments published in 1936 for the Coronation Planting Committee may once more be needed.

Urban Centres

The wide square surrounded by important architecture, such as Trafalgar Square or the Place de la Concorde, can be linked to main routes and planned on a grand scale in sharp contrast to the lesser urban spaces designed for other use (offices, shops, or dwellings). The need for paving or other hard surface in areas of constant heavy use applies to all these, but large extents of inorganic 'floor space' tend to be oppressive unless relieved by trees or plant-groups: the urban centre that can dispense with all natural forms is rare indeed. The need has found expression even in Moscow's Red Square, where conifers now nestle under the Kremlin's wall. Far from reducing its monumental character the trees effectively underline the height of the wall and the scale of the whole lay-out.

Increasing traffic in our towns, and the pressure of population on space has led to the revival of the 'precinct'. An interesting treatment in strong contrast to surrounding streets can be designed to suit its special use. Such an area is more like the market places in many small continental towns and may remind one of some of the Dalmatian coastal towns where motor cars are excluded. Seats, a few shade trees, some variation of level with shallow steps, and perhaps low walls or raised plant-groups, with textural interest in the paving pattern, can be introduced in these pedestrian precincts. Pools, fountains and sculpture may be appropriate in some cases, but over-all simplicity and clarity can often be overlaid by too much incident. Modern shopping centres lose quality through unrelated strident competition among the individual shop fronts, and in these cases the grouping and colour schemes of any planting lose their effect. There is a need for unity in the design of the whole to relate the planting to

Pedestrian street in Köln, W. Germany. Reconstruction following bomb damage in the Second World War retained the building lines of the old narrow streets in the centre but excluded wheeled traffic. The effect of modern buildings on the narrow streets is lively, and the pavements are constantly thronged. Vans are allowed to serve shops at restricted hours only, and this avoids the need for service approach roads behind the buildings. The scale of these streets is too small for trees, but how much they would contribute!

the architecture. Colourful groups in beds or boxes, if required, should be raised above ground level, to protect them from trampling feet, and their colouring should be related to that of the architectural setting.

Differing characters of urban centres, according to their use, can be reflected in the landscape treatment. Monumental squares of civic importance can obviously take richer detail and broader use of plant form than the shopping centre. The residential square or community garden can include areas of smaller, more intimate scale than any space planned for the general public. All such distinctions lend variety and charm to the whole. Where they can be linked by pleasant footways, so much the better not only for the children and mothers with perambulators but for all who live and work in the area. These are among the less obvious characteristics which endear a place to the inhabitants.

Cemeteries and Crematoriums

Human birth makes no impact on the landscape, but death has caused some terrible scars. The old-fashioned country churchyard, while the population remained small and before the days of Carrara marble monuments, was a natural and dignified setting for the church. But with the growth of the towns, the high population and death-rate in the larger centres led to overcrowded, insanitary churchyards, and eventually to the consecration of new sites in the suburbs. Even if this development had not coincided with the taste for elaborate and eccentric monuments of exotic marble, they could scarcely have had the simple dignity of the old churchyard: their primary function is different, being essentially places for corpses rather than part of the setting for the house of God.

Nevertheless, corpse grounds of a different kind have been more graciously dealt with in cases where the design provides for more orderly treatment. The worst effects are produced by the cult of individuality run wild: unbridled, irresponsible individuality, especially manifested in the memorials and headstones, whose lack of orderly unifying design makes eyesores of many urban cemeteries. Some have become historic museums, but their appeal is not to the eye.

An even more serious feature of our present burial system is the amount of land absorbed for this purpose. In a Broadsheet (No. 17. The Disposal of the Dead) published by the Association for Planning and Reconstruction after the Second World War, the subject was fully analysed and the figure of 500 acres estimated as the annual rate of extension of cemetery space in Britain. Since then the rate must be increasing significantly. The loss is nearly all land of the highest quality: the character of its new appearance is well seen from most of the railways approaching our cities, and they form part of the welcome offered to guests visiting this country for the first time.

Clearly cremation is a better solution in many ways. No additional space is needed beyond the original 'garden of remembrance'; it is a hygienic, economical system, almost free of the tombstone tradition. The crematorium can have a park-like open treatment and

Crematorium at Grantham, Lincs. Designed by G. A. Jellicoe. The firm angular architecture contrasts with sensitive ground modelling completely appropriate for its purpose. The Cross in a simple setting of hedgerow and trees is calm and comforting, and comes nearer to the feeling of a country cemetery than would be possible with more elaborate treatment.

be in appearance much like any public or private park. Properly designed, the crematorium can be a far pleasanter place to look at than the cemetery, and its maintenance is far easier and more economical because it dispenses with narrow footpaths and other obstructions breaking the simple stretches of grass. But in Britain the absence of an evolved ritual causes a lack of reality, at least in the design of the gardens, which tends to give a sense of aimlessness, or of frustration, for this reason. Either they look like nothing in particular, or else they suggest the private and rather theatrical abodes of wealthy ghosts. The 'Chapel of Repose', in lesser degree, has the same atmosphere: services conducted in a strange place, by a minister unknown to the bereaved, are cold and unreal. Perhaps nothing short of a genuine sense of community and shared reverence can give the depth of meaning felt in a country churchyard, nor anything short of an accepted ritual suited to cremation can overcome our embarrassment, and, in the case of the garden, give ease and simplicity in place of the self-conscious and perfunctory quality they tend to show.

Crematorium gardens in which individual enclosures can be purchased for a price which includes maintenance 'in perpetuity' do not solve the space problems, and, catering as they do for the rich, and drawing invidious distinctions between the incomes of the bereaved (through varying sizes of the allotted space), they are no answer to the problem, however sumptuous their gardens.

The problems seem to have been solved in other countries such

Highgate Cemetery, London. A historic monument of great character and charm. The encroaching forest is nature's way of softening the hard outlines of man's intention, making for the present a romantic scene.

as Sweden, Germany and Switzerland. In Basle an interesting plan has been adopted. All the dead of the Canton, of whatever denomination, are brought for burial or cremation to the Hornli Göttesacker. The rites are performed by the appropriate minister of religion, but the Council of the Canton provides the undertaker's services and, as owner of the site, exercises the necessary controls over memorials. The garden was laid out for this special purpose and is not to be enlarged. Graves are maintained free of charge for twenty years, after which they are re-used except in cases where the relatives by special request take over maintenance themselves.

The principle of planning control and the re-use of graves after twenty years are the outstanding points of this scheme. Under that system all sorts of designs become possible. It could be applied to that Spanish type of cemetery which consists of a rectangular garden enclosed in walls wide enough to contain rows of coffin-shaped cells opening at one end into the garden. These cells are sealed with the tombstone or inscription as they come into use, and the inscriptions then become a part of the wall face. Something of the same sort could be done even less obtrusively by arranging terraces on a sloping site, the retaining walls containing vaults; or by using such walls in conjunction with sunk gardens, so that the horizontal surface could be treated as part of the garden surroundings. Amongst all the astonishing monuments in Highgate Cemetery there is a circular group of sunken vaults which carries out this idea to some extent, though in the form seen there the proportions and details are unsatisfactory.

In London and in other cities there are old churchyards, disused for so long that no feelings can now be hurt by devoting them to new uses. Law forbids their further use for burials, or for building; and in many cases they are the only open space in an otherwise crowded area. Some of them have been used for children's garden plots or playgrounds, or as rest gardens for the general public. For such use no coffins need be disturbed, though records should be carefully kept for reference. Old headstones, which may be pleasing in themselves, can be ranged flat as paving stones or erect and linked to mark a boundary or division of space: their inscriptions then remain available.

17

Industry in the Landscape

Industry owns and uses a vast area of land in Britain: it is fair to regard the industrialists who administer all this land as the heirs of the former great landowners whose care for the beauty of their estates has left us so fine a heritage. In many cases private estates have been taken over directly from the former landowners with all their woods and farmland. Industry can make or mar the landscape of the future according to whether or not it accepts the responsibilities towards the land which were formerly assumed without question by the owners of fine estates. Productivity is a higher priority under present circumstances, and the produce is different, but productivity of a single item never was and never should be the only consideration. The whole of the land including 'non-operational' ground should be productive of something, even if some of it is of low economic value, or even, as in the case of landscape quality, of unassessable value—let us say an 'invaluable asset'.

We are now reaching a stage where human activity almost approaches a geological scale. Our extractive industry changes the levels and the ground forms over huge areas. We can even change the shape of our coast line, intentionally as in the case of the Wash or Morecambe Bay, or unintentionally by dredging gravel from the sea bed and so diverting existing currents and changing their effect on coastal erosion and sedimentation.

We have no alternative but to accept the necessity for change, but we have far greater powers of control over the changes than was formerly thought possible, and we are learning that the controls must be applied throughout the process of change and not as an afterthought.

Terrible legacies of waste land in the 'Black Country', and in polluted areas such as the Lower Swansea Valley, prove that it is far more costly and difficult, and in some cases well-nigh impossible, to

Industrial legacy: Llansamlet copper and arsenic works, Swansea. In this area the soil has been poisoned and made uninhabitable for human and other life. The condition is reflected in the visual air of dereliction. Scientific research and much expenditure is needed to restore the fertility and landscape. See *The Lower Swansea Valley Project* (Longmans, 1967).

restore land ravished by industry in the past, than to restore it to sound land use in the course of the industrial processes.

Planning controls in new developments, together with the growing awareness of responsibility on the part of industry itself and the use of new techniques for restoring land to fertility, combine to bring the possibility of fine landscape beauty in our industrial areas if industry appreciates its value and plans accordingly.

The scars of the past are a more intractable problem, and their continued existence is, to quote the Duke of Edinburgh's foreword to *The Lower Swansea Valley Project*: 'a stark monument to a thoughtless and ruthless exploitation . . . and a standing reproach to each generation which shrugs its shoulders and looks the other way'.

The possible means of restoration set out in the study illustrate the difficulties to be encountered in that task. Not only economic difficulties but also scientific and legal problems have to be overcome.

A Study Group set up by the Conferences on *The Countryside in 1970* (held under the wing of the Nature Conservancy in 1963 and 1965) reported on the hopes of restoring derelict land throughout Britain. Many excellent books on the subject have been published recently, such as those by the Civic Trust, and by John Oxenham, E. G. Barber and B. Hackett (see Reading List, p. 395).

All this proves that this generation is alive to the possibilities of restoring past dereliction, but is as yet unable to overcome its difficulties. The opportunity of restoring the land in the course of normal operations has been lost and the cost of restoration would now have to be met from taxation or government subsidies or loans. The value of the restored land and the amenities to be provided is not easily assessable: in the present-day climate of opinion the cost appears prohibitive, though posterity may have cause to see it in a different light. The worst areas of dereliction are the poorest, and, scattered as they are through so many different local authorities, the problem cannot be dealt with as a unified planning scheme.

Yet the black areas could become green and profitable. The experience and technical means are available. We should create new Corporations on the lines of New Town Corporations empowered to acquire and control whole regions where former devastation prevails.

If, or when, some such measures are applied, it is to be hoped that the need for fine landscape and healthy surroundings is fully appreciated. To do the work on the cheap, eliminating the refinements, has been tried in some cases, and low cost may be seen as a measure of success; but it is the landscape which then suffers. Recreation grounds and houses crammed on flat treeless planes may be worse, visually, than the dereliction they replace, where the encroaching weeds on broken ground had a nostalgic charm and at least held promise of nature's ultimate cure.

Atmospheric pollution and the pollution of coast and river contribute to the difficulties. The broader issues of over-population and the pollution of human environment are involved, and although they are beyond the scope of this book, such thoughts must be a back-

Town Moor, Newcastle. An area restored to agricultural use after opencast mining: flat, treeless and visually dull. The problem of more varied and valuable use is now being tackled. A town park including many kinds of use should restore an interesting landscape.

ground to our consideration of individual sites and their landscape treatment.

The restoration of land on a big scale, such as areas of opencast mining, extraction of gravel and sand, clay and limestone, is being done generally now, with varying degrees of success.

Experience and research has shown how to establish vegetation and to hasten the formation of soils on new surfaces of industrial wastes of many kinds from colliery shale to pulverized fuel ash, and the areas thus restored, whether to agriculture or to some new use, are capable of forming new landscapes of distinctive quality. The value of fine landscape, as one of the resources to be re-established, has yet to be fully appreciated, though in some cases this too has been well cared for.

The nationalized industries are showing their awareness of the need for restoring all land to new use in the course of industrial activity, and to the importance of the new landscape thus created. Opencast coal mining and iron ore extraction, which threatened vast areas when the big machines first made possible deep excavation from the surface, have now established systems of progressive restoration to agricultural use which quickly replace former landscapes with scenery not unlike the original, and in some cases even better adapted to its present use. The care taken by the National Coal Board Opencast Executive to preserve and replant trees on the restored land is a hopeful sign of the times and an example to some less discerning industries. Many individual collieries have given thought to the landscape effect of their sites. Careful modelling of the waste materials to form banks and screens planted with trees and shrubs improve their appearance from within and as seen from surrounding positions.

The Central Electricity Generating Board employs landscape consultants in connection with its new power stations, both nuclear and 'conventional', and also on its ash-disposal schemes which are larger in extent than the power stations themselves. Enormous quantities of pulverized fuel ash (p.f.a), usually called fly ash, are now used constructively instead of being dumped in unsightly heaps. Much is taken for road making and other commercial use, but the remainder is used for filling old derelict excavations and bringing them back to agricultural or other use. The old clay pits of the Peterborough brick works are being filled and restored by this means, with landscape advice from Mr Weddle. In Yorkshire, 700 acres of land liable to subsidence due to underground mining—land which would otherwise become marsh and swamp—is being turned into a hill farm, over a period of thirty years, by pumping ash slurry from two new coal-burning stations into lagoons whose banks are formed by coal waste from the mine below. As the ash dries out, new layers of lagoon are raised tier by tier till the final height of about 160 feet is reached. The sides will be grazed by stock, and the top plateau will be cultivated when the proposed shelter planting is established.

In size and height this new hill will be comparable with Brayton Barf and other local hills, and like them will be welcome in this flat and rather uninteresting area. The scheme represents considerable economic saving when compared with the far greater cost of transporting ash by road and dumping it out at sea.

Proposed new hill at Gale Common, Yorks. The intention to restore swampy land to agricultural use by means of a hill composed of fly ash from the furnaces of nearby power stations, together with coal waste from an underlying mine would have created a new farm of approximately 700 acres, having pasture, arable fields and shelter belts. The project was planned for economic use of industrial waste, consciously sculptured almost on a geological scale to create distinguished new landscape. The drawing, by Peter Swann, shows the hill as originally planned. Recent changes of policy and methods of ash disposal, however, may call for reconsideration of the original land form. Perhaps some different land use such as woodland or nature reserve rather than a hill farm may result.

Waste

Waste is a common cause of ugliness in the landscape. We must form a national habit of dealing constructively with waste materials instead of letting them lie around using up precious space and turning the countryside into rubbish heaps. The dumps of metal scrap, old bedsteads and wrecked cars, are bad enough; but industrial wastes are on a far larger and more serious scale. All waste, whether of ground surface, topsoil, smoke or other unused resources damages the landscape and upsets biological balance. It can all be used to create fine land form and valuable usable space if properly treated.

The control of smoke is an essential step towards better possibilities for industrial landscape, because smoke, polluting soil and atmosphere, acts deleteriously on life at each stage of the biological cycle. In the form of smoke, all that waste material is a poison: better uses must be found for it. If not required for other by-products it could at least be used in the landscape in a better way. Applied to the soil in a different form it might be valuable; or with pulverized city refuse and other so-called unusable wastes it could, under a proper plan, be used to create new contours, and, indeed, a new landscape.

Local authorities often use city refuse to raise the level of low-lying or swampy ground, making a well-drained area available for new use. When, as in the case of Brighton, the topsoil from the site is first stripped and then relaid on the surface, the area is made available for playing-fields, cultivation or tree planting, and a fine landscape treatment becomes possible.

New sculptured land forms can be created. It may often be practical to level up to a flat surface, but life on an endless flat plain is dull. Waste material is being used in various situations to create new hills and valleys of positive beauty. Totally new forms, depending on the system and machinery of the deposit, can be designed. It is unfortunate that past experience of monstrous spoil-heaps of slag and other waste has prejudiced the possibilities to a large extent. But the dump of brick rubble which was piled up in Hyde Park during the bombing of London in 1940–41 gave a glimpse of things that might be in the future. For some reason, possibly limited ground space, the ramp carrying lorry-loads to the top was made on curved lines, which, with the sharp escarpment at the top, possessed real beauty. Grassed over and crowned with a group of stately syca-mores—the tree which sprang up on all the bombed sites—it would have made a fine addition to the park landscape. Consisting as it did of London's crumbled homes, it would have become a war memorial having significance of a totally different order from any to be erected later.

Where a site devasted by abandoned industries is to be used for new buildings, there will, in any modern planning scheme, be a high proportion of open space, and this, if it is to provide fine landscape, ought to give interesting land forms as well as trees and grass and fresh air. Flat areas are best for housing and other buildings, and for playing-fields: for these, old spoil-heaps would be removed or flattened, either in the process of using the material for industrial purposes, or by pushing it back into hollows or disused pits, or by rolling it out on the surface by bulldozer. But where public open spaces and parks other than playing-fields are to be included, the bulldozer needs very careful handling. To roll everything out flat would be to miss a great opportunity; and though old spoil-heaps may be unpleasing in their present form, they can become the basis for new and better contours well related to the new building lay-out.

In almost every case of industrial damage to the scenery, it can be shown that waste is a main cause of the resulting ugliness. Whether it be gravel and sand working, brick works, iron ore, slate or china clay, waste of space and waste of material contribute to the sense of devastation. During the actual working, some unsightliness is usually inevitable, but careful planning of the routine adapted to the final restoration can reduce that to minimal proportions, and restoration can proceed, section by section, until at the end of the operation all scars are healed.

Design for Extractive Industries

At Hope Cement Works in Derbyshire, an early example of such improvement was put in hand. Mr G. A. Jellicoe prepared a fifty-year plan, which recognized the main limestone quarry high on the hillside as a feature to be seen in its full grandeur, but which reduced the quarry mouth to conceal the inner clutter of rail tracks and equipment. Waste from the workings was to be moulded into the existing outer contours of the hillside, and trees planted to link the quarry with the 'tamer' valley landscape where the factory buildings lie amongst sports fields and trees. Clay pits in the low-lying excavations were to become boating and fishing pools—to be seen against the wooded hills beyond.

Since that time very many similar schemes have been put in hand by Mr Jellicoe and by many other members of the Institute of Landscape Architects. Landscape consultants are being appointed in ever-growing numbers as industry awakens to the new potential of intelligent design.

Conservation of Soil

Waste of soil should be regarded as a criminal offence, even though modern methods of mechanical seeding and fertilizing make it possible to establish vegetation on many waste materials and on subsoil without humus. Humus is essential for productive soils: the world in general, and Britain in particular, is in no position to squander this stored-up asset of topsoil. The use of processed sewage or other organic wastes can doubtless be more fully exploited in the future. Further ecological research can show the best means of using these wastes and of establishing vegetation on them, and of creating new soils.

Existing geological formations are in some cases (e.g. chalk or coal) of organic or animal origin. We scarcely think of man as a builder of geological strata in this sense, yet he is constantly adding material to the earth's surface. Where his waste products have to be disposed of they should be used not to destroy but to raise the quality of life. For healthy life it is necessary to preserve a state of biological balance in the surface, with soil, bacteria, plants and animals in concert. Full use of the land to ensure stability of the balance conduces to civilized life and pleasing landscape. Man's needs may be paramount, but his needs include fine surroundings as well as food and material comforts.

Reservoirs and Water Catchment Schemes

Hydro-electric installations can mar or in some cases even improve the highland areas where they appear. Their buildings are comparatively small. Well designed, they fit very happily into the valley scenery, and their associated lakes and reservoirs can be pleasing additions to the scene. The siting of the water pipes connecting the installations is all important, and underground pipelines are obviously desirable. Staff buildings, car parks and offices have in some cases intruded on the sense of remoteness more than the actual installations. The sight of a suburban dwelling complete with standard roses and colour borders in such positions, incongruous as it is, typifies the British love of gardening, and the individuality of the staff members. Only in this country do we find this display of horticultural skill in such inappropriate positions. Where staff cottages, gardens and car parks can be sited in a village or hamlet they can be

Hydro-electric power station at Ffestiniog, North Wales. Firmly of this era, yet built with deference to the character of its surroundings, this structure with its storage lake is not an unwelcome feature of the landscape. The pale colour of the upper dam, however, appears as an intrusion. The banks of the lower dam, composed of loose stones or 'rip rap', are not unsightly at low water but the landscape suffers loss when the reservoir is empty.

absorbed happily enough—it is in the case of isolated buildings that the contrast is most obtrusive.

Reservoirs supplying urban areas, when sited in wild hilly land-scapes, can look natural enough if the details of their design are well considered. In addition to their storage purpose, these reservoirs can prevent flooding of rivers at lower levels, and check erosion in the high valleys. For these reasons many small and 'natural' dams form-ing a chain of pools along the valleys, are better than very large dams at lower levels.

The large reservoirs with vast dams and pumping stations and other functional installations present many landscape problems. Con-crete-lined reservoirs show an ugly rim at periods of low water, and the appearance of some of the earlier installations has created a very

A hydro-electric storage dam. It has been introduced into a wild landscape with infinite care and accuracy. The subtle curve and the even flow of water over the dam relate it happily to its context. Below the rim the rocks break the water up to splash and bubble in contrast to the smooth surface above and the even ripples below. (Landscape architect: Colwyn Foulkes).

bad image in the public mind, which probably contributes in no small degree to public resistance to new enterprises.

Recent reservoirs, made with more thought for visual results, can go far towards alleviating public dislike of dams and reservoirs. The advice of landscape consultants has been sought and some of the worst features of the installations have been modified. The appearance of the rim at low water is one of the worst problems, but this has been met to some extent by varying the treatment at different points. Some stretches of the bank can have the concrete formed to contain rocky 'rip rap' giving the effect of a shingle beach, while other lengths may be given a vertical face of a different material, with grass or herbage right up to the rim.

Buildings incorporated in the structure of the dam are to be preferred, but where isolated ancillary buildings are essential, their design and colouring should be subdued, and subsidiary. Modelling of the ground forms of the land below the dam, and of all areas affected by roads and other new structures, when shaped to flow into existing contours, looks far better than the uniform slopes and rigid lines so often seen. The new forms should be linked to the surrounding land-use pattern, by connecting new plantations and pasture with those existing beyond the site. Pasture, with farm animals grazing all open areas, is economic in maintenance and appropriate visually, particularly if woodland for shelter is included in the scheme.

The tendency to convert reservoirs into play parks (now that improvements in water treatment processes make it possible to permit public access) can hardly be indulged in the wilder areas without an urbanizing effect. Car parks, club houses, restaurants and all the rest of the 'amenities' must inevitably create an inappropriate intrusion to the scene, and kill any sense of remoteness in our small-scale land. The extreme contrast between the engineering structure and the wild surroundings can only be effective in very large-scale landscapes, such as we see in the Tennessee Valley scheme, U.S.A.; and in these cases also it may be possible to lose sight of car parks and other amenity features in the folds of the ground combined with suitable planting.

In Britain, lowland reservoirs, especially those in the gravel areas near large towns where the natural scenery tends to be uninteresting and uneventful, are obviously a better choice for play parks, boating, fishing and swimming facilities than the remote highland reservoirs. In such places the additional buildings, roads and car parks can be grouped and well designed to create interesting new landscape and to provide for the needs of the urban population within easy access of their homes. These small-scale features are not incongruous in an area already almost urban in character.

Reservoirs drawing their supplies from a river are sometimes sited above the surrounding levels, as in the case of those near the A30 road at Staines. If enough space is available around the brink to allow for pleasing modelling of the contours, this rather awkward effect of a raised reservoir can be overcome. But if the space is limited to the engineering necessities, the steep straight banks are ugly, and no strip of small-scale planting will camouflage the effect. Some extra space is needed from the landscape point of view, and the problem of providing and maintaining such space must be faced. At Trimpley, near Bewdley in Worcestershire, the Birmingham Water Board lets the land on the banks between the reservoir and the river Severn for sheep grazing. The treatment of the contours and the planting groups (protected by fencing) were designed with this intention. The public is not excluded but is requested to keep to the footpaths provided.

Dams collecting water to irrigate comparatively flat areas of tropical lands allow for cultivation of the banks as the water level falls, and this use of the area between high and low water makes interesting seasonal variation in the appearance of the reservoir. In some instances in India the dam itself has been used as the terrace of a fine garden, or in others as a holy place with temples sited on stepped terraces leading down to the water—a place of pilgrimage and worship. It must be acknowledged that such uses contribute more to the quality of the landscape than do car parks and ice-cream booths.

Major Structures in the Rural Scene

Many of the major industries have to be sited in open country, near sea, river or the source of supply such as coal, clay or limestone. These overwhelming functional requirements limit the choice of site, and often indicate areas of exceptional landscape beauty.

Isolated human structures in remote places have, in the past, contributed to the grandeur of the scene. Our power stations, oil refineries, factories and water-works must take their place, in time, with the pyramids, castles and temples of the past. Perhaps they may succeed, visually at least, if something more than sheer materialism enters into their making. Some care for their effect on their surroundings—at least some simple recognition of man's place in nature and of his responsibility to the land and to the future—is needed.

There are sites where a vast structure can rest sublimely on a rocky base or on a flat expanse without the cushioning of vegetation. The effect then depends on the shape of the structure in relation to ground form, and on the direct simplicity of that relationship. There must be no clutter or intermediate incident. The role of plants in the majority of industrial sites is to serve as screen for the inevitable clutter that accumulates on the ground around the buildings.

Milford Haven, Pembroke. The refinery is built on the site of a disused eighteenth-century fort. The landscape architect, Colwyn Foulkes, advised using the old buildings for storage, and siting the tanks in a lower position stepped down towards the harbour. Thus an interesting skyline has been enhanced and the silhouette of the tanks is contained unobtrusively within the group.

In the case of power stations or other buildings with very high chimneys and towers, massed planting of trees or shrubs can give firm horizontal base lines to balance the height of the structures whilst concealing only the ground and the lower items of the group. All the car parks, sheds, roadways and other incidental or ancillary items if seen from outside the site, destroy the simplicity of the group. The main structures, rising high above the trees, may be fine features in themselves, and they can be best appreciated if set on a strong horizontally extended base of foliage form undisturbed by clutter.

In areas where trees seem inappropriate or where they cannot be grown—for instance, on open stretches of coast and moor or above the tree line—the direct relationship between structure and ground form may be brought about by modelling of the contours to screen the clutter where necessary. Low shrubs such as heather or gorse may help this effect without reducing the simplicity of the group.

Individual Industries in the Landscape

As industry encroaches on the fields and woods, as new roads, runways, car parks, houses, factories and warehouses swallow up the open space, the creation of new landscapes to meet the needs of modern life becomes the responsibility of each individual project, to compensate in some degree for the loss of former landscape. This surely applies whatever the previous merit of the site. Each concern has some effect on the national scene, and all have a part to play in the broader biological sphere.

Short-term economics often seem to conflict with the wider long-term view, but a fine landscape has certain practical advantages for industry, now more generally understood. The effect on public relations, on staff and labour attitudes, is not negligible. A fine building in a fine setting can be seen as a status symbol, or just as a form of advertisement. Whatever the motive, each individual site can contribute something to the green mantle of vegetation on which the health of the community depends, and the treatment of each site will express much of the character and 'image' of the individual enterprise.

Factories and other industrial buildings dominate their sites and occupy a large proportion of their land, but nearly all have open space or 'non-operational' land within their boundaries which provides their landscape setting: such space can be used to relate the buildings and installations to their surroundings. That this is best done by means of trees, shrubs and grass with suitable ground modelling, rather than by a blaze of seasonal bedded-out plants, has yet to be fully appreciated by many concerns. We in Britain are so fond of our 'pop-gardening' that too many opportunities for creating fine enduring landscape are missed. Time and money are often misspent on the care of subtopean sub-parks.

All the 'non-operational' space should contribute positive value. In most cases the spaces are obviously too small for full productive

Aust power line, Severn Bridge, Bristol Channel. The great pylons carrying power lines across the river estuaries have majesty whether seen in industrial surroundings or, as here, in isolation. The single high tower lends vertical value to the flat horizon.

value as forest or farm, but trees can often be planted for rotational felling so that some timber can be recovered. Except near the buildings, large open spaces should be grazed rather than mown. Only in very small grounds is it wise to regard the space purely for its ornamental value; but where that is the case, such ground can at least contribute beauty to the surrounding areas better by its important trees than by small flower-beds seen only at close range. Flowers can give of their best in very small but critical positions, near the main entrance perhaps, and preferably in containers related to the architecture, so that the simplicity of the ground forms is unbroken.

From the largest to the smallest industries, the landscape presented is of importance to the nation as a whole. Intentionally or unintentionally, all contribute to the impression of those who see the site, whether the next-door neighbours or the visitors we hope to attract from afar.

Heinz research and administration centre, Hayes, Middx. Good existing trees have been preserved around the new building and pasture is retained close to it. Maintenance of lawn and garden is minimized, and the setting made more interesting and pleasing by this use. Small decorative garden trees and flower-beds would ruin the simplicity of a group such as this. Industry, heir of the land-owners of the past, can enjoy equally fine parkland prospects.

Nuclear power station, Chinon, France. The composition of contrasting shapes creates a stimulating landscape without the use of tall tree forms. Low groups are enough to conceal clutter, and the river boundary prevents sprawl, at least in this direction.

Cement works, near Westbury, Wilts. An industry situated in an agricultural setting. The well-related but varied shapes of the roof lines correspond happily with the surrounding hedgerow pattern and with the rising contours beyond.

Hamburg oil refinery, W. Germany. Seen from a well-to-do suburb on the opposite bank of the river Elbe, it provides a fine and enviable view. Only the silver cylinders appear above the forest belt along the river; all clutter is contained behind the trees. A sandy shore line between river and tree belt, kept strictly in its natural state, enhances the dramatic quality of the industrial scene.

18

Communications and Services

The great majority of people see the country mostly from roads, railways and footpaths. These points of view are those of the population in general, and are of national concern—for the sake of our own people, and also because they represent an important aspect of the country displayed to visitors from abroad.

Railways

It is unfortunate that railways present the most intractable problem of all. Not only their rigid, uncompromising lines, but all that goes with the railways combines to make them apparently a hopeless case. All the worst untidiness, the worst aspects of industry, collect along the line and become accepted as an inevitable corollary of railways: they are the outstanding example of the result of assuming that useful things must necessarily be ugly, and they serve to spread that belief till it is ingrained in the minds of the people. And so visitors arriving for the first time in England, unless they travel by air, or come by night, or step into a car at the quayside, are presented, as a first introduction to this country, with some of its very worst aspects.

Electric railways with overhead gantries look worse than in the old days of steam. Some improvement in the design should be possible. Electrification, avoiding the smoke from engines and reducing the noise, is an important step towards eventual improvement. But drastic architectural and planning changes are needed too, allowing room for planting. Above all, improvements would depend fundamentally on an acceptance by British Railways of definite responsibility for the appearance of the railways. Such a possibility seems remote unless the public becomes far more allergic to ugliness than it appears to be now.

Ouse Viaduct, Sussex. This viaduct crossing the Ouse between Balcombe and Haywards Heath was built in 1841. Its grand arches linking the two sides of the valley with graceful strength bring welcome enrichment to the scene, and may be taken to counteract, in some degree, the squalor we too often associate with railways.

There is, however, room for improvement at small expense even under existing conditions. Much of the waste space near stations and marshalling yards could be planted with trees which would help to screen the railway from the surroundings and the surroundings from the railways. Such planting would be a small item and would make a good skyline and background in places where at present all is drab dullness.

Disused Railways

The case of the old disused railway lines seem to be an exception to the rule that waste space makes poor landscape. These strips of neglected solitude are not, however, sterilized. They become quickly clothed by vegetation and are a haven for all the wild life excluded from the surrounding territory. The tracks make good footpaths and might well be regarded (together with canal towpaths) as the basis for a countrywide footpath system. But there are problems of fencing, gates, etc., and of danger from derelict bridges and other structures to be overcome in this connection.

Power Lines

The number and complexity of overhead power lines grows constantly, draping the skylines like a spider's web. Either they numb our senses till we cease to notice them, or we hate them to the point that we become blind to the beauty that certain well-sited high power lines have. The tallest towers carrying power across the estuaries or over wide flat land lend a strange quality of magnificence to their surroundings, as in the case of the Aust tower on the banks of the Severn. (Photograph on p. 347.)

Careful siting can reduce the impact of these lines, especially in the case of the high power cables, as Sylvia Crowe has shown in *The Landscape of Power*. The low power lines are the worst offenders. They are ubiquitous, clumsy and usually sited with little regard for visual effect: they are seen near eye-level in direct conflict with views and sight lines. The immediate obvious need for electric power in every household justifies their existence, while the cost of putting them underground is, it seems, prohibitive, though it is low by comparison with main cables. Perhaps the best we can hope for is a future when improved systems of cable insulation, together with the rising cost of crossing valuable property, may drive power lines underground. Or may we look to a yet more distant future when new systems of power storage and transmission may render cables obsolete, so that pylons will join the telegraph poles as forgotten curios of the twentieth century?

Roads

Roads present a far more cheerful prospect. We are becoming alive to the great possibilities of making beautiful roads, and each new main road shows improvement of design and landscape treatment. There is hope for this generation to prove that ugly roads are an anachronism.

Country lane, Little Sark. The charm of the old country lanes is worth preserving for they are unrepeatable. They suit slow local traffic and can be used as foot-paths. Road widening in such cases invites dangerous driving and wastes a valuable asset of the countryside. Trees in this exposed area are sculptured by the prevailing wind, proving the value of their shelter for those using the lane.

Most of the old roads are beautiful, and when vandalism has occurred in the course of road widening, active protests have been made, showing that the public resents the idea of a purely utilitarian road. Unfortunately the public seems to be less active in those cases of unnecessary widening and straightening of minor roads where the existing old road is adequate for present use. There is really a good case for preserving the traditional character unchanged in the case of country by-roads which carry little traffic and where speed is of secondary importance, yet many of these local authority roads seem to be aping the treatment of new main roads unsuccessfully and for no apparent reason. They become more dangerous by encouraging unnecessary and inappropriate speed, particularly when the widening

Mittenwald, W. Germany. A road crossing reservoirs and curving along the banks above the new high water level. It seems to respond to the shapes of mountain and water surface in a charming dialogue or counterpoint.

is on short lengths only, interspersed with twists and bottle-necks, and they cannot compensate for loss of the former beauty (as do many of the new trunk roads) by breadth of treatment and close adaptation to their surroundings. A sharper distinction between the character of main roads and secondary roads would be better both from the landscape point of view and that of road safety. Many country lanes could become bridle and footpaths to their great advantage, wheeled traffic being prohibited, or limited to inhabitants with private right of access.

Improvements in technical construction of the main roads have gone hand in hand with finer adjustment to landscape and ground forms: fresh views of our countryside have been opened up and many new highways relate happily to their context. It has been recognized that roads made on gradients and curves like those of a railway are not suited to ordinary motoring. In Germany, the early autobahns constructed for military purposes were found to be dangerous because dreary, while those made more recently were

New York State Thruway, U.S.A. The widely diverging traffic lanes make a more interesting landscape than when they are closely parallel (as at the top left) and form a wide striped ribbon. In the heavily populated land of Britain, however, this system is impracticable. Access to the land between is too difficult, and there are too many cross roads requiring bridges across both lanes.

designed to keep the motorist awake by providing interest and variety of scene. The same thing has been proved by experience on the Pennsylvania Turnpike and other roads of similar type in the U.S.A.

The American parkways have contributed greatly to present-day thinking on the siting and construction of roads, and it is worth noting that landscape architects are largely responsible for the fine features of American parkways. Olmsted and others showed the way to a construction adapted to modern motoring—differing from the railroad lines on one hand and from the old coaching road on the other: a system which provides the easiest and most efficient driving conditions for the ordinary motorist and also gives pleasing landscape results. This 'fitted highway' has curves and gradients allowing for safe motoring speeds of seventy miles per hour: yet it follows in general the indications of the contours, curving gently in response to

Road widening, Mickleham, Surrey (1939). By making a new lane, the line of the old road with its roadside trees has been preserved for one-way traffic: the new lane alongside is built on a lower level, so that both are fitted closely to the land form. The varying width of the central reservation accommodates trees on the sloping bank. Modern speeds demand more drastic alterations.

the undulations of the ground in preference to driving straight across them. The length may be slightly greater than that of a railway or speed track, but since it avoids unduly deep cuttings and high embankments it is less costly both in construction and in maintenance than a straight track over-riding the contours.

The general direction of any road is, of course, governed by the points to be linked together, but the detailed siting along the route may be largely influenced by landscape considerations, and in the case of American parkways this aspect of highway design is recognized as being largely a landscape problem. In our country, where the undulations of the ground are an outstanding characteristic, it is clear that any important line, such as that of a road, adapted to those undulations will fit more happily into the general scene than one which disregards them, unless the road is built above ground as a viaduct.

Where the contours are not the main factors, other existing features may indicate the best position for a road: the line of a river or coast, even the edge of a wood, spinney or shelter belt. The boundary between hill grazing and cultivated land may be suitably emphasized by a road, and where such siting is possible the road will seem to belong happily to its surroundings.

Where embankments and cuttings become necessary they need not blatantly emphasize or repeat the parallel lines of the road: careful modelling of the ground can merge the angle of slope easily into the unchanged contours on either side. The angle of slope on British roads, up to the present, is treated in an unnecessarily rigid way. The single angle produces hard lines at top and bottom. Some of the European slopes, given three changes of angle from top to bottom, link the slopes more naturally with adjoining contours; and although this appears to require more roadside space than would a single steep slope, it would, in practice, make it possible to set the fences closer to the road, leaving more space in agricultural use. Temporary arrangements with adjoining land-users to allow for construction beyond the ultimate fence position would be necessary but this can scarcely be an insurmountable difficulty.

Independent alignment of dual carriage-ways reduces the amount of embanking and cutting necessary, as the opposite streams of traffic can be on different levels and part of the fall goes into the central strip—which, in these conditions, is of variable width. This reduces the danger of headlight glare at night, and it also means fewer parallel lines—it is those endless parallel lines which are so unpleasing in many of the existing new roads.

There are, however, some serious objections to independent alignment of the two carriage-ways in country areas in our highly populated land with its small-scale undulations; for the land between the two roads becomes an inconvenient island, whose size and importance may not justify bridges or underpasses, yet access from the main road is prohibited. If the land is not used for agriculture or forestry its maintenance becomes an 'amenity' chargeable to the road authority. These considerations greatly limit the possibilities of separating the two traffic streams. The maintenance problem closely concerns also the width of the roadside reservations. Travelling abroad, the British observer is struck by the absence of fences and

Widford, Herts. Forest trees preserved in the central reservation. They mark the line of an old hedgerow, and contribute their mature beauty to the new two-lane road.

roadside reservations. The cultivation extends to the road itself in many places. A farmer wishing to graze cattle in such areas evidently has to provide his own fencing. Grazing is far more general in British farming, and uniform fencing along our roads is clearly needed: visually it is far preferable to the medley of fencing which results from the varying standards of the farming community. Distances between settlements are greater in most European countries than in Britain, a factor which reduces the need for fencing. Nevertheless, greater flexibility of the width of the roadside reservation inside the fence would be welcome: on balance, it might result in less ground to be maintained. The monotony of the road width is emphasized by the fence lines, and the changes made necessary by embankments and cuttings are welcome. Small corners of fields cut off by the new line of the road can be taken in to accommodate a group of trees, and compensation could be made by narrower roadside reserves in flat areas.

Roadside rests or stopping places on motorways are needed at fairly frequent intervals, and can be made attractive if there is room to separate them from the main carriage-way. There are some excellent examples on the German autobahns, providing space for several

Zion Canyon, Utah, U.S.A. An unobtrusive parking place and look-out point where motorists stop to enjoy the scale of the canyon and its massive rocks.

family cars to picnic in comparative seclusion and peace. Simple benches and tables are provided, with unobtrusive litterbins, grouped naturally amongst mature trees and shrubs in a way to provide maximum rest and comfort as a change from fast travel.

Roundabouts

The large areas enclosed within the junctions of roads and on the verges should be modelled and planted to merge with the surroundings, especially in open country. Even in town or suburb there is no justification for treating the island sites as parks when no access is available for pedestrians, and where the motorist's attention should not be distracted from the road. Of all the inappropriate places for bedding out annuals, these are perhaps the worst. Nor is there any need for a central pudding-shaped mount. Curved banks, to block headlight glare, can usually be sited on the island to appear as natural outliers of adjacent high contours. Simple plant groups of trees or shrubs can contribute to this general effect. The roadside reserve areas at a roundabout provide opportunities for interesting ground modelling, especially where there are underpasses or 'fly-over' roads on different levels.

We are seeing exciting new developments of fly-over roads crossing open valleys or built-up areas—their further evolution will

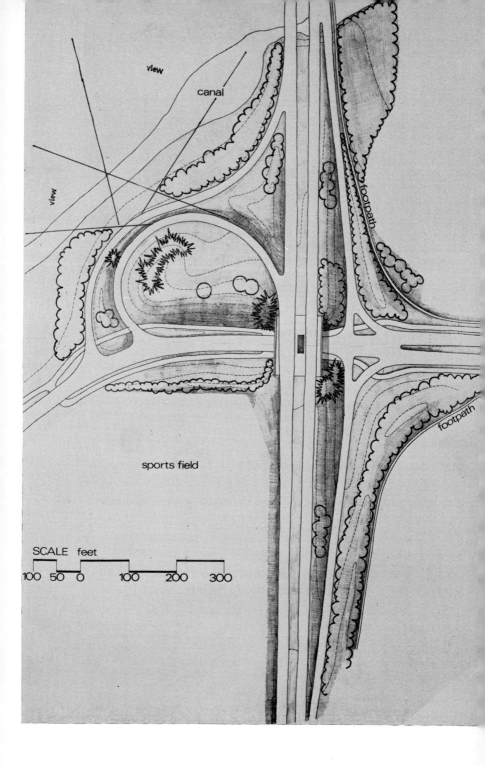

view

canal

view

footpath

footpath

sports field

SCALE feet

100 50 0   100   200   300

Thelwall Viaduct, Cheshire. The M6 is carried over the railway and the Manchester Ship Canal here. Curving in plan and elevation, the structure relates well to its context—a pleasing example of twentieth-century engineering skill. One could perhaps wish for more sympathetic treatment of the embankment on the right of the picture.

be interesting. The open park flowing under main roads in Dusseldorf, the Bristol road junctions and the Thelwall Viaduct where the M6 road crosses the Manchester Ship Canal, are recent examples. Each new structure shows finer adjustment than the last, but the supporting pillars still provide an inelegant frame to the views beyond.

Roadside Planting

Planting of main roads is an important, but secondary aspect of their landscape setting. No roadside planting, however good, can compensate for bad siting or inelegant ground shapes. If the road itself affronts the major features of the country through which it passes, roadside planting may serve only to emphasize its faulty position. Siting and design of roads is a more important landscape matter than the planting of the road verges, though the two things

Dual carriageway (A325) and underpass (opposite). Soil excavated from the underpass is used to model flowing contours to link the new road levels naturally to their context. The saving on transport of material by using the surplus on site contributed to the cost of the modelling.

should be considered together from the outset. It was emphasized earlier in this book that of the two natural materials of landscape, land and vegetation, the land is always the more important, and that plant masses should be related to the land forms. Nowhere is this more clearly evident than in the case of the highways.

We have often heard it said of a new road that it looks 'like a great scar' across the face of the country. The harsh parallel lines, cut straight across convexities and vales, are typical of the scar-like effect. But a road can be, on the contrary, a feature belonging as if by right to that face, having the type of modulations and curves which mould a living feature and relate it to adjoining forms, making it a logical part of the whole. This calls for quite different treatment from that of covering up the scar and hiding it (as much as possible) after it is irreparably made.

Nevertheless, the planting of the roadside has a vital part to play when the siting and alignment of the road *is* appropriate to its surroundings. Good planting contributes interest and variety to the road which helps to keep the driver alert and vigilant. This interest and variety should be as great as possible, since it should serve to cancel the mechanical monotony of engine sound and road surface. Correct planting is thus an important functional feature of the design.

It was shown in an earlier chapter that avenue planting, or any regular spacing of trees, is unsuitable for fast-moving traffic, since the trees pass at such a rate that the eye is irritated—or in some cases the repetitive monotony of regular spacing is found to have a hypnotic effect, inducing drowsiness in the driver. Even if widely spaced, regular repetition of trees or shrubs becomes monotonous and tiresome, in the same way as the repetition of parallel lines becomes boring.

Planting can be used to draw attention, in advance, to curves in the road and to cross-roads. It can give warning of the approach to built-up areas: it is frequently used to prevent the risk of headlight glare, though if this is done by means of a continuous ribbon of nearly equal height and width, as so often seen on existing by-pass roads, it emphasizes undesirable parallels and becomes monotonous.

Roadside oaks. Probably survivors from an old hedgerow, they enliven the road and lift a horizon which might otherwise be flat and monotonous.

It can be used to frame, and so draw attention to, a distant view, or it can screen out unpleasing features, or obviate the parallel position of the road boundary on either side.

Planting, automatically done just for the sake of planting, often increases the parallel effect of the road; but if it is planned in relation to the surrounding features, that effect can be, to some extent, dispelled. It is unfortunate that the strips allotted for roadside planting have to be of such even widths. It would be far better if they could be variable in width and shape so that the boundary of the total width was not parallel to the line of the road itself. There are many parts of the road which require little or no roadside space or planting, though provision against future contingencies and changing land use may be necessary. There are other road stretches where wide irregular-shaped space on one side would be more pleasing visually.

Even if the actual width available is a ribbon strip of regular width, its apparent width can be varied by the planting treatment. Where the road passes near a wood, the roadside strip, planted with the same trees, becomes in appearance an extension of the wood.

Where the character of the country is open, the roadside treatment can retain that character. Existing trees and hedges help this effect when they can be preserved, giving immediate maturity, whereas new planting takes time to grow. Independent alignment of the two traffic streams makes it possible to save many existing features which would have to be sacrificed for a wide 'all-in-one' road; and such features may often provide indications for the siting and curves of the two carriage-ways. An existing hedge, even if it emphasizes the line of the road for a short length, may help to tie it in to the field pattern and can therefore be valuable, though if it were extended for a greater length without regard to the field pattern it might become monotonous. Where the road passes through stone-wall country, such as the Cotswolds or the Pennines, the same remarks apply to wall boundaries.

The broad variations in our countryside, depending on geological and soil types, on elevation, aspect and other local climatic influences —all of which have so much bearing on the agricultural pattern or general land use—are on a scale beautifully suited to fast travel. In a run of an hour or so, one may see the sharpest contrasts of natural vegetation and landscape, passing over river silt, chalk downs, sandy ridge, rich clay, and damp peaty ground. These major dramatic variations, unless deliberately emphasized by the treatment of the roadside, can too easily be blurred and lost to the motorist by a lavish use of trees and shrubs of exotic or garden type—many of which tolerate a wide range of soil conditions. The smaller-scale variety given by flowering trees of garden type—however interesting and ornamental in themselves—is mediocre and insignificant by comparison with the strong natural variation between one district and another. Horticultural variety is suited to gardens where things are seen at a walking pace or at greater leisure, but not to motor travel. In order to emphasize and underline the wealth of natural landscape variety along the roads, it is necessary, paradoxical though it may seem, to limit the species to those of the local type. In other words, vegetation of the same sort as that growing naturally in the neighbourhood is the most suitable for the roadside itself in open country.

This is not to say that introduced plants and striking unfamiliar effects can never be appropriate: they are peculiarly appropriate when we leave the open country for the built-up areas. The more striking and different such areas can be made, the greater the contrast, and the greater the invitation to slower speed—suggesting a different type of appreciation. The grouping should still be simple and broader in treatment than that of park or garden—relative speeds being taken into consideration—but the change from natural to 'domesticated' vegetation, if treated broadly enough, may correspond to, and underline, other contrasts between open and built-up areas, giving a foretaste of the still richer or more decorated treatment of parks and gardens within the town. From every point of view it is surely a mistake to extend the richer garden treatment far beyond the town: the eye is easily glutted with too much garden, and the spirit longs for the simplicity of the open country in contrast. But on returning to the fold, with uncloyed vision, the contrast again is stimulating and appropriate. Moreover, exotic and garden plants requiring a higher degree of care can be dealt with more easily if confined to the built-up neighbourhood. The English have become too garden-city-minded, and there is a real risk that the enthusiasm for planting the roadside might overlay the native variety of our landscape with a monotony not to be compensated by horticultural variety.

The ubiquitous suburban mixture of lilac, laburnum, double pink cherry and rhododendrons is the result partly of lack of space for more dignified effects, and partly of poor imagination and ignorance. The 'domesticated planting' recommended as suitable for heralding the approach to town or village could be of an altogether different and grander calibre if space limitations were less exacting, and they could be planned to mark the individuality of each town or district instead of being all much alike. The use of *Pinus radiata* and arbutus in certain south-coast towns *does* give this special character, and the idea is applicable elsewhere. A moist, acid soil might suggest the use of liquidambas and maples to give special autumn colour effects, massed against the dark green of redwood, or some other fine conifer not easily grown elsewhere. A town on a light, dry soil could show what can be done with the less-common grey-leaved shrubs, sheltered and set off by pine or evergreen oak. The idea is capable of endless expansion and should appeal to local patriotism and pride.

The widest possible range of size, both in the material used (from turf and low shrubs up to the tallest forest trees) and in the size of the groups—depending on the numbers and spacing of a given species forming each group—is clearly necessary for roads in open country, particularly on long straight lengths. The scale of grouping in relation to traffic speed calls for practical research; for example, what length of open road, free of trees, is needed for the appreciation of a distant view in the case of passengers in a car travelling at, say, fifty-five miles an hour? Obviously the space must be far wider than would be needed by a cyclist. But in either case the open view will be more welcome for appearing in contrast to a massive, compact group of trees near at hand, so that it is first seen through a frame of foliage and shadow.

A road in Derbyshire. Tree groups beside the road frame the view of distant skylines, adding drama and height in the foreground. Trees on the bend would spoil this view: the length of open road after passing the trees is long enough to allow appreciation of the view in pleasing contrast to the planted length.

A good view available on one side of a road can sometimes be improved by a screen or shelter belt on the other side of the road, but on high heath land, mountain roads above the tree-line, or in other positions where no trees grow naturally, open treatment on both sides may be more appropriate.

Where the distant or middle-distant view indicates absence of trees by the road, there may yet be the need for groups of dwarf shrubs below eye-level, not interfering with the line of vision but serving to give variety of form, and to key in with the surrounding vegetation.

At high speeds the outline or silhouette of the roadside planting is more important than the details of flower or foliage, and gives a more constant effect throughout the seasons; but contrasts of foliage and texture, if boldly conceived, are very noticeable at certain seasons and in certain lights. Service areas, roadside rests and other stopping places could be marked by special groupings of this type. The shape of the roadside groups and the height of the lower branches can be related to more distant features and to the horizon or general skyline in the way referred to in Chapter Twelve.

The view of the road from the country through which it passes is equally important. The means here suggested, of giving large-scale variety for the motorist is also the best way of blending the road into its surroundings when seen from those surrounding areas. Gentle curves and a minimum of cutting and embankment help the road-way to merge into and become a feature of the countryside and not a scar. Wide irregular alternations of tree groups and low plants help this effect, whereas regular avenues or continuous planting of any sort would mark the line of road too much from a distant view. Low shrubs muffle the hard edge of the road when seen from a distance, and serve as effectively as trees to break the road-line and key it in to its surroundings. Planting in harmony with the local vegetation also helps to make the road seem to belong to the rest of the landscape.

Of the two points of view, that of the road-user can, therefore-on this system, be given first priority in the assurance that the treatment will not conflict with the view seen from afar.

A footpath through beechwoods on the Chiltern escarpment. Well separated from the road with which it connects, it provides fine views and easy walking without loss of rural character.

Footpaths

The siting of footpaths should be governed by the pedestrians' needs and in general this indicates their complete separation from wheeled-traffic routes. This is safer and more pleasant than pavements adjoining wheeled-traffic roads, and even in towns where there may be some necessity for footpaths adjoining roads, separation is to be preferred wherever possible both for safety and appearance.

With the possible exception of the family party walking out, complete with pram, on Sunday afternoons to see the world, walkers in the country prefer quiet, independent tracks away from wheeled traffic. The Sunday promenade is only a very short length; it needs to be wide and to have a smooth dry surface, whereas the rambler or foot traveller who goes for greater distances prefers the natural surface. Where the footpath beyond the built-up town follows the line of a highway, it would be better if they were separated by a hedge or other planting.

The footpath system should be country-wide rather than local.

Local footpaths in agricultural areas too easily fall into disuse. If linked to a national hikers network they would be more regularly used and would enjoy better status. Short rights of way, serving only local inhabitants, depend on regular use—otherwise their maintenance is no one's responsibility. A network of paths, if well planned on a national basis with connecting links between the districts would be an asset to the whole country, providing healthy outdoor recreation of a popular kind, particularly useful for the industrial centres. Such a network would relieve congestion in holiday districts and would meet the growing need for understanding and contact between town and country.

The usual difficulties of litter, open gates and desecration of the countryside is best overcome, not by excluding town-dwellers from agricultural country, but by developing their appreciation and understanding of it—not by segregation of the two communities, but by emphasizing mutual obligations and responsibilities. Educational campaigns, Wild Life and Nature Study Clubs, need controlled access to agricultural as well as to 'wild' country.

Map-reading, as Sir G. Stapledon pointed out, is an important element in the training of landscape appreciation. A map-conscious

Kennet and Avon Canal near Wilcot, Wilts. The towpaths of the canals provide another country-wide chain of footpaths removed from wheeled traffic; they too can be linked with a general system to enable walkers to do long journeys away from roads.

The Pennine Way. Originally a Roman road, this part of the Way is still in use as a footpath and farm track. The Way leads through unspoilt, almost wild country and could be made to link with a nationwide footpath system.

public would learn to understand and value good landscape in a far more logical way than is possible for those who know only the names of places and the bus routes linking them. Good maps, showing the contours and configuration in attractive colours, should be available at hostels, cafés, pubs, garages and other focal points linking the footpath and highway systems. It is a pity that geological structure and surface configuration cannot be shown well on the same map, but they *can* both be shown by means of models, whose educational value is perhaps even greater than that of maps. Such models might with great advantage be introduced, or made, in schools, and they would be an attraction if displayed also in cafés and hostels.

The old green roads, pack-horse tracks, canal towpaths and the disused railways could form the backbone of the footpath system, and any existing rights of way or narrow lanes unsuitable for fast traffic could become part of it. Additions would undoubtedly be needed to improve cross-country walking generally: but the landscape of Britain deserves recognition, and even if we cannot compete with the Tyrolese Alps and other places which regard their scenery as a major resource, at least we could make the most of our own characteristic landscape for the benefit of our people.

Along the footpath system, spaces might be allotted in odd corners, or on soils too poor and dry for cultivation, for picnic places and small camps, which would be an added attraction. Much would depend on the siting and planting of these if they are to give pleasing results. There are places where a few tents can be inconspicuously placed under trees or near hedge and spinney, and there need be nothing significant to mark the place in their absence. The control of these could either be the charge of the farmer on whose land they occur, or of a national holiday organization which could exercise some influence over its members in return for the advantages of membership.

Footpaths, in the nature of things, tend to add interest in the country scene. They draw attention to the landscape insinuatingly rather than aggressively; and there is little to be said about their design. The oldest ones have survived—almost unchanged—longer than anything else of human creation in this country; and the only reason why new ones should differ structurally is that, not being confined to dry ground as were the old green roads, they often require special drainage and surface. The nearer they can keep in appearance, however, to the old models, the more they will be used and appreciated.

Bridges and viaducts have been telling features of landscape since the earliest days of human travel.

(*above*) The clapper bridge in Crummack Dale, Yorks, is one of the earliest, and has remained in use throughout our history. It is still much used by hikers and others who enjoy walking in the country.

(*below*) The stone bridge at Cassiobury Park, Herts, is typical of many eighteenth-century bridges designed as landscape features in parkland. Its curves respond tunefully to one another and emphasize the contrast between the flat horizontal water surface and the vertical tree stems.

(*above*) The Union Chain Bridge, Horncliffe, Northumberland, crosses the river Tweed with a light strength like a cobweb. Built in 1820, it is the earliest suspension bridge in this country.

(*below*) A road bridge of recent construction at Fairburn, Yorks. The single span and delicate parapet frame the curve of the road beyond. The junction of the parapet with heavier fencing at the top of the embankment could be screened with advantage by low planting.

See also pp. 351 and 361 for the Ouse railway viaduct and the Thelwall viaduct spanning the Manchester Ship Canal.

Harbours, whether we look at the little village harbour on a Scottish loch or at busy developments such as Southampton Water or Milford Haven, are very representative of the nation's landscape. Easedale in the west of Argyll (*below*) holds to its simple character with happy self-assurance, in firm contrast with the wild surroundings. The Bay of Naples as seen idealized in the water colour by Francis Towne (*above*) is again a compact group, absorbed in romantic surroundings of the type which inspired the English landscape style. Dover with its busy spread (*lower right*) has so far managed to preserve the open country near the White Cliffs, while Southampton (*upper right*) threatens to outgrow its landscape setting.

London (Heathrow) and Zurich Airports. It is unfortunate, though perhaps in-evitable, that built-up areas and housing of undistinguished type tend to cluster around airports, yet the apparently haphazard clutter on the sites themselves adds to the confusion. The layout of Zurich (*opposite*) suggests a more logical and flowing circulation than Heathrow (*above*), an impression gained also on the ground.

Zurich is also fortunate in having a better natural setting and some woodland preserved in the region greatly helps the general effect.

Aerial View

At the opposite extreme, in the scale of speed, air travel may affect the ground landscape in various ways. Quite apart from the necessity for dealing with the aerodromes themselves, occupying as they do such large areas of valuable space, there is the aerial view-point from low levels to be considered. On approaching and leaving the airport, travellers get a unique view of surrounding areas. Vertical forms lose significance from this aspect, the ground pattern becomes all-important and the scale values are altogether different from those we are accustomed to. This might indicate very broad colour effects in the ground material of areas near aerodromes or on the ground of the aerodrome itself. Such effects are possible by the use of different types of turf, crops or other ground cover, and though such ideas are as yet perhaps no more than an amusing speculation, they might well come to be given more consideration in the future. Aerodromes cover so much space and can spoil large areas of landscape around them. If vertical take-off and descent should ever become general, we might feel more keenly the need to tidy up and re-arrange the clutter that now collects in the hinterland of runway and airport buildings.

The dreary look of British passenger airports ruins the surrounding scene for many miles. They give little cheer to homecomers, and if we think of them as shop windows displaying the attractions

of this country to tourists from abroad, they probably deserve the world's booby prize, though few of the world's airports can as yet claim to have landscapes of marked distinction.

As technology increases in scope and influence, and new land uses develop, new landscapes inevitably emerge. We fail to appreciate the importance of their visual impact on the general quality of life. The drab undistinguished environment of new features, lacking a traditional background, is too readily accepted.

The shapes of new structures and their detail design is perhaps of less significance in the general effect than their grouping and their relationship to the surroundings. Conscious aesthetic design of the whole complex, integrated in a wide landscape concept, is needed if we hope to prevent debasement of the landscape in the world of the future.

Epilogue

The cycle of life between soil, plant and animal is an essential condition of life—including human life. The response of human consciousness to scenery which expresses a balanced and enduring aspect of that cycle is therefore a normal instinct to be cultivated and refined to the fullest extent.

Man, the dominant animal, is no less dependent on sound ecology than any other form of life. He has greater power to alter and control his surroundings, but is endowed through his sense of natural beauty with a direct vision and appreciation of the balance on which such beauty depends. His responsibility towards the future grows in proportion to his increasing powers of understanding and control of his environment.

Longer views built on a wider foundation than we have been accustomed to, are called for in planning. Calculations and policies should embrace the future as well as the present, and piecemeal solutions to immediate problems must give way to regional or national consideration. The emotive power of natural beauty should be given scope, and humanity should cherish all the relationships binding us to the rest of creation, knowing that an independent existence is impossible, and would be unendurable even if it were possible.

We reach a stage when adolescent humanity, ceasing to be cradled in nature's arms, becomes aware of the power to will and control. We must advance quickly through this dangerous rebellious stage to a mature appreciation of the laws ensuring balance and duration.

The landscape humanity creates will reflect the condition of human ecology: only in landscapes reflecting healthy balance can human life remain worth living.

Landscape Architecture Today

Landscape Architecture is the youngest of the professions, and has yet to establish its position in relation to the many other professions concerned with land use and design. These other professions fall into two main groups: scientific subjects, including geology, geography, road engineering, biology, agriculture, forestry, Nature Conservancy, horticulture, sociology and town planning on one hand; and design subjects of which, perhaps, art and architecture are the most outstanding, on the other. All these impinge on the landscape in one way or another. At the outset, each and every one of them is inclined to assume that landscape design is a minor aspect of their own profession, and it is only after deeper study of the issues involved that the realization dawns that specialization in positive landscape design is a valid need in these days of rapid change.

The recognition of this fact has been advanced by the formation of professional Institutes in many countries, and by the International Federation of Landscape Architects founded in 1948, which unites the member bodies from every country that can meet the requirements of its constitution. There are at the time of writing 24 National Institutes represented on the Grand Council of the International Federation of Landscape Architects, and a few individual members from countries whose Institutes have not yet been formed. The Federation was founded in Cambridge, the Institute of Landscape Architects acting as convenor and host. The fourteen Foundation member countries were:

Portugal	Poland
Great Britain	Sweden
Belgium	Spain
United States of America	Holland
France	Norway
Denmark	Switzerland
Italy	Finland

Since then an international Congress has been held in alternate years, different member Institutes acting as hosts and organisers, so that members have special opportunities to see the landscape of other countries and the work of their colleagues under varying conditions. Working parties of the Federation study special problems of various regions and compile reports on matters of general interest. The Education Committee publishes a list of Universities and Schools where courses in Landscape are available throughout the member countries, and is working towards recognized international standards of training and qualification.

The International Federation of Landscape Architects (usually referred to as 'IFLA' for short) has in recent years been operating from Portugal, at the Centro de Estudos de Arquitectura Paisagista, Tapa da Ajuda, Lisboa, but the Secretariat may move to a new address having closer links with other international organizations such as IUCN (International Union for the Conservation of Nature) or UNESCO, which has recently promoted IFLA from Category C to Category B. The Federation hopes eventually to qualify for Category A.

Landscape Architecture in Britain

The love of landscape, its portrayal, care and development through human use is profoundly characteristic of the British people.

In the arts of painting and poetry, as in the land based sciences such as geology, geography and ecology, and in the skills of husbandry including farming, gardening and land management, the love of landscape has been a dominating theme. Landscape is as a central node of life in Britain.

The profession of landscape architecture, or as we are coming to think of it, landscape design—aims to unite these different facets of this theme in its work.

When *Land and Landscape* first appeared in 1948, the profession of landscape architecture was almost unknown to the British public; now the term is familiar and in general use. This is due in large part to the work of the Institute of Landscape Architects and its members; to the practical demonstrations of this work for public authorities and industries; to their teaching in the all-too-few centres where the subject is taught and in public speeches and lectures. Above all, the writings of experienced members of the Institute have made an impact; Geoffrey Jellicoe's *Studies in Landscape Design*; Sylvia Crowe's *The Landscape of Roads*, and *The Landscape of Power*; B. Hackett's *Man, Society and Environment*; J. R. Oxenham's *Reclaiming Derelict Land*; to list a few which have appeared in the last twenty years and have helped to bring the subject to public notice. The progress made in this period can be seen as a renaissance—a reflowering of the New Art, as the poet Gray called it in the eighteenth century. In his time this art was trying out its paces on a comparatively small scale, in the gardens and estates of private land-owners. In 1947 *Land and Landscape* was written in the realization of the new and wider role which it was to play, but with little actual experience in that wider field. Since then landscape architects have been employed by Government Departments, Local Authorities, Nationalized and other Industries.

The New Towns Corporations employ landscape architects in their planning teams with town planners, architects and engineers. These Authorities employ members of the Institute both as consultants and as salaried staff:

Industrialists are realizing that the proper use and appearance of the landscape setting is not only their responsibility as landowners, but has positive value for public relations and work satisfaction for employees. There is also a considerable demand for landscape consultants from amenity societies and private individuals.

The need for qualified members of the Institute grows faster than their numbers. Because it is a new profession, schools and teaching staffs are inadequate for the present need for training. The complexity of the subject and the vast field over which it ranges are only now being realized; those who have not had actual experience of its problems tend to think that the subject can be tacked on to other basic professions. Existing post-graduate courses, following other qualifications have done excellent work, and many leading members of the profession have taken up landscape studies after following other disciplines and so have helped to advance the landscape profession. Exceptionally gifted people entering landscape design from allied fields such as architecture, planning, horticulture and geology have been welcome when their understanding of the relationship of design and land sciences has been proved, but it is recognized that the subject really calls for the combined study throughout the student's most formative years.

Up to the present the courses available at various universities and training centres vary widely in their approach to the subject, in the length of training and in depth of study. Postgraduate courses in landscape design for students whose main interest may be architecture or some other related discipline do not meet the need for dedicated landscape architects: full time undergraduate courses still need to be further developed if we are to prevent the loss of good candidates to oversea universities. Now that graduate courses are available in two British universities the situation is improving but the profession still expands too slowly to meet the rapidly growing demand.

It is becoming increasingly evident that many people qualified in related professions, either in the fields of art and design, or in one of the land-based sciences, have much to contribute to the changes of our landscape. Although their training and experiences may not as yet have linked art and science, they realize the need for appreciation of both and see their responsibility to the landscape of the future.

For this reason the Institute of Landscape Architects is now considering the formation of what may become a new and more widely based organization: a multi-disciplinary body contributing various professional services by teamwork under different headings. Each profession within such a body would maintain its own identity and qualifications but they would share a common principle of responsibility towards the land, both in its health and in its appearance; recognizing human responsibility for manmade change, and the visible evidence of sound land use in the appearance of the new humanized landscape now being created.

This proposal is being studied by an ad hoc committee of the

Institute as I write. Co-opted members from other interested disciplines concerned with land use (not represented already by established professional institutes) contribute to this task which may lead, if the idea develops, to a new 'Landscape Institute'.

The Institute of Landscape Architects, 12, Carlton House Terrace, London S.W.1., can give information about existing courses in Britain and particulars of its own syllabus of training and of its examination leading to associate membership. Its journal *Landscape Design*, published quarterly, is available to all who wish to follow events.

Soil and Vegetation

An understanding of soil is essential for the landscape designer, and although the subject is beyond the scope of this book, a brief outline account of soil structure and its relationship to plant growth and planting design is given here to help the general reader to an appreciation of its significance.

Only the surface soil has the capacity of supporting plant life. This topsoil, usually about nine inches deep in Britain, may be deeper in silty valleys or very much more shallow on porous slopes and uplands. The shallow layer of living soil is far less static than we imagine. Plant roots, earthworms, mice, moles, insects, bacteria, fungi and all the myriad forms of life it contains keep the soil in movement, aerating it and preventing stagnation. In water-logged or completely dry conditions this movement is lacking. Well-balanced soils develop only where some moisture and air are retained without stagnation. A fairly regular movement of water through the soil is essential to the health of soils and the plants they support.

Soil Structure

Fertile soil consists of rock particles of mixed sizes, with decaying vegetation (in the form of humus) and living organisms in varying quantity. Bacteria and fungi are the chief living elements of the soil whose function is intimately connected with its fertility: most of them live on decaying vegetation and animal wastes, producing humus; and the proportion of humus contained or held in any soil depends not only on the amount of organic material it receives from plants and animals on the surface, but also on the conditions of moisture, drainage, temperature and other climatic factors affecting the life and structure of topsoil.

Well-balanced soils, with mineral particles of mixed texture and plenty of humus, have a structure which holds both air and water in the proportions needed by plant roots. The roots of some water-plants are specially adapted to saturated or submerged soils, but the majority of trees and dry-land plants require aerated soil.

The 'crumbly' soil texture beloved by farmers, which can only develop under well-drained conditions, allows air space between the 'crumbs', but the crumbs themselves, ranging in size from about that of a pin's head to that of a pea, are bundles of mineral particles encased in moist humus. Each crumb is a reservoir and store of food and drink for plant roots. Fine fibrous plant roots grow freely through the air spaces between the crumbs, and their root hairs penetrate the crumbs, absorbing from them mineral in solution, or 'sap'. The sap rises through the sapwood, is digested or 'processed' under the action of sunlight in the leaves, when carbon is absorbed from the air. The resulting carbohydrates, now available as plant food, pass back and are distributed to the growing cells and other parts of the plant under a strict system of priorities, and finally, when the leaves fall or the plant dies, all is returned to the soil, becoming humus if the climatic conditions remain favourable to the action of soil bacteria.

Animals are utterly dependent for food on the power of plants to absorb carbon. Nature plans for the return of all the waste material rejected by the animals to the soil as dung to stimulate new life in the soil. (Man would do well to find means of implementing this plan under civilized conditions, through the use of composted sewage sludge and other wastes.)

Excessive grazing, or any other treatment which denudes the surface of its protective vegetation and its supply of humus, leads in time to the death of the soil. It becomes infertile, and the mineral particles, no longer held together by humus and roots, get blown or washed downhill, exposing the underlying rock. On flat areas the constantly moving mineral particles or 'sand' form desert which may encroach over and bury fertile soils around it.

Erosion of the rocks accounts for the mineral content of the soil: the action of water, grading the particles by weight, accounts for different textures giving different mineral soils their characteristic qualities, by which they are commonly classified.

Acid and Alkaline Soils

Peats, in extreme cases, have little or no mineral content. They are purely organic soils formed by decaying vegetation. Their chemical acidity is a main characteristic, and the degree of acidity governs the range of plants which will grow in them. Calcareous soils, on the other hand, are alkaline in reaction and are colonized by distinctly different vegetation. They also are of organic origin, but the limestone and chalk giving rise to calcareous soils have no remains of ancient humus, and their soils are as dependent on current supplies of humus as are the soils of mineral origin. Limestone and chalk were deposited in the form of shells in deep seas.

Soil Fertility

The size of the mineral particles in a soil whose mineral content is high affects the structure and physical conditions of the soil.

A gravel or sandy soil having a high proportion of large mineral particles presents less surface for chemical action, so releasing less for the current account. Moreover, its moisture-holding power is low, its air content is high, and such compounds as are brought into current circulation get washed quickly through the surface by rain water and are lost to use. The humus content tends to drain away by the same process, known as 'leaching'. In periods of drought plants in such soils suffer seriously from thirst and hunger. At the opposite extreme, heavy clays having a high proportion of very fine material, though presenting the greatest possible surface to the chemical action of soil water, and therefore capable of a rich yield of plant foods, hold too much water and too little air for free penetration by plant roots. The small mineral particles pack tightly together, leaving little possibility of organic life in the soil. Clay soils tend to be infertile, though rich in plant foods, because their mechanical structure does not favour root growth. They are literally 'heavy' to work because they are more closely packed and because intercellular spaces retain water instead of air for long periods: and if compacted by cultivation, or heavy equipment, or even if trodden when in this condition, they tend to pack even more closely and to become sticky and more impervious. When such soils do eventually dry out in a spell of drought, the particles do not fall apart as in lighter soils, but shrink together, forming large clods with wide cracks or fissures between—a process which tears asunder the scarce, stringy roots of plants struggling to find a livelihood under difficult conditions.

Loam is a general term applied to soils which are well mixed in mineral texture and which contain enough humus to support a wide range of plants. They are described as light, heavy, medium, sandy, or chalky loams; acid, alkaline, or neutral loams, according to the proportion of their constituents; but the word, though extremely loosely used, implies a reasonable degree of *mixture* of constituents, and no soil deserves to be called a loam unless it has the crumbly structure described earlier. Fertility depends much more on the structure and condition of the soil than on its actual constituents; a soil that is full of vitality and life will be fertile even though not rich in mineral constituents.

We have seen how the size of the mineral particles affects the structure and physical condition of soils having a high mineral content largely through the water-holding capacity of the soil itself. There are, however, other conditions where the amount of water present in the surface soil depends, not on the soil texture, but on other factors such as porosity of the underlying rock, the amount of rainfall, or the position and elevation of the land. Badly drained conditions tend to increase soil acidity to the point where plant growth is restricted or inhibited. The accumulation of vegetable residues in a perpetually acid condition may become so high in proportion to the mineral content as to outweigh the chemical reaction of the latter. Alternatively, quick decay of organic matter on sharply drained soils produces a shallow soil, low in humus content, so that the reaction of the mineral content remains the dominant factor. The degree of acidity produced by decaying vegetation varies with the rate of decay. Slow decay, arresting bacterial activity, increases the acidity to the point where plant and animal life ceases. Rapid decay of well-aerated leaf mould and other surface deposits, on the other hand, encourages earthworms and other living organisms of the soil.

Constant stagnant water in the soil and sub-soil, arising from whatever conditions, arrests the rate of decay of dead leaves and other organic material and increases the acidity. Excessive acidity checks the growth of animal and bacterial life in the soil. These are the conditions that give rise to peat soils. Lack of animal and bacterial action, or movement of any kind, leads to consolidation, which in course of geological ages becomes a rocky sediment, or 'brown coal'.

Two main types of peat are found. Bog peat, consisting of the residues of heather and mosses (particularly sphagnum moss), is found in damp, exposed positions where nothing but these dwarf acid-loving plants can survive. Decay proceeds to a certain stage and then ceases, and the material reaches a degree of acidity so high as to preclude earthworms and most of the other living organisms which would otherwise aerate and stir the soil. The resulting compression makes such peat totally unsuitable for any but a very limited range of plants. It is this arrested decay which has preserved intact the wind-borne pollen grains from trees of surrounding areas, for thousands of years, as described in Chapter Two, so that they are still identifiable under a microscope, thereby adding to our knowledge of climatic and geological changes since the Ice Age. This kind of peat occurs on exposed sites in Britain where there is a high rainfall and moist atmosphere, with an impervious formation underneath, or impeded drainage of any sort. It is the peat used for fuel in districts where it occurs, burning with a slow even heat, without flames.

Fen peat, the second type, composed of residues of reeds, rushes and other water plants, is formed at the edges of slow-moving or choked-up rivers and streams. The difference in the conditions producing this and those producing bog peat is that whereas fenland conditions are even wetter than bogs, the moisture in the former is not entirely stagnant and the soil never becomes tightly compressed. The water, unlike rainwater, has collected mineral salts and other materials in the course of its travels, all of which serve to fertilize and keep alive the soil through which it passes. Decomposition of the vegetable matter in this case is far more complete than in the bog peat; and such soils, when drained, are light, friable and fertile, particularly when, as is usually the case in England, the areas where they form are drained by rivers which have previously passed through limestone districts. Much of the peat of the Lincolnshire fens actually shows an alkaline reaction due to the amount of lime present in the drainage water, and so favours lime-tolerant (or calcicole) plants.

Fenland areas spread and increase as the material accumulates, and the course of their sluggish rivers is often deflected unless kept open by man. At some periods of our history the amount of water-logged fen country must have been far higher than at present—this is borne out by the huge preponderance of alder pollen found at certain levels in the bog peat. Alder woods are the characteristic 'climax' of fenland. Fenland can, in the course of time, give rise to bog peat through the formation of 'raised bogs', which form when an acid accumulation of decaying water plants rises above water-level, or to mixed woodland of other types where the rising accumulation is not too acid.

Alkaline or Calcareous Soils

Just as the degree of moisture governs the formation of peat soils, so the sharp drainage provided by limestone and chalk governs the formation of calcareous soils. These are usually inclined to be shallow, owing to the fact that the decay of vegetation (leaf-mould, etc.) is hastened by the presence of lime: when well-decayed, the resulting humus leaches away through the porous rock. The soil depth tends to be determined by the depth to which roots of plants growing in it are able to penetrate.

The fact that chalk country is porous and evenly drained has led to its use for grazing. Early man grazed his cattle on the chalk downs, and in the historic period they have been used for sheep-grazing. Sheep relish the short springy turf—the fescues and bents which are native to the chalk, though those produce less leaf or food value than the coarser, succulent grasses of meadow land. The drier ground of the chalk is better for the feet, and the health of the flock is easier to maintain than on the richer land; therefore much chalk land has been kept open and free of forest. The soil of the steep chalk pasture may be only a few inches deep. On the chalk plateaux, particularly where forest has been allowed to develop, as in Grovely and other woods of Salisbury Plain, the soil is much deeper, and a heavy loam frequently develops. Mechanization and other recent changes have brought much land on the alkaline plateau areas into arable cultivation.

Much of the chalk land of England is overlaid by drift soils deposited by glaciers during the Ice Age. Glaciers formed in the highland areas of the west and north, moved south and east, collecting boulders and grinding down rock as they moved. Masses of loose material froze up with the moving ice and were carried long distances overland, to be deposited when the ice melted. The extreme southern limit of the ice in this country was roughly a line drawn between the Bristol Channel and the Thames Estuary. All over the midland lowlands and eastern counties glacial soils occur, mostly boulder clay (fine soil containing boulders rounded by their movement under the ice), and in many cases these deposits are found in such depth as to counteract any influence of the local rock underneath. For this reason very little of the chalk lands of Essex, Suffolk and Norfolk show the same characteristics as the chalk of Salisbury Plain and the North and South Downs.

Calcicole and Calcifuge Plants

Vegetation falls into three main groups determined by the degree of tolerance of plants to alkaline or acid soils. Firstly, there is a large majority of plants whose preference is for neutral or nearly neutral soils, but which will tolerate some degree of either acidity or alkalinity. This includes most of our native trees and a very large number of shrubs both native and exotic. Secondly, there is a group of lime-loving plants (known as calcicoles) happiest in alkaline soils though some trees and shrubs of this group are tolerant of a slight degree of acidity. The group includes most of the vegetables and farm crops, stone fruits and berrying shrubs and trees. Thirdly, there is a 'calcifuge' group, intolerant of lime, whose range is more limited than most of the plants in the two other groups; even they do not tolerate extreme acidity. This calcifuge group is composed largely of ericaceous plants, including rhododendrons, azaleas and heaths.

In the case of productive crops, where the harvested plants are removed from the site, the farmer must restore the equivalent soil constituents, mineral and organic, in the form of manure, lime or fertilizers: or, if his soil is not by nature properly suited to the crops he wishes to grow, he can in many cases add the constituents needed. But in the case of non-productive planting with which the landscape designers may be chiefly concerned, there is little need to alter the nature of the existing soil, because plants naturally adapted to the site conditions can be used, and these have the additional merit of being in harmony with their surroundings. The improvement of the physical condition of soils is, however, likely to produce better effects through more luxuriant and faster growth. In so far as this can be done by control of moisture and drainage conditions or by cultivation, planting and the addition of humus, it is well adapted to the wider landscape schemes, and produces results more appropriate than the effects obtainable by the use of chemical fertilizers. The art of manuring for crops is essentially designed to replace losses, and these do not occur in normal landscape planting.

Selected Reading List

Books and publications dealing with technical aspects of landscape design will not be found here. They are listed in *The Techniques of Landscape Architecture* compiled by the Institute of Landscape Architects (Heinemann, 1968).

Books and pamphlets by government departments, national undertakings and voluntary societies will be of much help, but are too numerous to list. A useful survey of the organizations concerned with the land will be found in the *Proceedings of the First 'Countryside in 1970' Conference, 1963* (HMSO, 1964). I would single out for special attention the publications of: British Waterways Board, Civic Trust, 'Countryside in 1970' (Nature Conservancy), Forestry Commission, International Federation of Landscape Architects, Ministry of Agriculture, National Trust, Water Resources Board. Many are listed in the useful *Countryside Booklist*, compiled by R. Bloxam (Murray, 1966).

HISTORY

Bacon, Sir F. (1612), *On Gardens. Works*, ed. Spedding et al., 1905.
Brett, L. (1965), *Landscape in Distress*. Architectural Press.
Cary, J. (1798, 11th ed. 1828), *Cary's New Itinerary*. London.
Chadwick, G. F. (1966), *The Park and the Town; public landscape in the 19th and 20th centuries*. Architectural Press.
Clark, H. F. (1948), *The English Landscape Garden*. Pleiades.
Cobbett, W. (ed. 1912), *Rural Rides*. Dent.
Crisp, Sir F. (1924), *Mediaeval Gardens*, 2 vols. Bodley Head.
Fiennes, C. (ed. 1948), *The Journeys of Celia Fiennes*. Cresset.
Fox, H. M. (1962), *André Le Notre*. Batsford.
Gibberd, F., Holford, W. G., Sharp, T. (1953), *Design in Town and Village*. HMSO.
Gothein, M. L. (1928), *A History of Garden Art*, 2 vols. Dent.
Green, D. (1956), *Gardener to Queen Anne; Henry Wise and the formal garden*. OUP.
Hadfield, M. (1960), *Gardening in Britain*. Hutchinson.

Harada, J. (1956), *Japanese Gardens*. Studio.

Hawkes, J. (1951), *A Land*. Cresset; Penguin, 1959.

Higgs, J. (1964), *The Land; Visual History of Britain*. Studio.

Hoskins, W. G. (1955), *The Making of the English Landscape*. Hodder.

Hussey, C. (1927), *The Picturesque*. Putnam.

— (1967), *English Gardens and Landscapes, 1700–1750*. Country Life.

Jellicoe, G. A. (1932), *Baroque Gardens of Austria*. Benn.

Jourdain, M. (1948), *The Work of William Kent*. Country Life.

Loudon, J. C. (1940), *The Landscape Gardening and Landscape Art of the late Humphry Repton*. Black.

Malins, E. (1966), *English Landscaping and Literature*. OUP.

Massingham, B. (1966), *Miss Jekyll; portrait of a great gardener*. Country Life.

Massingham, H. J., et al. (1939), *The English Countryside*. Batsford.

Orwin, C. S. (1938), *The Open Fields*. Clarendon Press.

Piper, J. (1948), *Buildings and Prospects*. Architectural Press.

Quarterly Review (1966, April), special issue, 'The Countryside'. Murray.

Robinson, W. (1870), *The Wild Garden*. Murray.

— (1883), *The English Flower Garden*. Murray.

Seebohm, F. (1884), *The English Village Community*. Longmans.

Sharp, T. (1950), *English Panorama*. Architectural Press.

Shepherd, J. C. and Jellicoe, G. A. (1953), *Italian Gardens of the Renaissance*. Tiranti.

Shepherd, W. (1963), *Looking at the Landscape*. Phoenix.

Sieveking, A. F. (1899), *The Praise of Gardens: an epitome of the literature of the garden-art*. Dent.

Siren, O. (1949), *Gardens of China*. Ronald Press, New York.

Sissons, J. B. (1967), *The Evolution of Scotland's Scenery*. Oliver & Boyd.

Sitwell, Sir G. (1909), *On the Making of Gardens*. Murray.

Stamp, L. D. (1955), *Man and the Land*. Collins.

Stewart, C. (1948), *The Village Surveyed*. Arnold.

Stroud, D. (1950), *Capability Brown*. Country Life.

— (1962), *Humphry Repton*. Country Life.

Tipping, H. A. (1921), *English Homes*, 5 vols. Country Life.

— (1925), *English Gardens*. Country Life.

Trent, C. (1956), *The Changing Face of Britain*. Phoenix.

Trevelyan, G. M. (1944), *Social History of England*. Longmans.

Triggs, H. I. (1906), *The Art of Garden Design in Italy*. Longmans.

Villiers-Stuart, C. M. (1913), *Gardens of the Great Mughals*. Black.
— (1929), *Spanish Gardens*. Batsford.
Weaver, L. (1914), *Houses and Gardens by E. L. Lutyens*. Country Life.
Young, A. J. (1962), *Poet and Landscape*. Hart-Davis.

URBAN LANDSCAPE

Abercrombie, Sir P. (1945), *Greater London Plan*, 1944. HMSO.
Allen of Hurtwood, Lady (1968), *Planning for Play*. Thames & Hudson.
Ashbee, C. R. (1917), *Where the Great City Stands*. Batsford.
Beazley, E. (1960), *Design and Detail of the Space between Buildings*. Architectural Press.
Chadwick, G. F. (1966), *The Park and the Town; public landscape in the 19th and 20th centuries*. Architectural Press.
Eckbo, G. (1964), *Urban Landscape Design*. McGraw Hill.
Geddes, P. (1968), *Cities in Evolution*. Benn.
Gibberd, Sir F. (1953), *Town Design*. Architectural Press.
Mumford, L. (1938), *The Culture of Cities*. Secker & Warburg.
— (1961), *The City in History*. Secker & Warburg.
Sharp, T. (1968), *Town and Townscape*. Murray.
Unwin, Sir R. (1909), *Town Planning in Practice*. Fisher Unwin.
West Midland Group (1948), *Conurbation: a planning survey of Birmingham and the Black Country*. Architectural Press.

AGRICULTURE AND LANDSCAPE

Best, R. H. and Coppock, J. T. (1962), *The Changing Use of Land in Britain*. Faber.
Caborn, J. M. (1965), *Shelter Belts and Windbreaks*. Faber.
Howard, Sir A. (1940), *An Agricultural Testament*. OUP.
Huxley, E. (1965), *Brave New Victuals*. Chatto & Windus.
Jensen, M. (1961), *Shelter Effect*. Danish Tech. Press, Copenhagen.
Ministry of Agriculture (1961), *Shelter Belts for Farmland*. HMSO.
Skilbeck, D. (1961), *Country Planning and the Farm*. TPI Summer School, University of Reading.
Stapledon, Sir R. G. (3rd ed. 1944), *The Land Now and Tomorrow*. Faber.
Sykes, F. (1946), *Humus and the Farmer*. Faber.
Sykes, F. (1959), *Modern Humus Farming*. Faber.
Wibberley, G. P. (1960), *Agriculture and Urban Growth*. Michael Joseph.

GEOLOGY, ECOLOGY, CONSERVATION

Arvill, R. (1967), *Man and Environment*. Penguin.
Barr, J. (1969), *Derelict Britain*. Penguin.
Carson, R. (1963), *Silent Spring*. Hamish Hamilton; Penguin.
Commoner, B. (1966), *Science and Survival*. Gollancz.
Crowe, S. (1966), 'The Nature of the English Landscape'. *Quarterly Review*, Countryside Issue, April.
Hyams, E. (1952), *Soil and Civilization*. Thames & Hudson.
IUCN (1957), 'Relation of Ecology to Landscape Planning'. *Proceedings* of Sixth Technical Conf. Edinburgh, Nature Conservancy.
Manley, G. (1952), *Climate and the British Scene*. Collins; Fontana.
Miller, A. (1961), *Climatology*. Methuen.
Olgyay, V. (1963), *Design with Climate*. Princeton University Press.
Pearsall, W. H. (1950), *Mountains and Moorlands*. Collins.
Pfeiffer, E. (1947), *The Earth's Face*. Faber.
Russell, E. J. (1957), *The World of the Soil*. Collins.
Shepherd, W. (2nd ed. 1963), *The Living Landscape of Britain*. Faber.
Stamp, Sir L. D. (5th ed. 1960), *Britain's Structure and Scenery*. Collins; Fontana.
— and Beaver, S. H. (5th ed. 1964), *The British Isles*. Longmans.
Stapledon, Sir R. G. and Waller, R. (1964), *Human Ecology*. Faber.
Tansley, Sir A. G. (1939), *The British Islands and their Vegetation*, 2 vols. CUP.
— (1949), *Britain's Green Mantle*. Allen & Unwin.
Tennessee Valley Authority, *The Story of TVA*.
Trueman, A. E. (1949), *Geology and Scenery in England and Wales*. Penguin.

MODERN LANDSCAPE DESIGN

Allen, Lady and Jellicoe, S. (1956), *The New Small Garden*. Architectural Press.
Church, T. (1956), *Gardens Are For People*. Chapman & Hall.
Crowe, S. (1958), *Garden Design*. Country Life.
— (1961), *Space for Living*. Djambatan for International Federation of Landscape Architects.
Crowe, S. and Miller, Z. (1964), *Shaping Tomorrow's Landscape*. Djambatan for International Federation for Landscape Architects.
Eckbo, G. (1964), *The Art of Home Landscaping*. McGraw Hill.

Gruffydd, B. (1967), *Landscape Architecture for New Hospitals*. King Edward's Hospital Fund.

Hackett, B. (1950), *Man, Society and Environment*. Marshall.

Howard, E. (1945), *Garden Cities of Tomorrow*. Faber.

Jellicoe, G. A. (1960, 1966), *Studies in Landscape Design*, 2 vols. OUP. (3rd vol. in preparation).

Jellicoe, S. & G. A. (1968), *Modern Private Gardens*. Abelard-Schuman.

Kassler, M. (1964), *Modern Gardens and the Landscape*. Museum of Modern Art, New York.

Olmsted, F. L. (ed. 1922), *Professional Papers*. Putnam.

Shepheard, P. (1953), *Modern Gardens*. Architectural Press.

Shepherd, J. C. and Jellicoe, G. A. (1927), *Garden Design*. Benn.

Simonds, J. O. (1961), *Landscape Architecture*. Iliffe.

Tunnard, C. (2nd ed. 1948), *Gardens in the Modern Landscape*. Architectural Press.

PLANTS AND PLANTING

Bean, W. J. (7th ed. 1950), *Trees and Shrubs Hardy in the British Isles*, 3 vols. Murray. (8th ed. in preparation.)

Caborn, J. M. (1965), *Shelter Belts and Windbreaks*. Faber.

Colvin, B. et al. (1961), *Trees for Town and Country*. Lund Humphries.

Crowe, S. (1966), *Forestry in the Lanscape*. Forestry Commission.

Edlin, H. L. (1956), *Trees, Woods and Man*. Collins.

— (1965), *Know Your Conifers*. HMSO.

— (1968), *Know Your Broadleaves*. HMSO.

Forestry Commission (1956), *Shelterbelts and Microclimate*. HMSO.

Jekyll, G. (1904), *Wood and Garden*. Longmans.

— (1913), *Wall and Water Garden*. Country Life.

Ovington, J. D. (1965), *Woodlands*. EUP.

Rowe, W. H. (1947), *Our Forests*. Faber.

Salisbury, E. J. (1935), *The Living Garden*. Bell.

Searle, S. A. and Smith, L. P. (1958), *Weatherwise Gardening*. Blandford.

Sueur, A. D. C. le (1951), *Hedges, Shelter Belts and Screens*. Country Life.

INDUSTRY AND COMMUNICATIONS

Barber, E. G. (1963), *Win back the Acres: Ash and Agriculture*. CEGB.

Bracey, H. E. (1963), *Industry and the Countryside*. Faber.

Crowe, S. (1958), *The Landscape of Powers*. Architectural Press.

— (1960), *The Landscape of Roads*. Architectural Press.

Maré, E. de (1950), *The Canals of England*. Architectural Press.
— (1954), *The Bridges of Britain*. Batsford.
Oxenham, J. (1966), *Reclaiming Derelict Land*. Faber
Turner, E. J. (1962), *Electricity and the Land*. CEGB.
University College of South Wales & Monmouthshire (1967), *The Lower Swansea Valley Project*. Longmans.
Verulam, Ld and Youngman, G. P. (1955), *Factory Gardens*. Industrial Welfare Society.
Vyle, C. J. (1963), *Industrial Waste Land, its Afforestation and Reclamation*. Landscape Research Project, University of Newcastle.
Williams-Ellis, C. (1967), *Roads in the Landscape*. HMSO.

RECREATION AND THE LANDSCAPE

Browning, N. (1950), *National Parks and Access to the Countryside*. Thames Bank.
Central Council of Physical Recreation (1964), *Inland Waters and Recreation*. CCPR.
Christian, G. (1966), *Tomorrow's Countryside*. Murray.
CPRE (1965), *The Future of National Parks and Countryside*. CPRE.
Dower, J. (1945), *National Parks in England and Wales*. HMSO.
Jellis, R. (1965), *The Countryside for Use and Leisure*. BBC Publications.
— (1966), *Land and People*. BBC Publications.
Land Use Planning and the Social Sciences (1930–63). Centre for Urban Studies, University College, London. (A selected bibliography.)
Lederman, A. and Trachsel, A. (1959), *Playgrounds and Recreation Spaces*. Architectural Press.
Ministry of Land and Natural Resources (1966), *Leisure in the Countryside: England and Wales*. HMSO.

LANDSCAPE PAINTING

This field is well worth extensive study, as painters often select the essential elements of landscape for their compositions. The following titles might serve as an appetiser, to lead on to other periods.

Arts Council (1952), *Early English Landscapes from Col. Grant's Collection*. Catalogue.
Bury, A. (1962), *Francis Towne, 1740–1816*. Skilton.
Butlin, M. R. F. (1962), *Turner: Watercolours*. Barrie & Rockliff.

Clark, Sir K. (1949), *Landscape into Art*. Murray; Penguin.
Constable, W. G. (1953), *Richard Wilson*. Routledge.
Eates, M. (ed. 1948), *Paul Nash*. Lund Humphries.
Hofer, P. (1967), *Edward Lear as a Landscape Draughtsman*. Harvard University Press.
Hughes, C. E. (3rd ed. 1950), *Early English Water-Colour*. Benn.
Hutchings, G. E. (1960), *Landscape Drawing*. Methuen.
Lhote, A. (1950), *Treatise on Landscape Painting*. Zwemmer.
National Museum of Wales (1960), *Ideal and Classical Landscape*. Catalogue.
Ogden, H. V. S. and M. S. (1955), *English Taste in Landscape in the 17th Century*. University of Michigan; Cresset.
Röthlisberger, M. (1961), *Claude Lorrain: the Paintings*, 2 vols. Zwemmer.
Turner, A. R. (1966), *The Vision of Landscape in Renaissance Italy*. Princeton University Press; OUP.

Index